This notebook belongs to:

_____

Published by: Character Designs

WHO IS YOUR AUDIENCE?

PROJECT:_____   DATE:_____

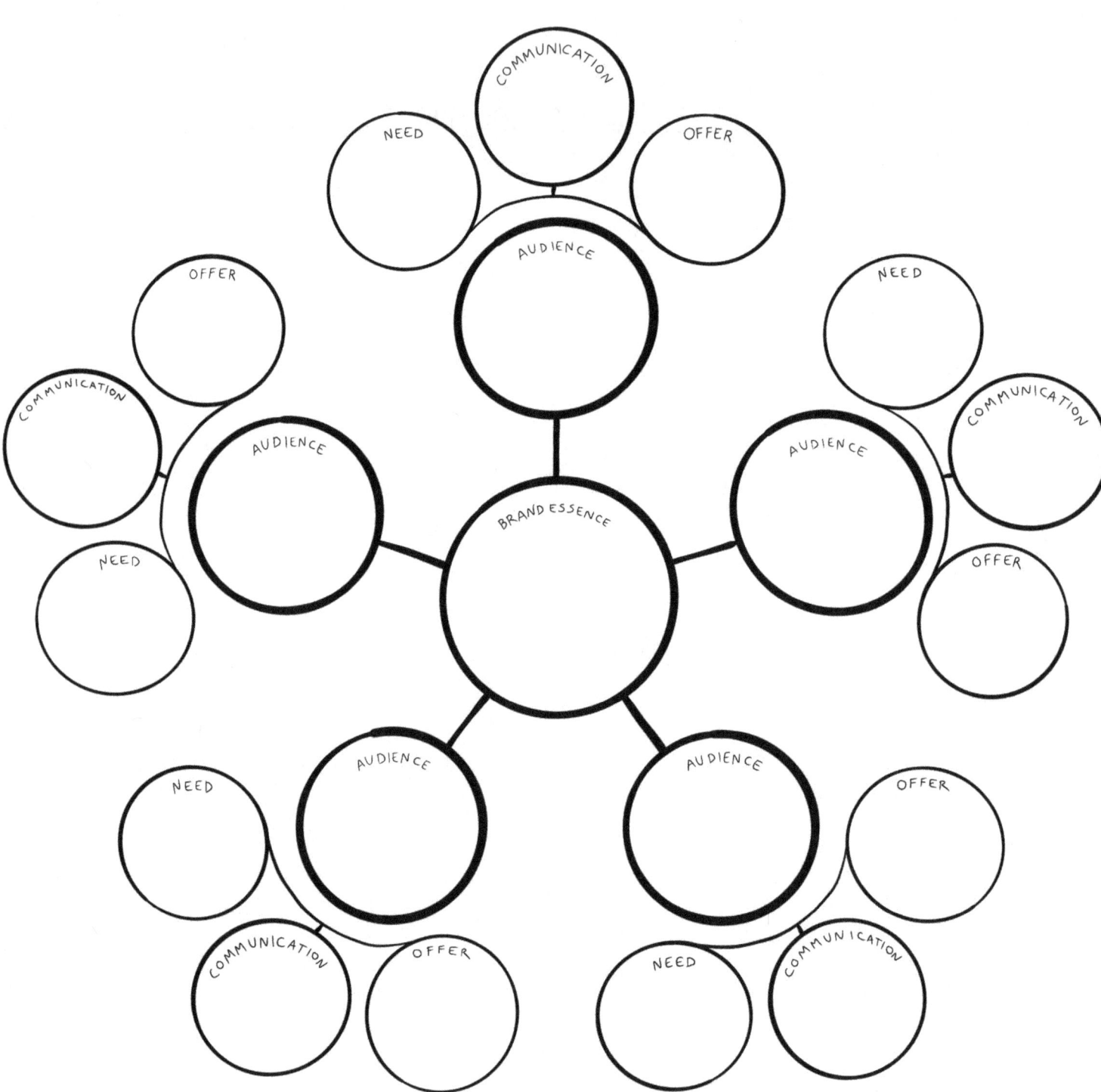

WHO IS YOUR AUDIENCE?

PROJECT:_____   DATE:_____

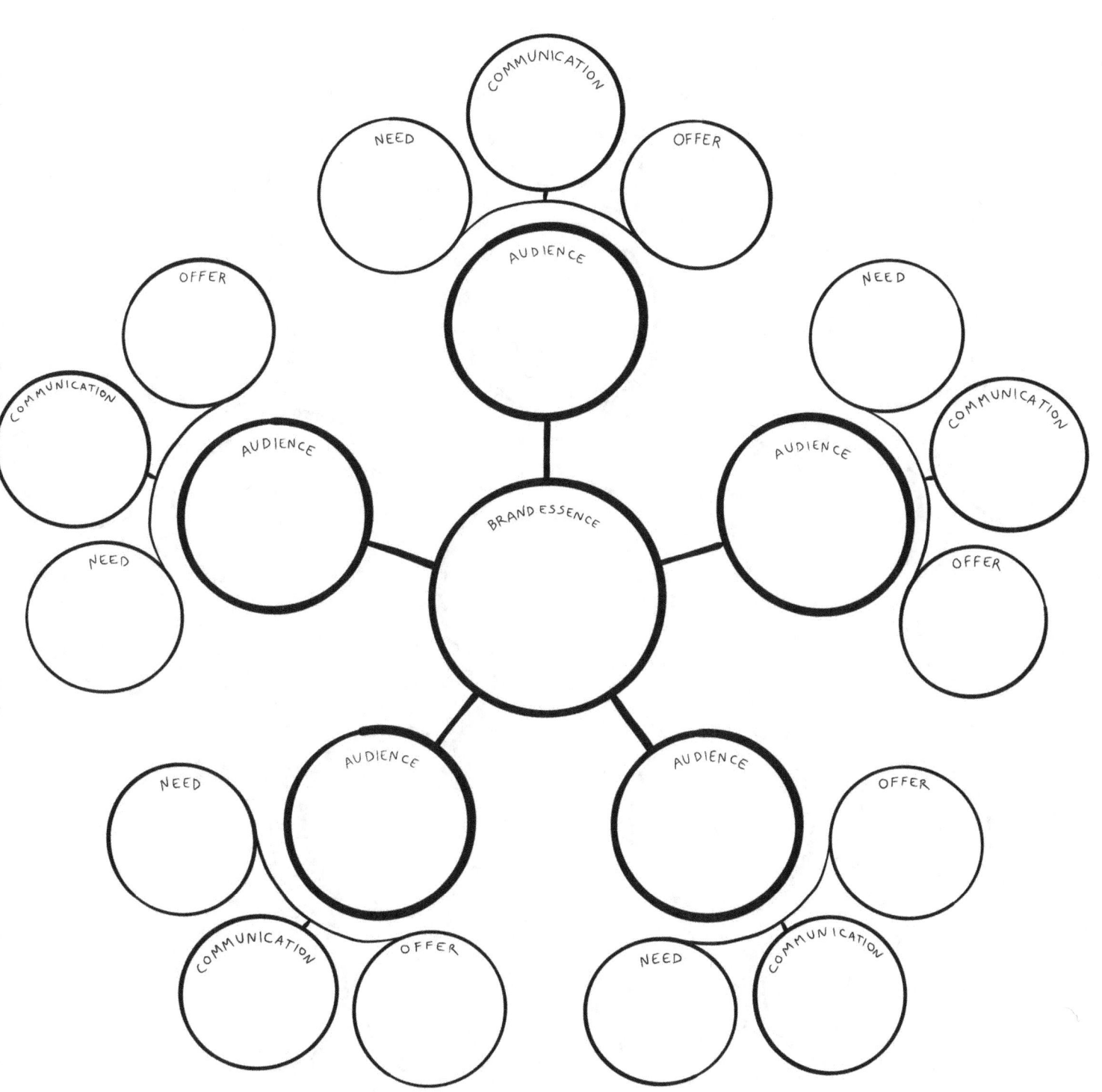

WHO IS YOUR AUDIENCE?

PROJECT:_____   DATE:_____

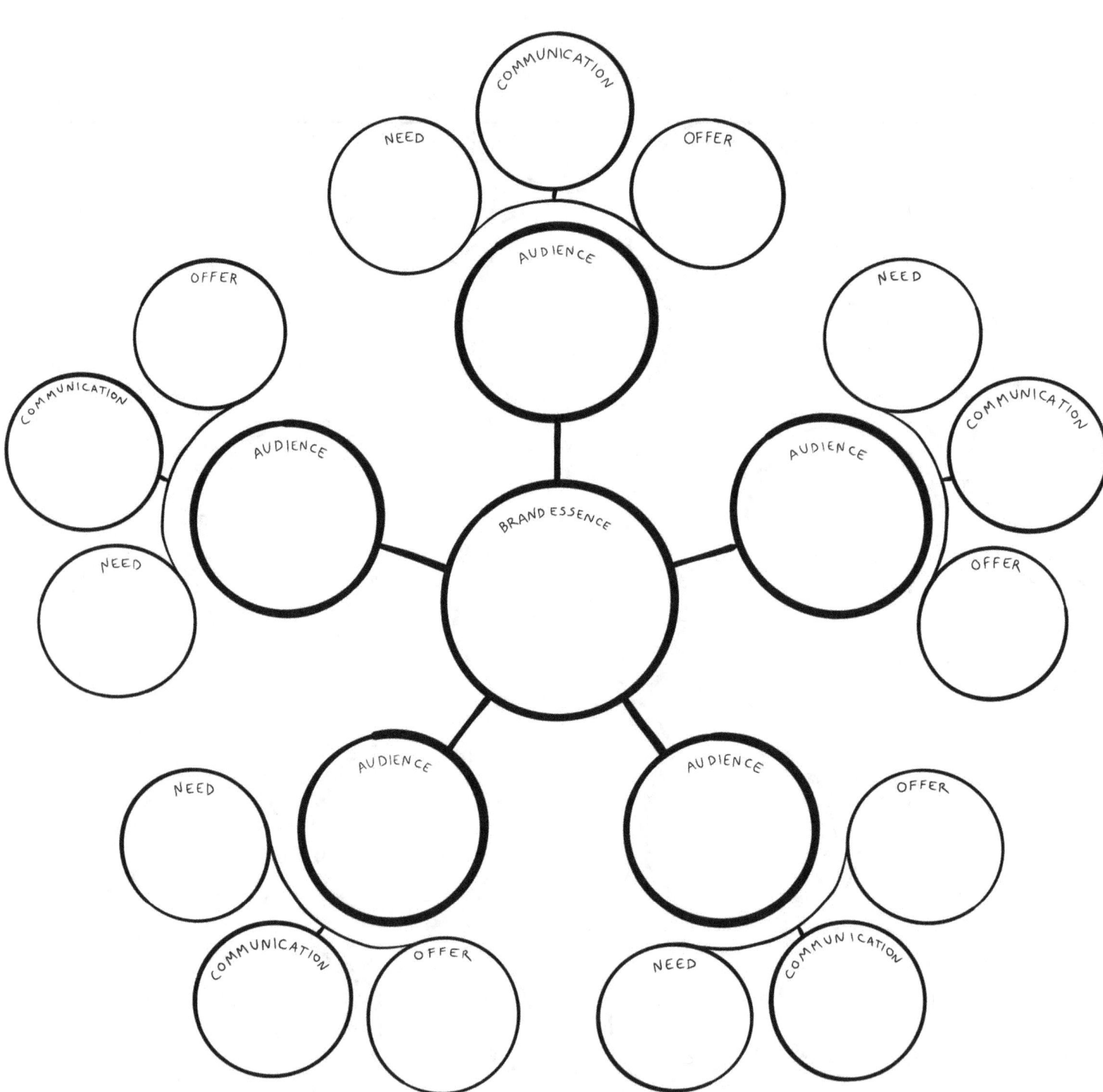

WHO IS YOUR AUDIENCE?

PROJECT:_____   DATE:_____

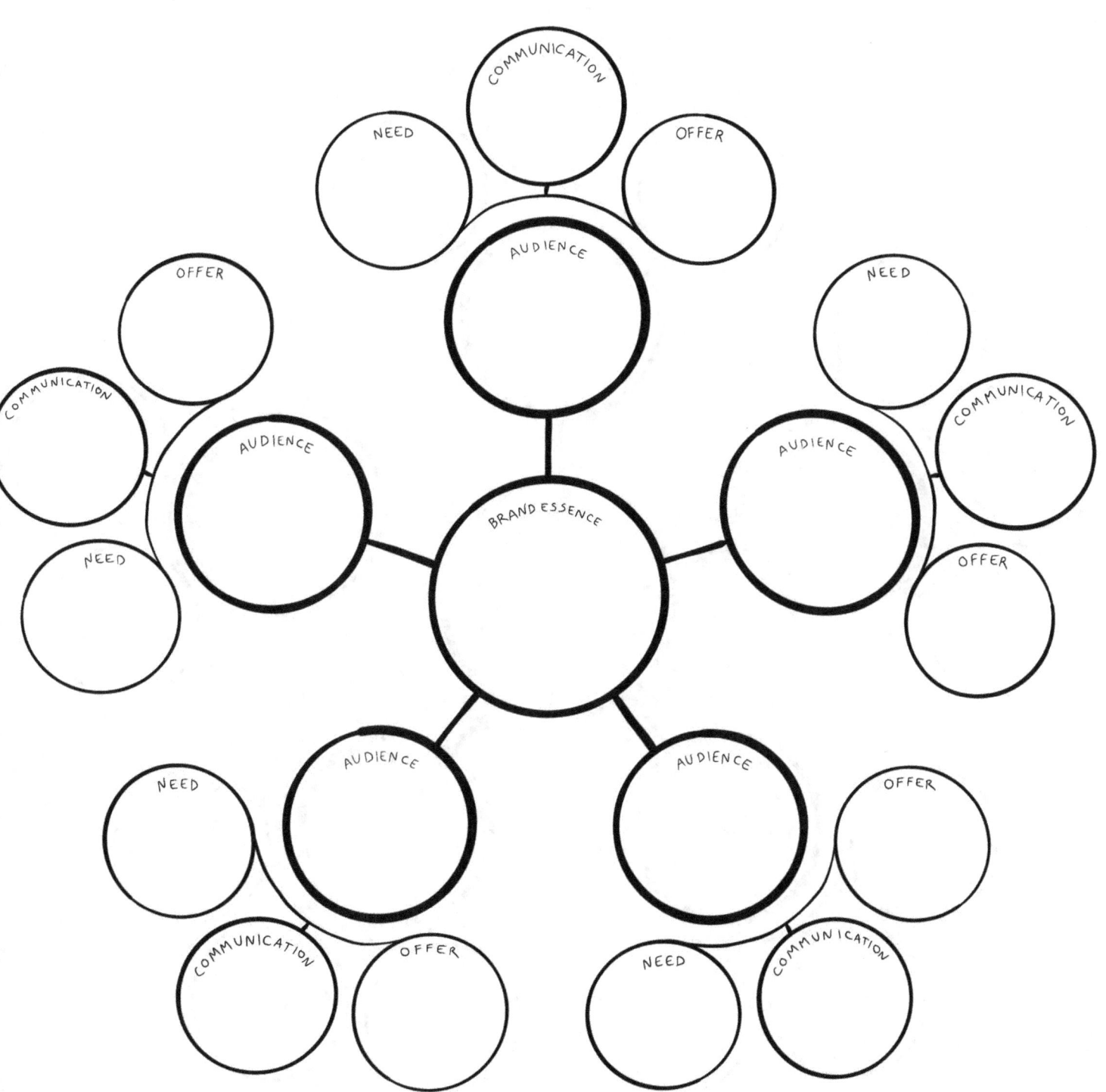

WHO IS YOUR AUDIENCE?

PROJECT:_____   DATE:_____

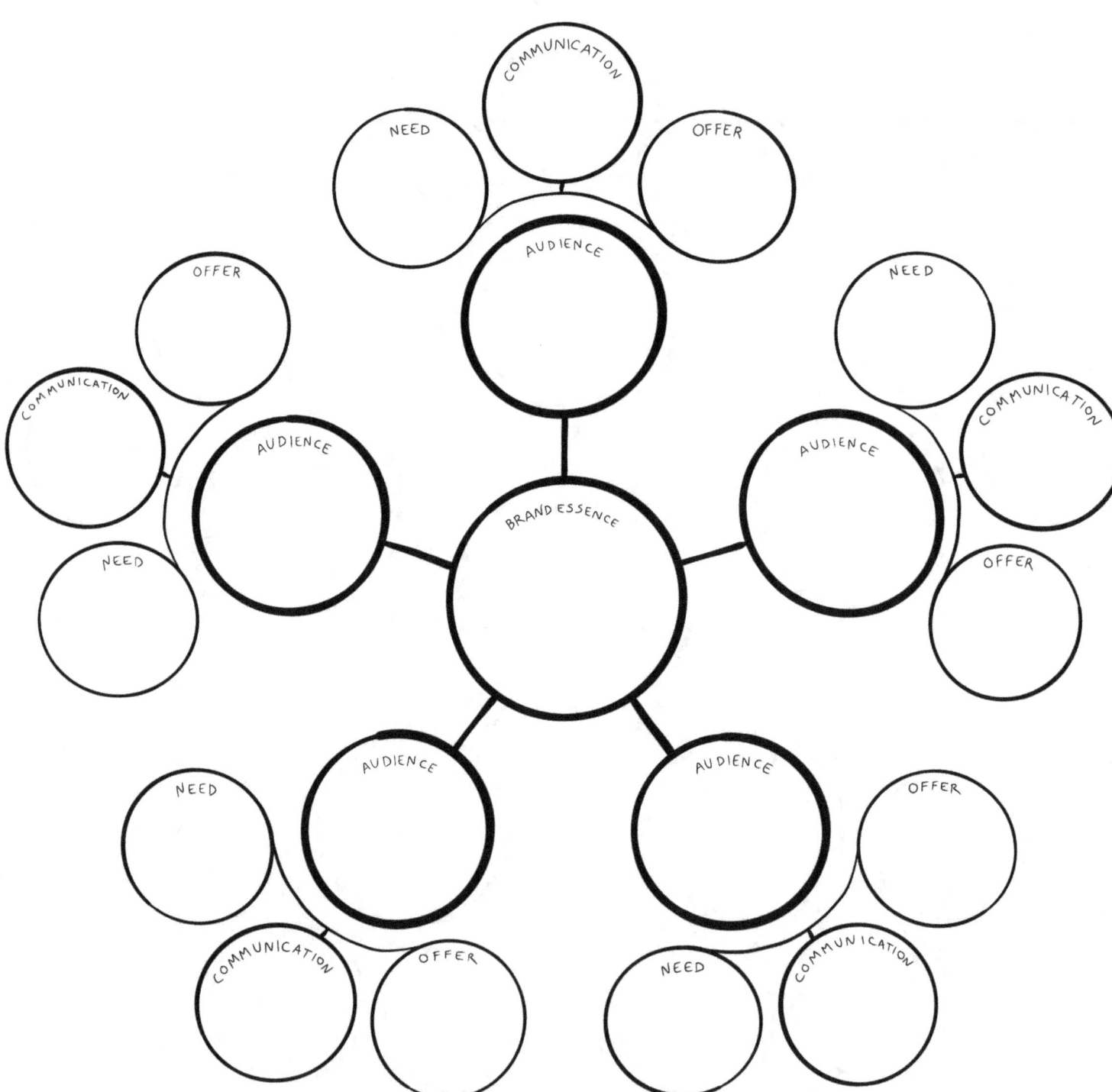

WHO IS YOUR AUDIENCE?

PROJECT:_____   DATE:_____

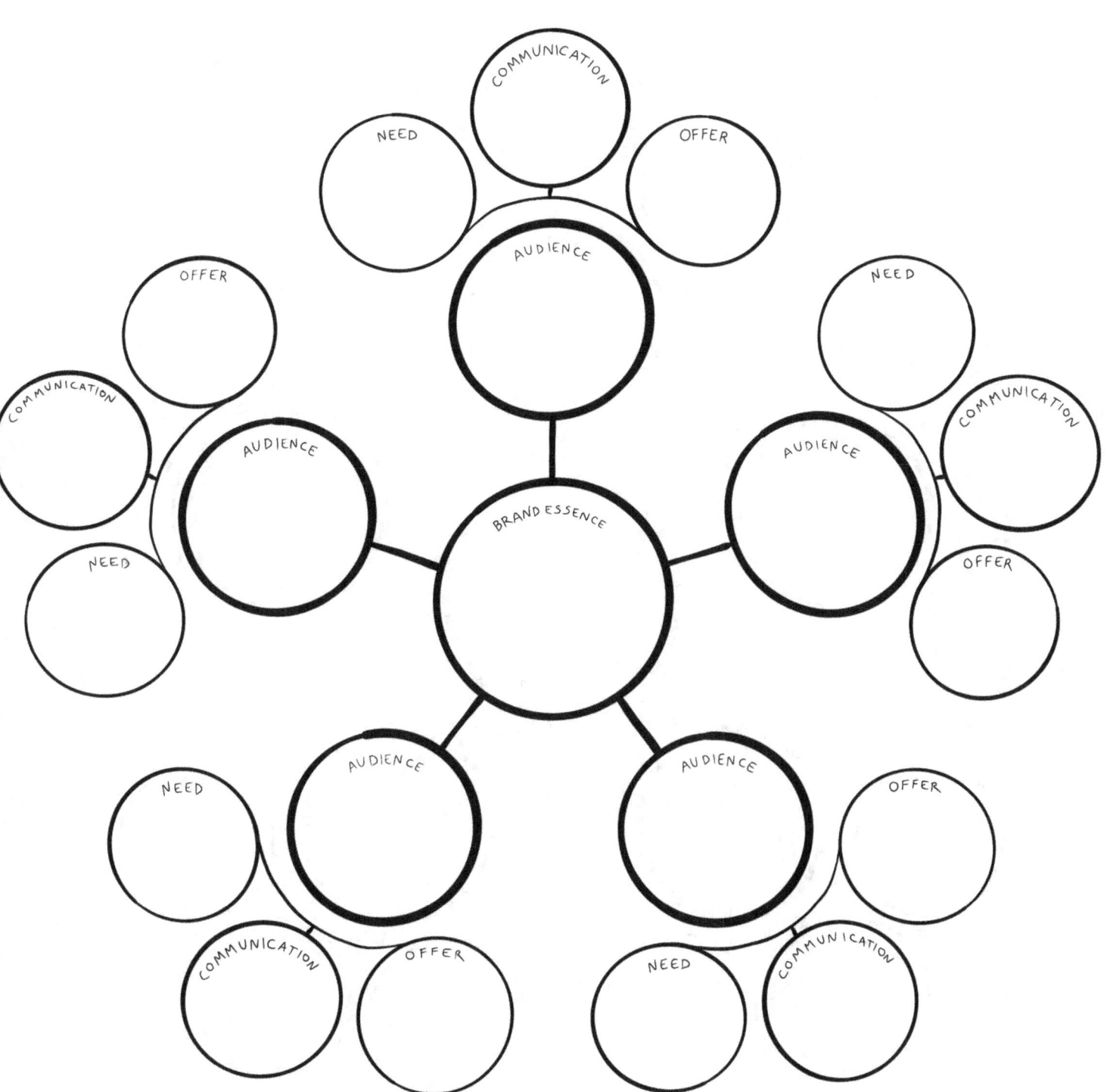

WHO IS YOUR AUDIENCE?

PROJECT:_____   DATE:_____

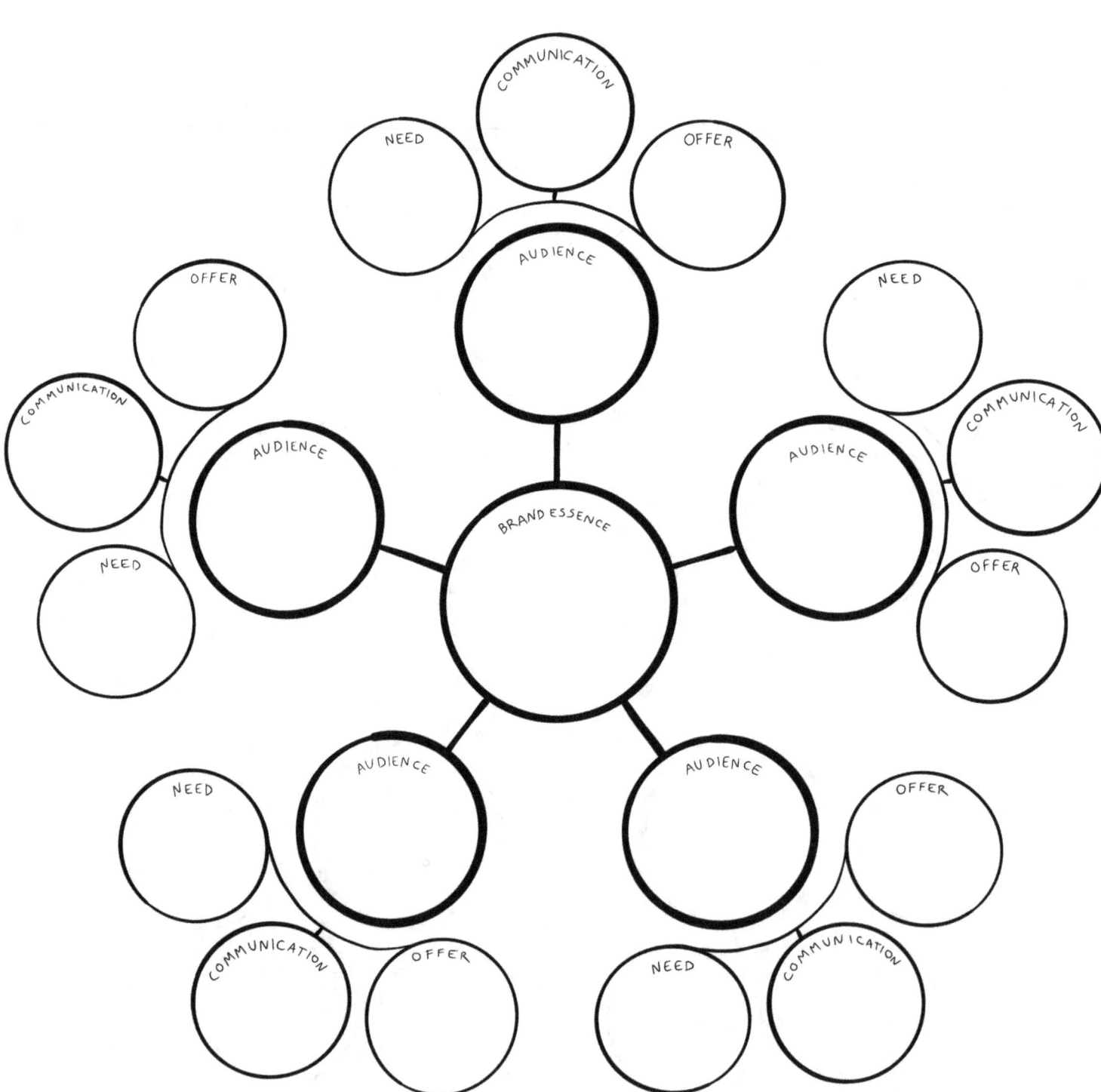

WHO IS YOUR AUDIENCE?

PROJECT:_____   DATE:_____

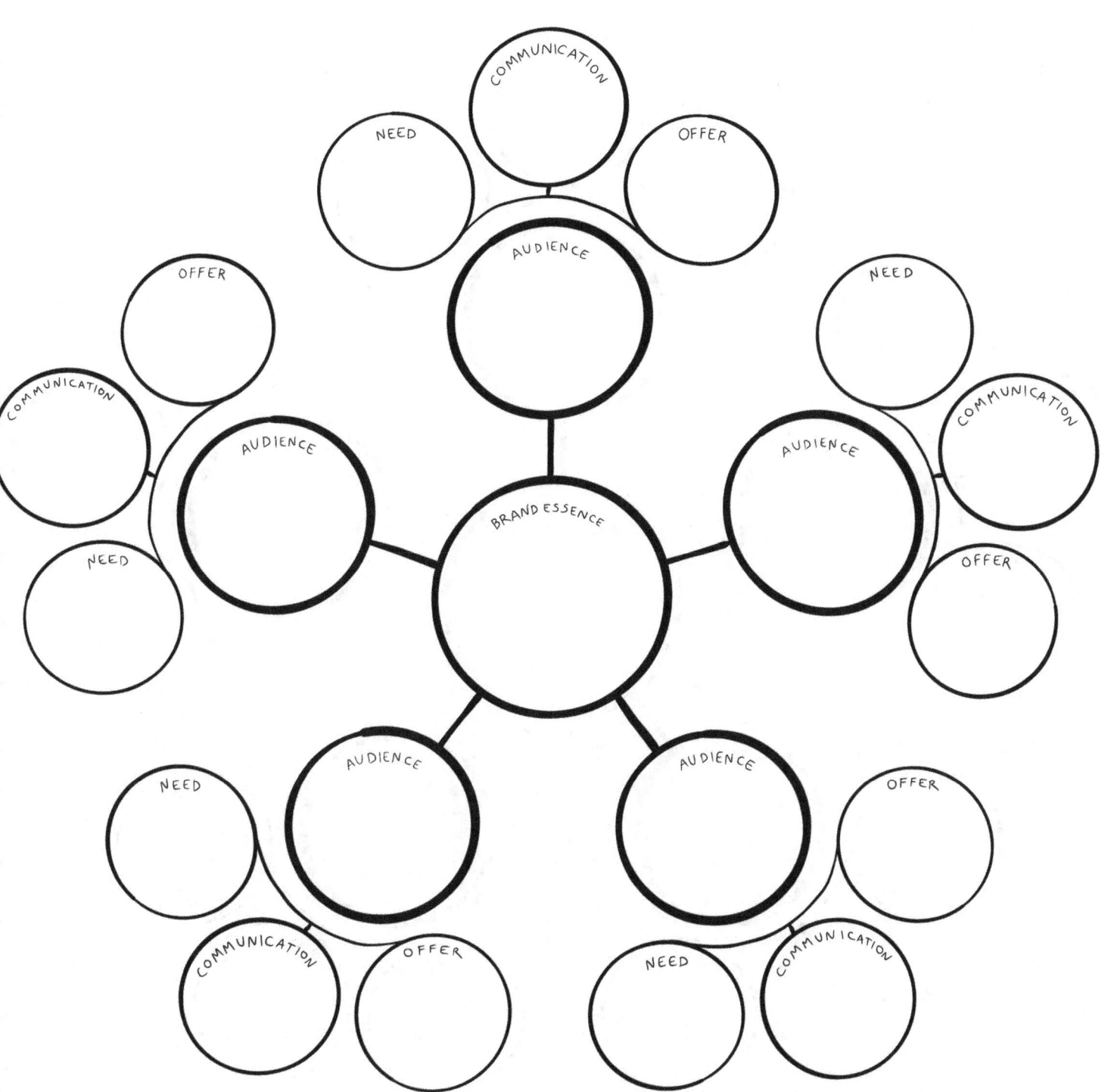

WHO IS YOUR AUDIENCE?

PROJECT:_____   DATE:_____

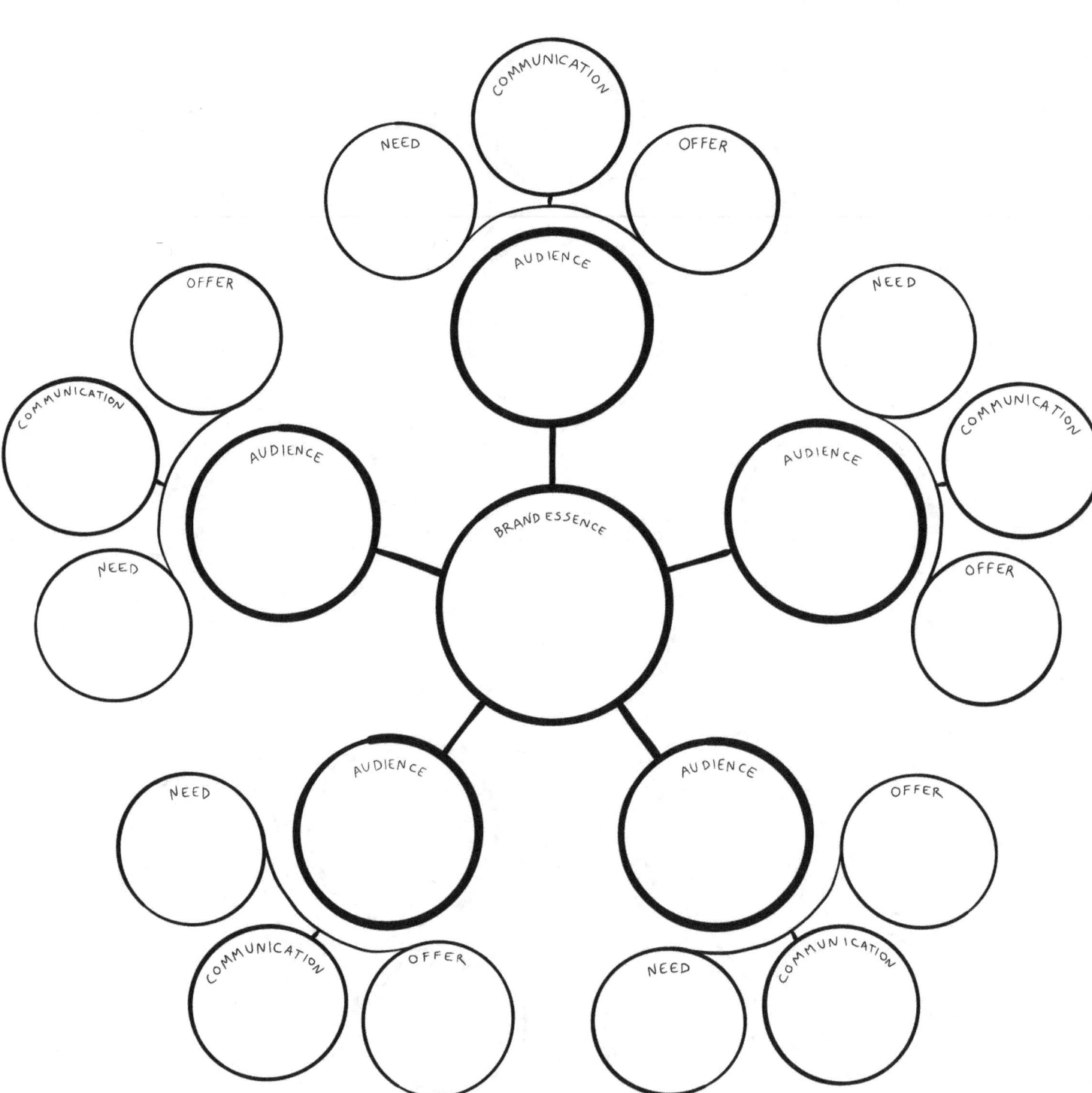

WHO IS YOUR AUDIENCE?

PROJECT:_____   DATE:_____

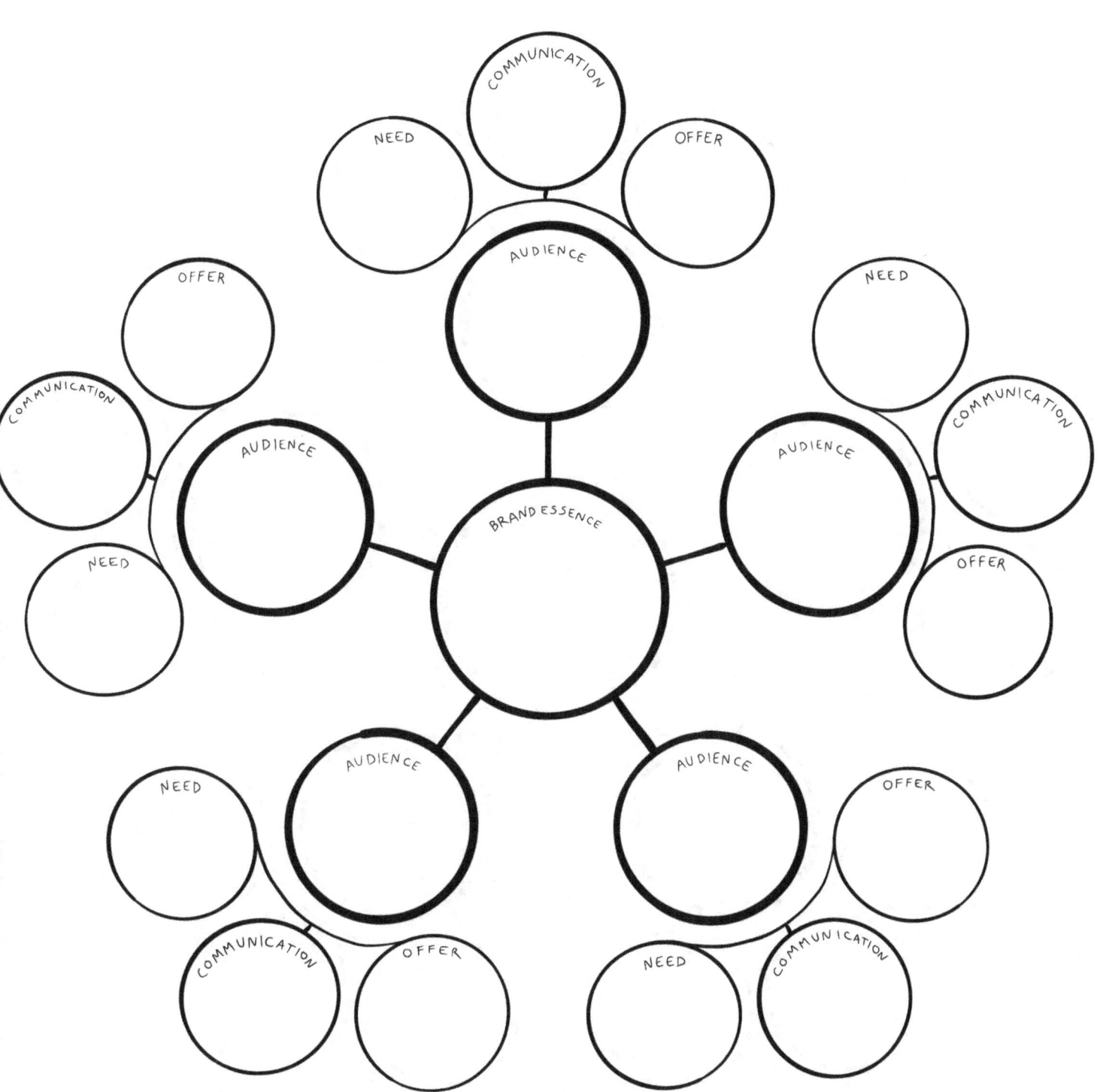

WHO IS YOUR AUDIENCE?

PROJECT:_____   DATE:_____

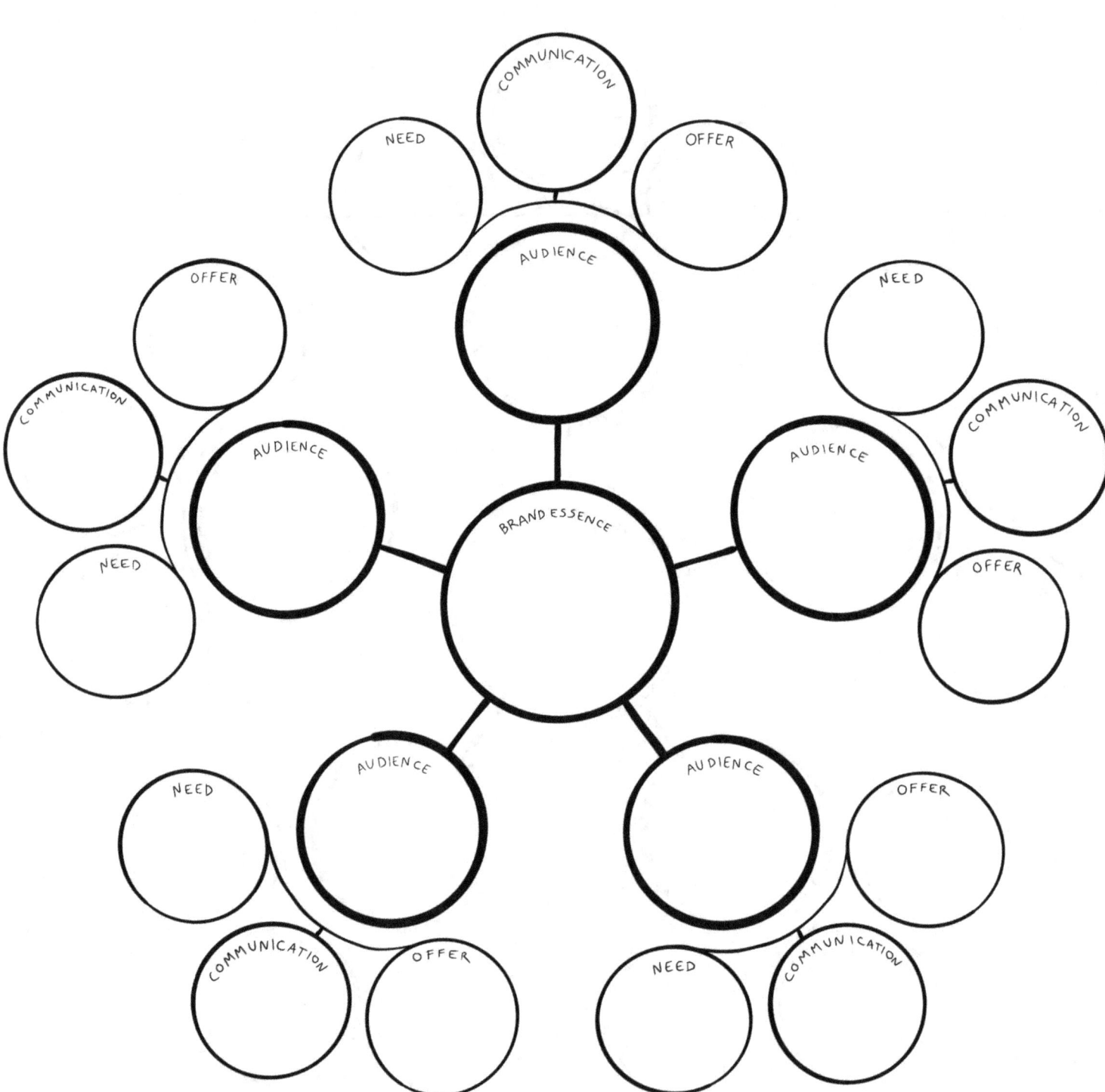

WHO IS YOUR AUDIENCE?

PROJECT:_____   DATE:_____

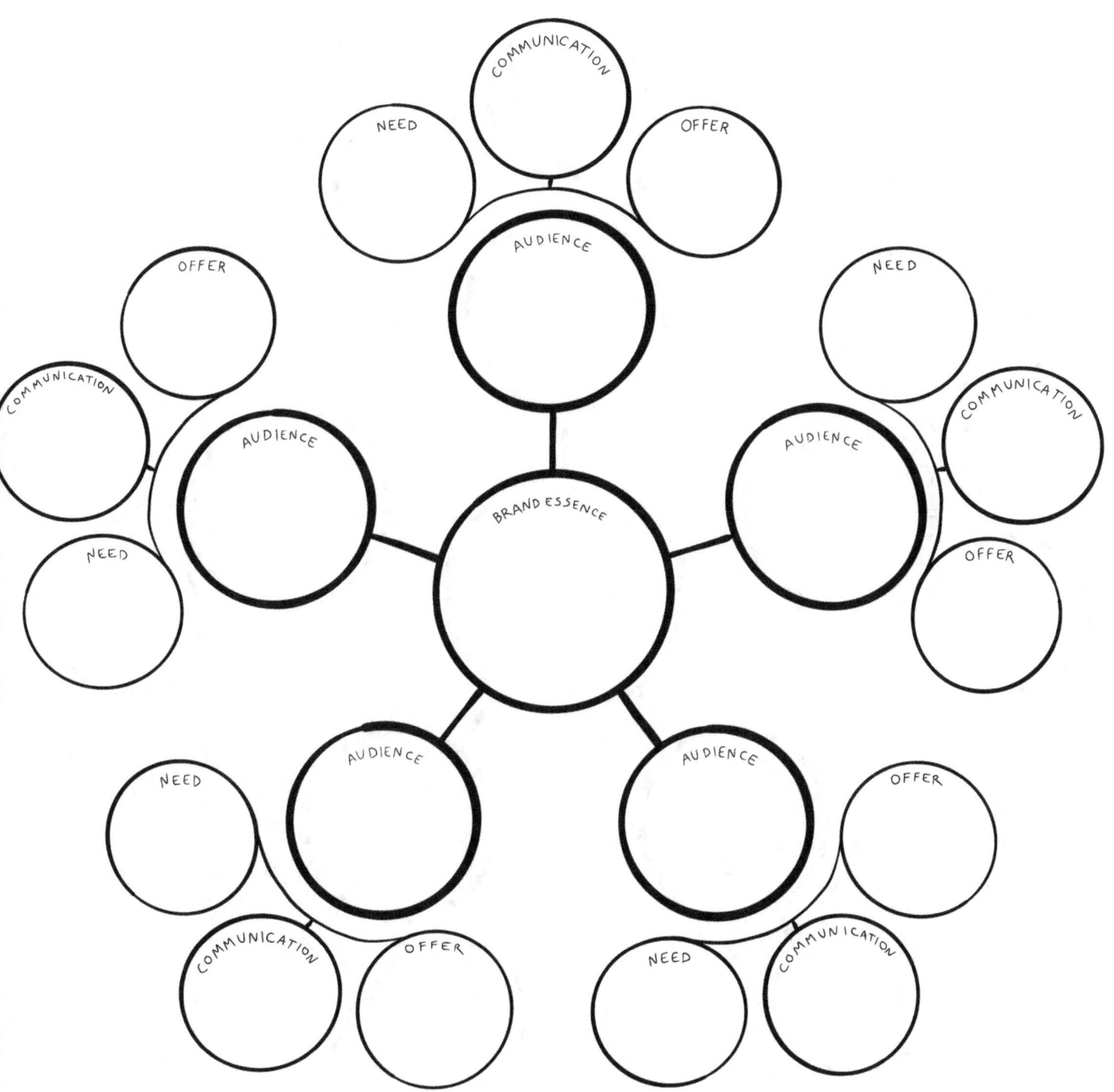

WHO IS YOUR AUDIENCE?

PROJECT:_____   DATE:_____

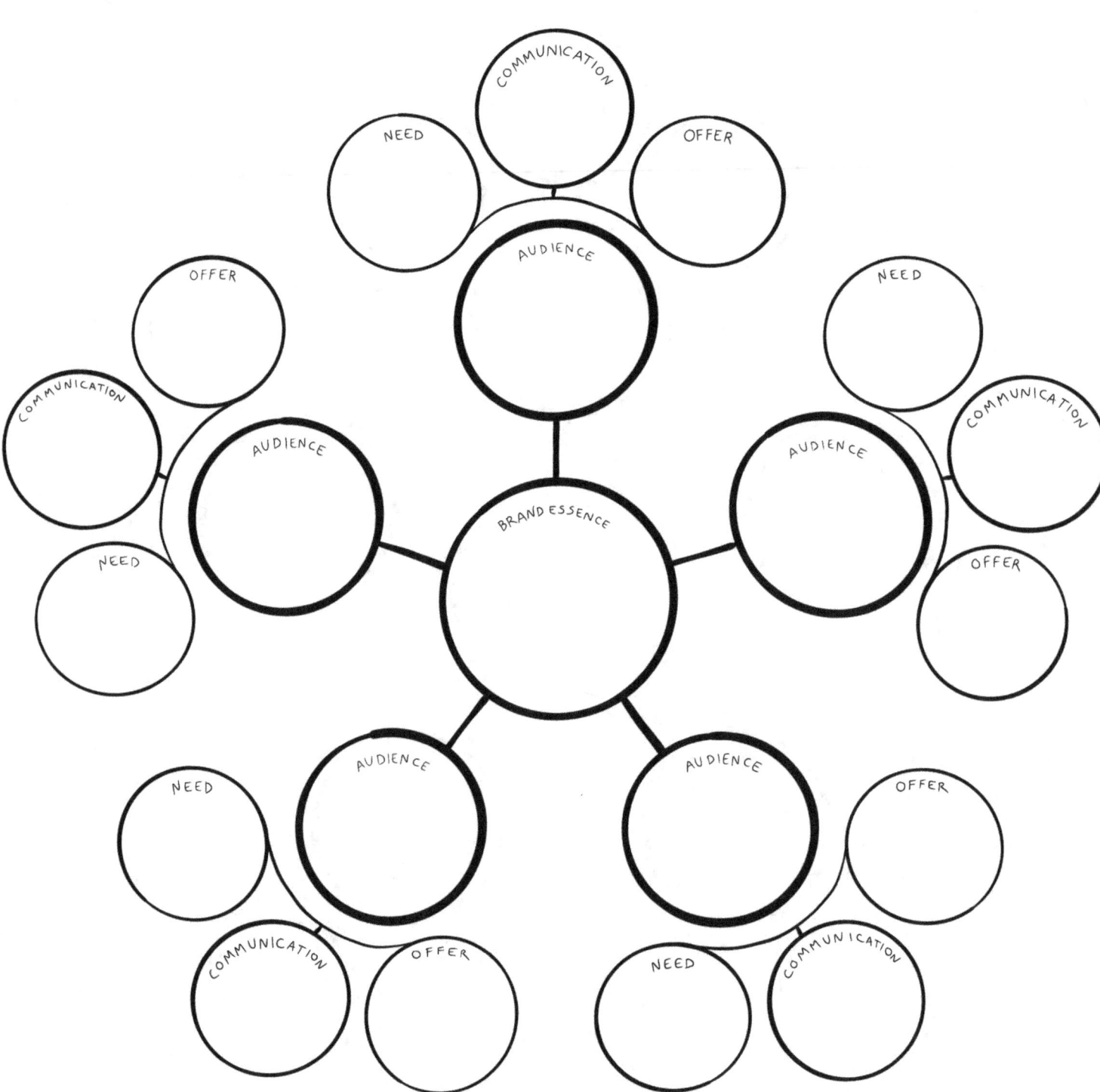

WHO IS YOUR AUDIENCE?

PROJECT:_____   DATE:_____

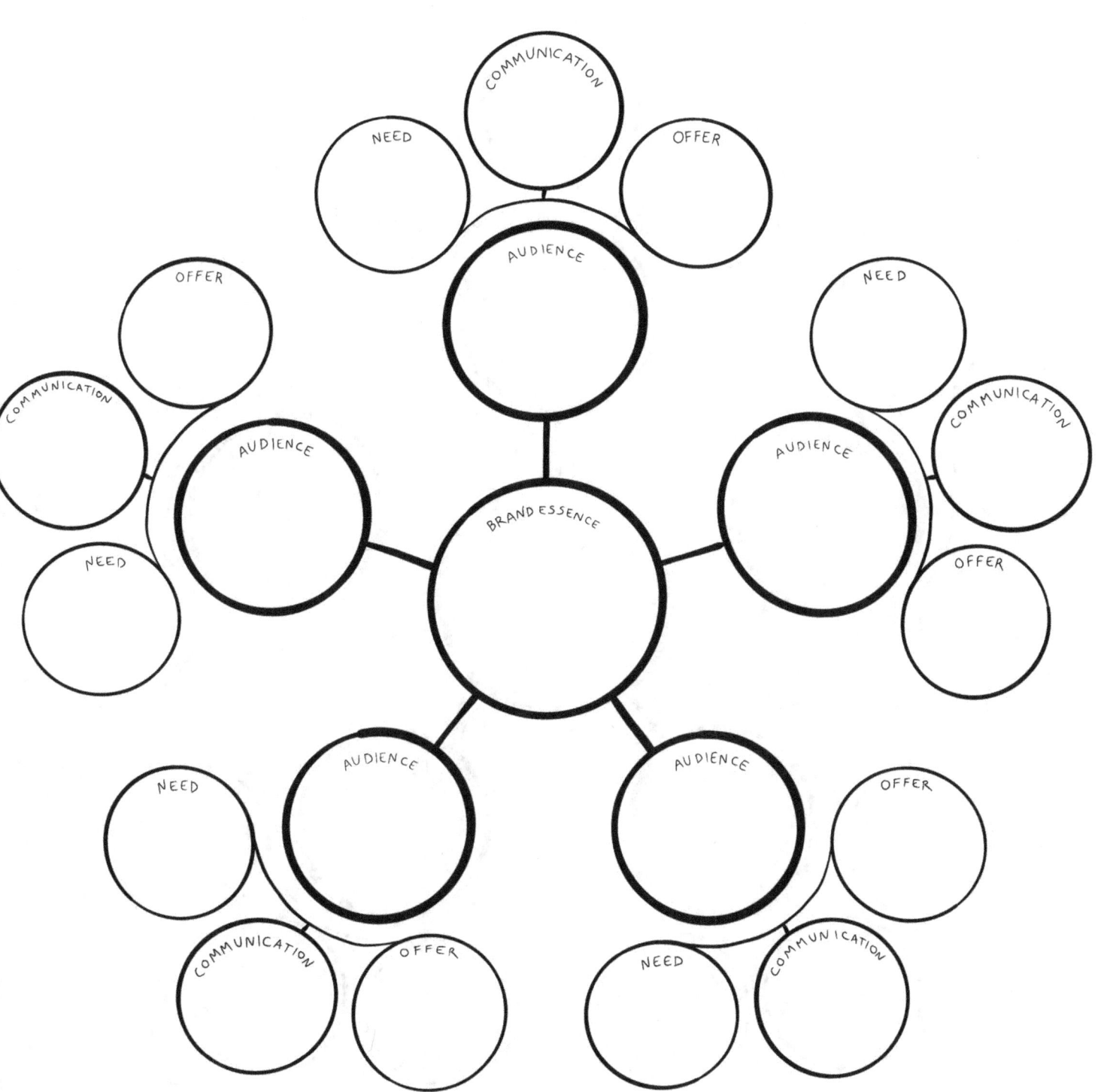

WHO IS YOUR AUDIENCE?

PROJECT:_____   DATE:_____

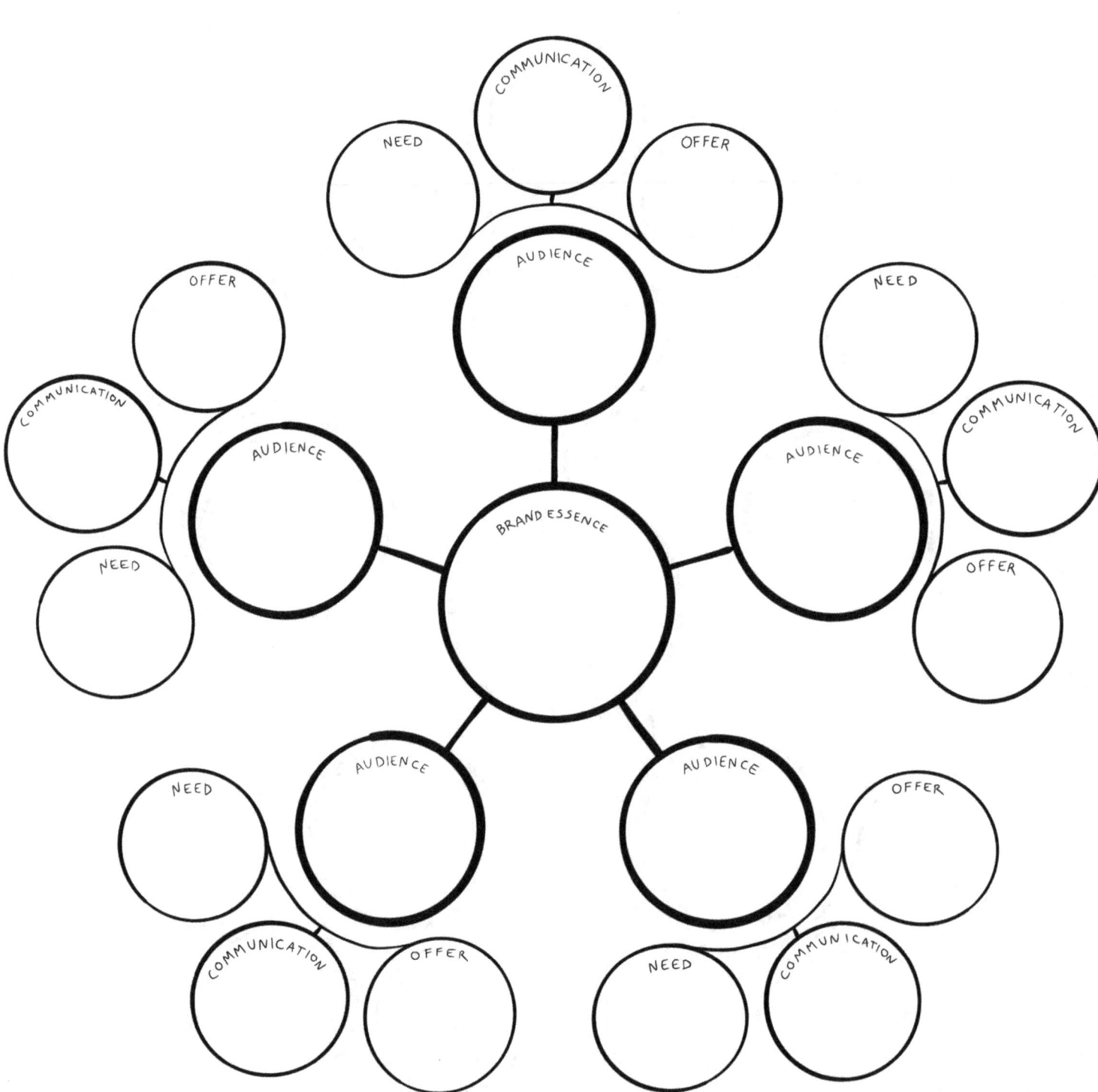

WHO IS YOUR AUDIENCE?

PROJECT:_____   DATE:_____

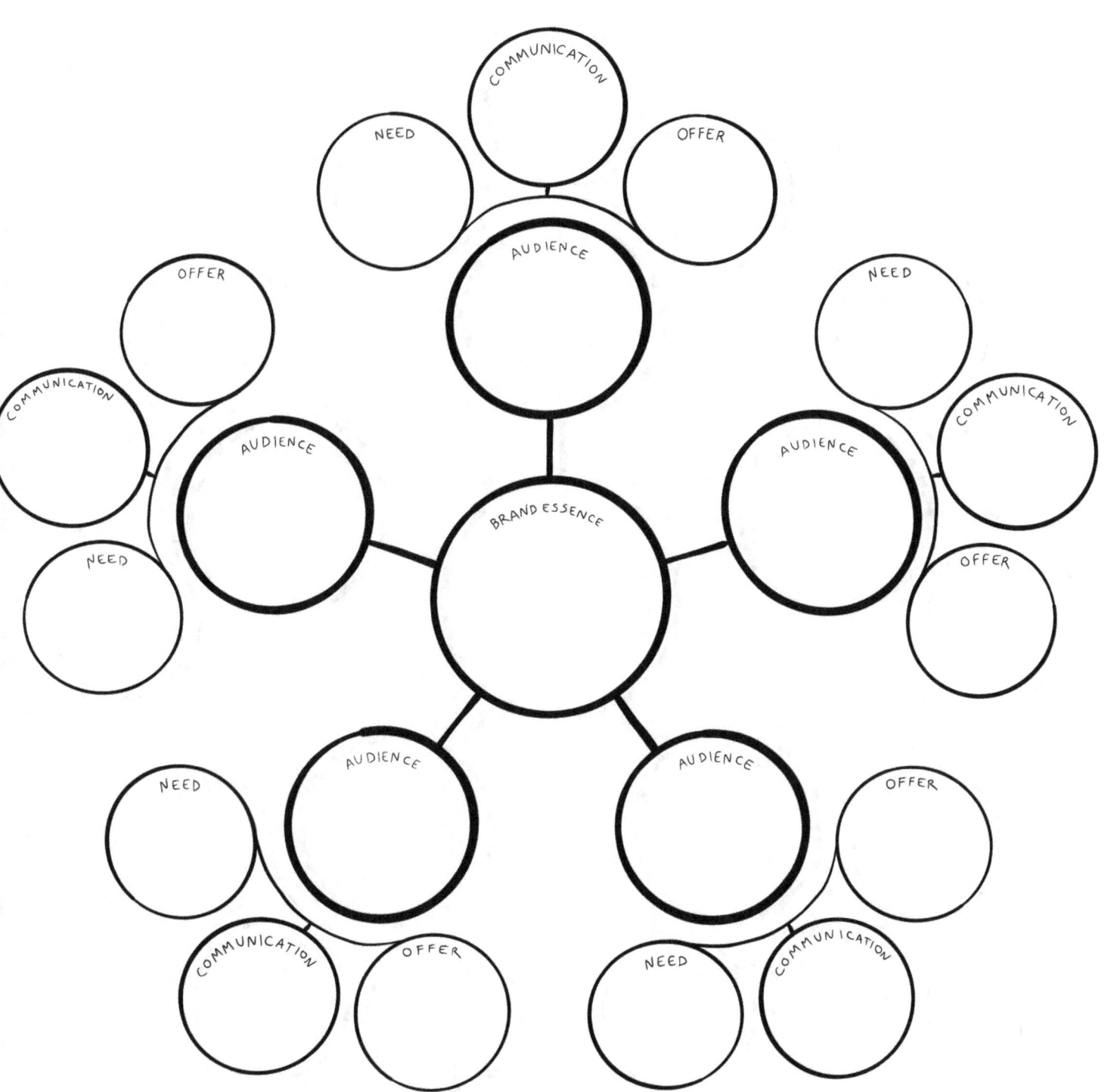

WHO IS YOUR AUDIENCE?

PROJECT:_____   DATE:_____

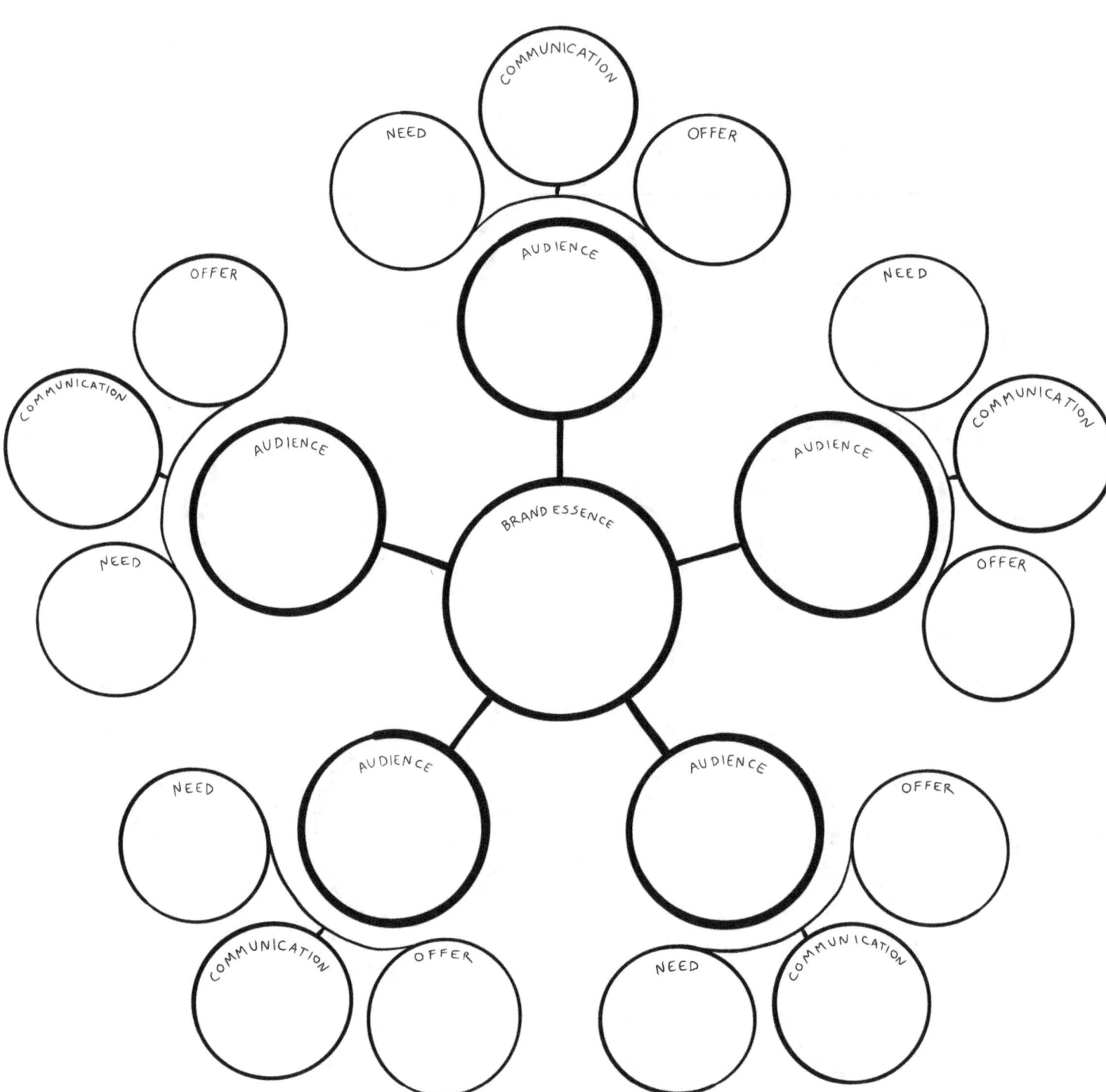

WHO IS YOUR AUDIENCE?

PROJECT:_____   DATE:_____

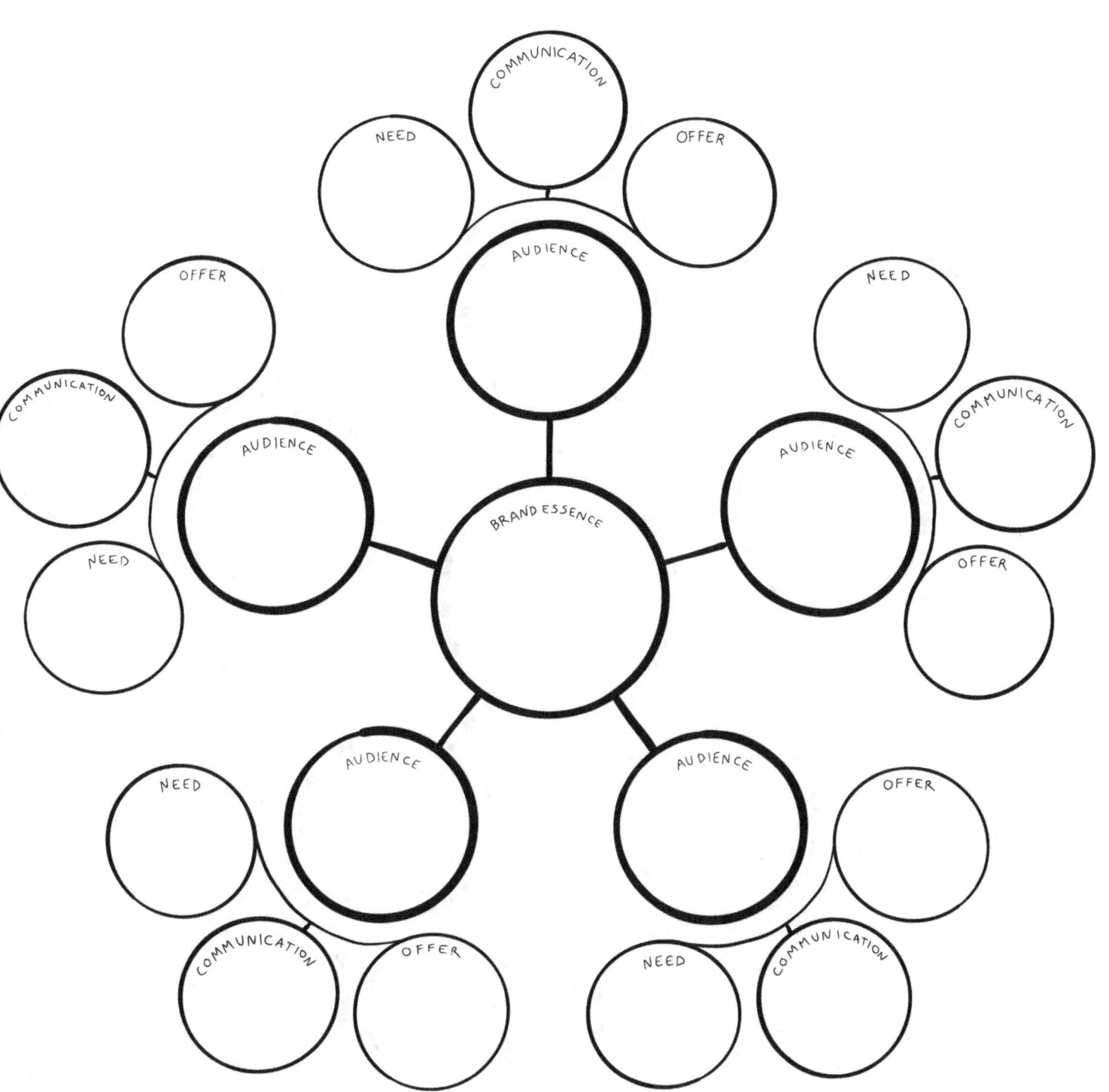

WHO IS YOUR AUDIENCE?

PROJECT:_____   DATE:_____

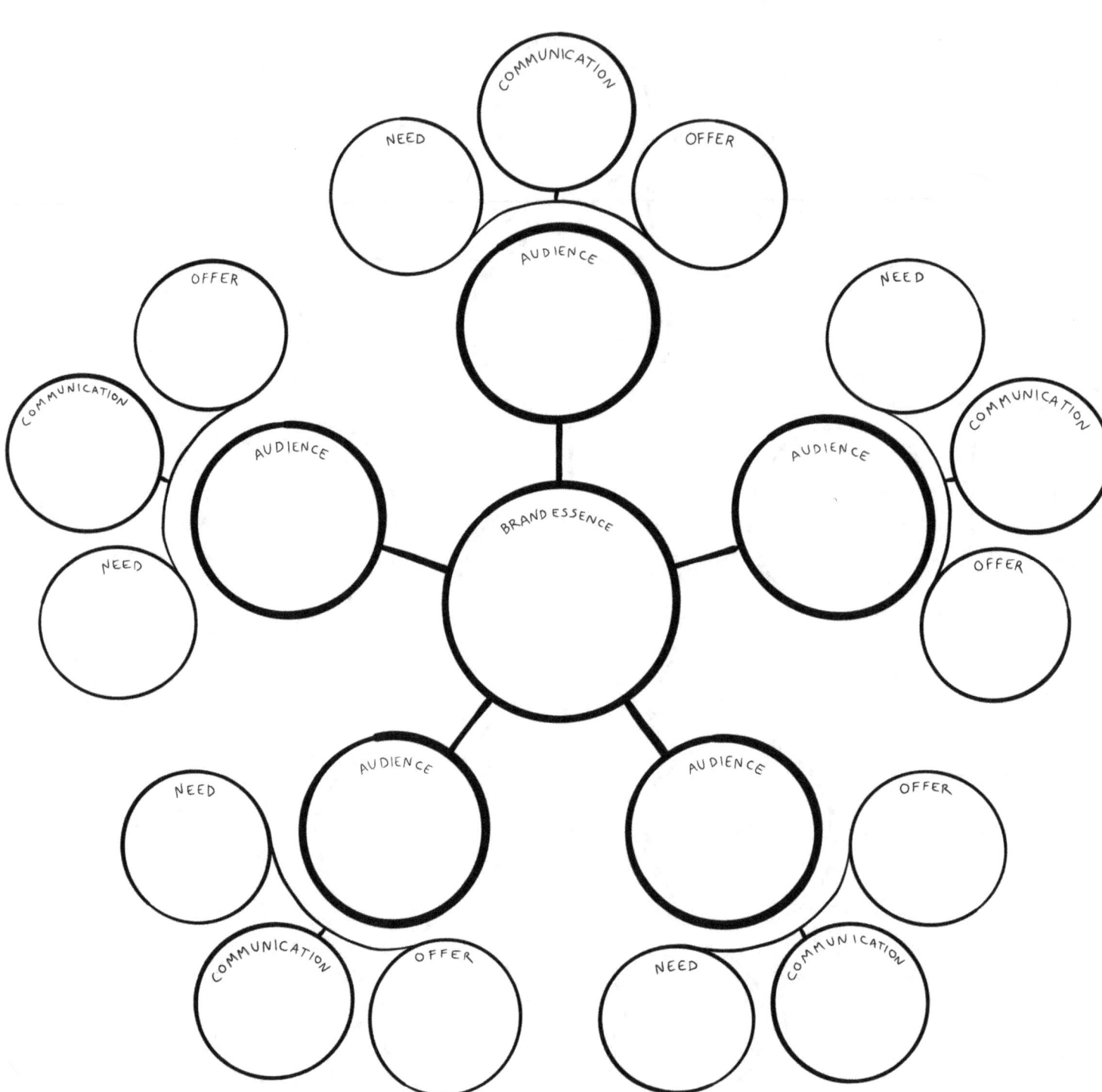

WHO IS YOUR AUDIENCE?

PROJECT:_____   DATE:_____

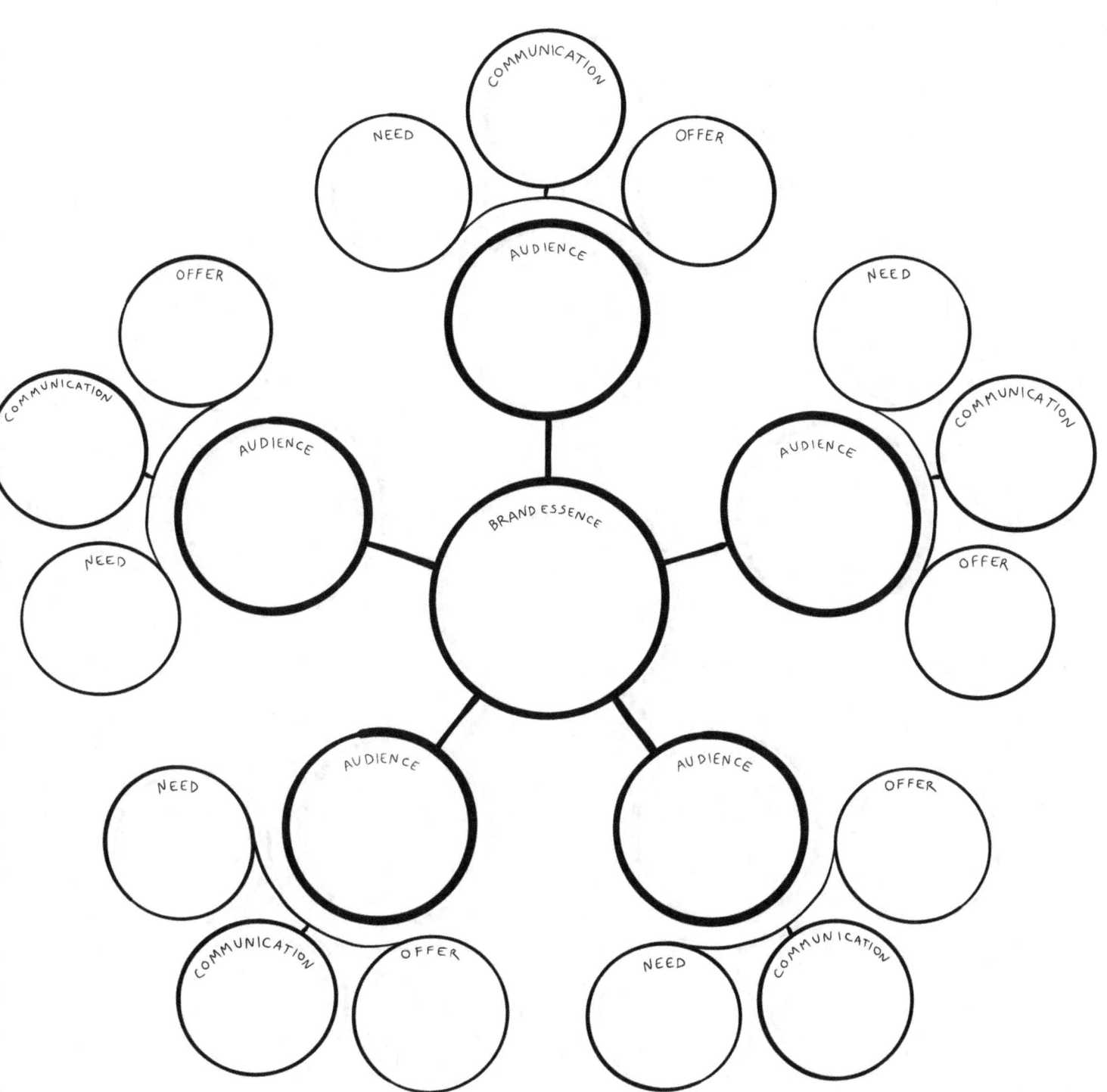

WHO IS YOUR AUDIENCE?

PROJECT:_____   DATE:_____

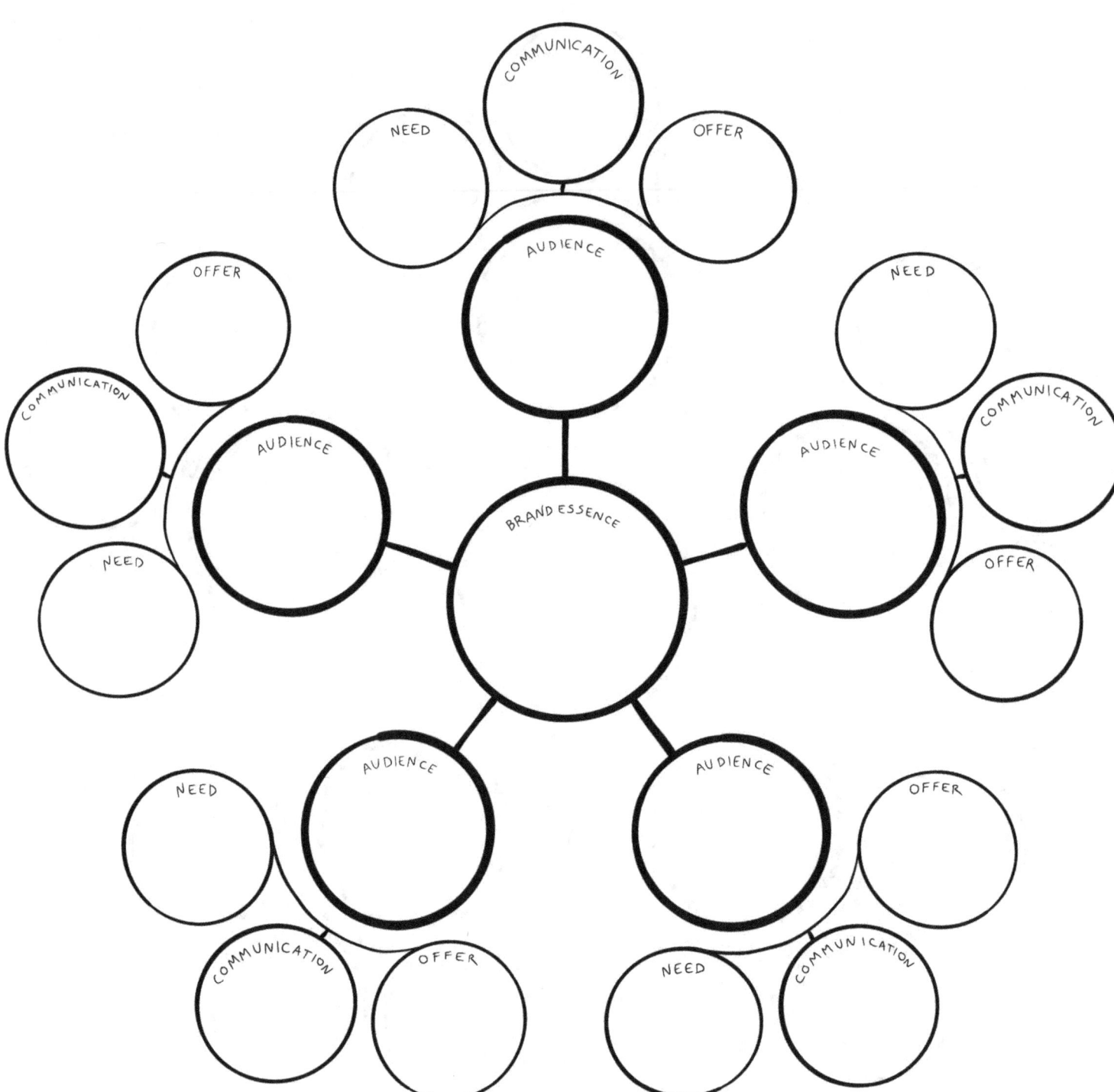

WHO IS YOUR AUDIENCE?

PROJECT:_____   DATE:_____

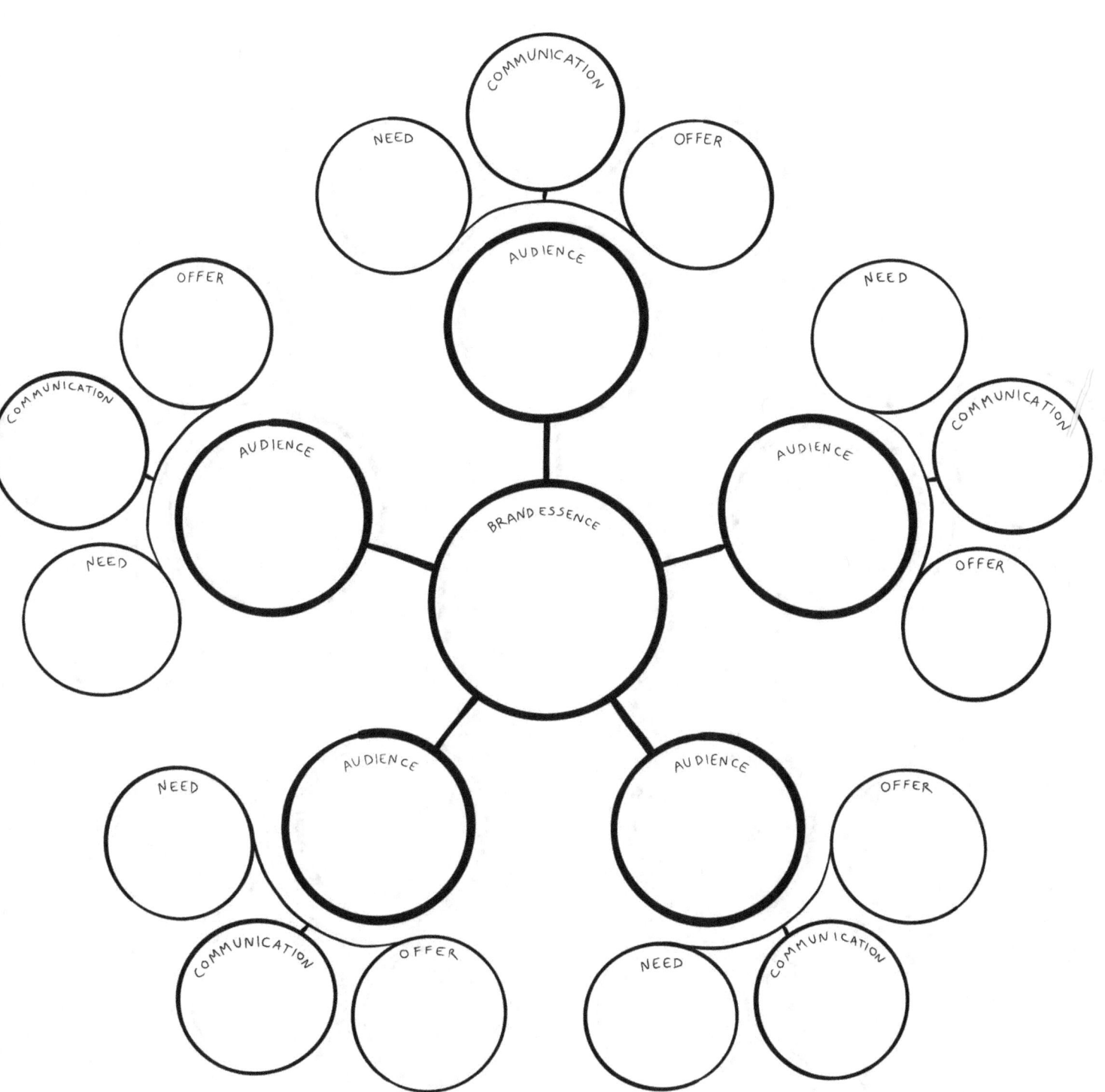

WHO IS YOUR AUDIENCE?

PROJECT:_____   DATE:_____

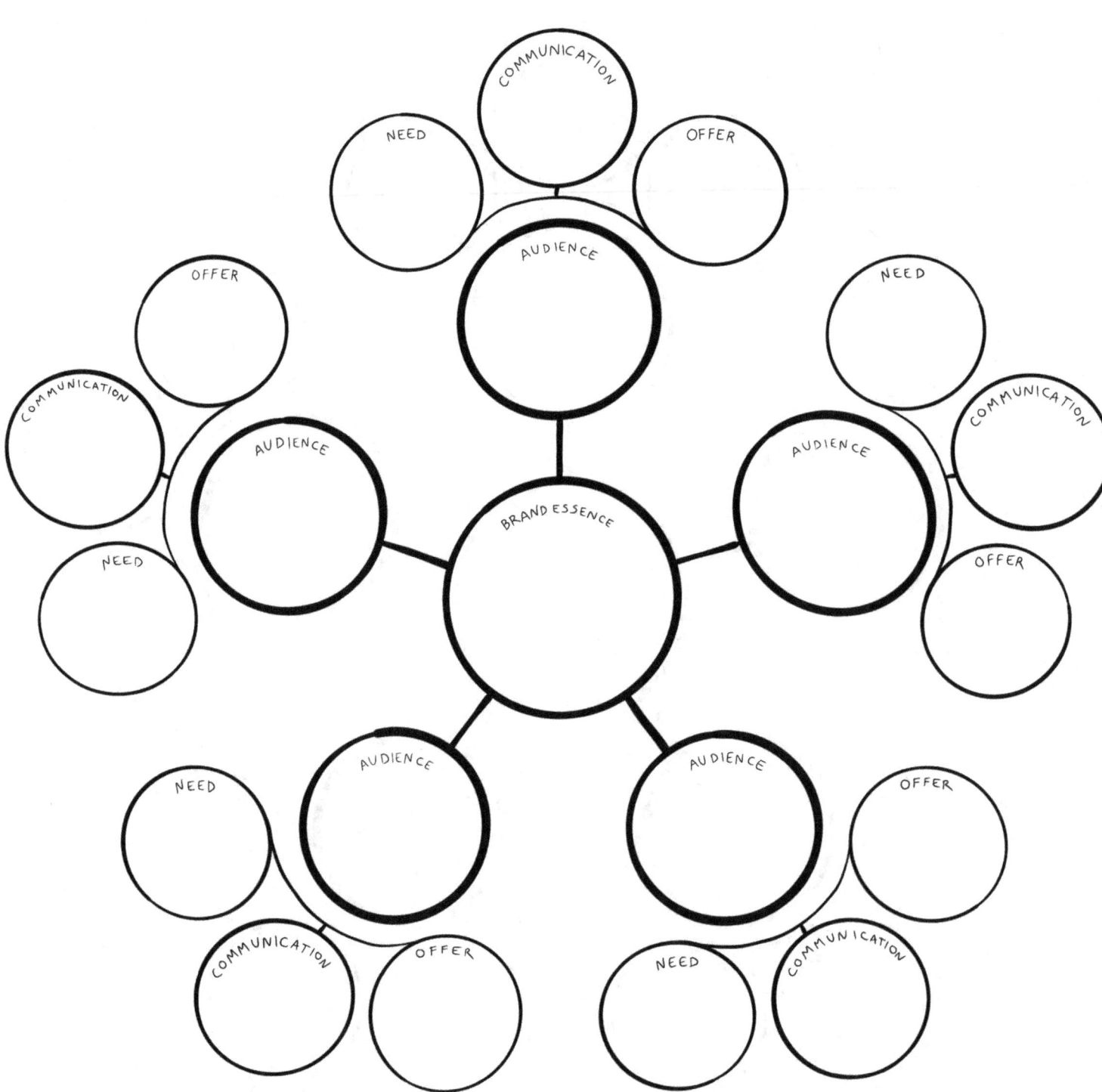

WHO IS YOUR AUDIENCE?

PROJECT:_____   DATE:_____

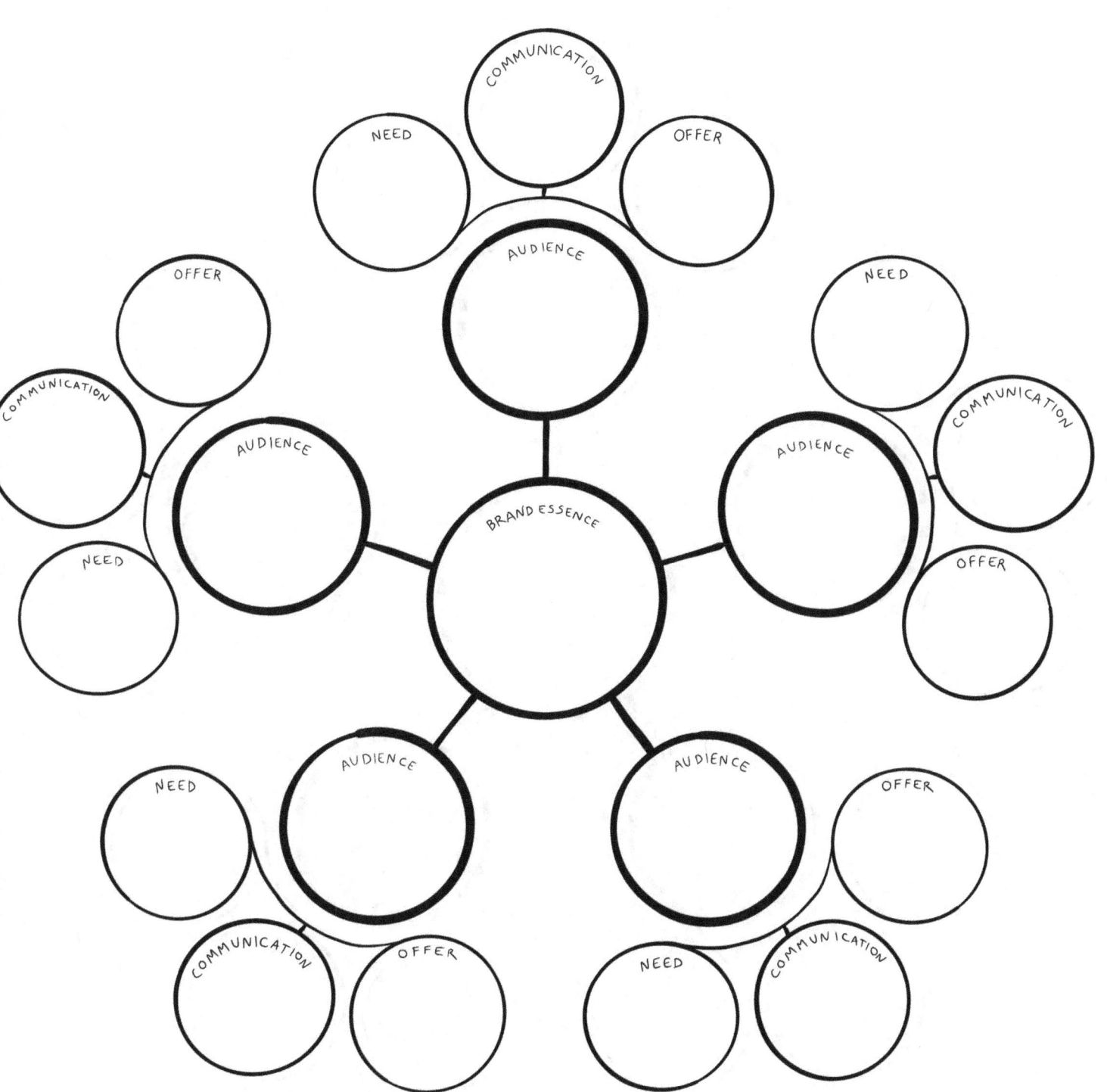

WHO IS YOUR AUDIENCE?

PROJECT:_____   DATE:_____

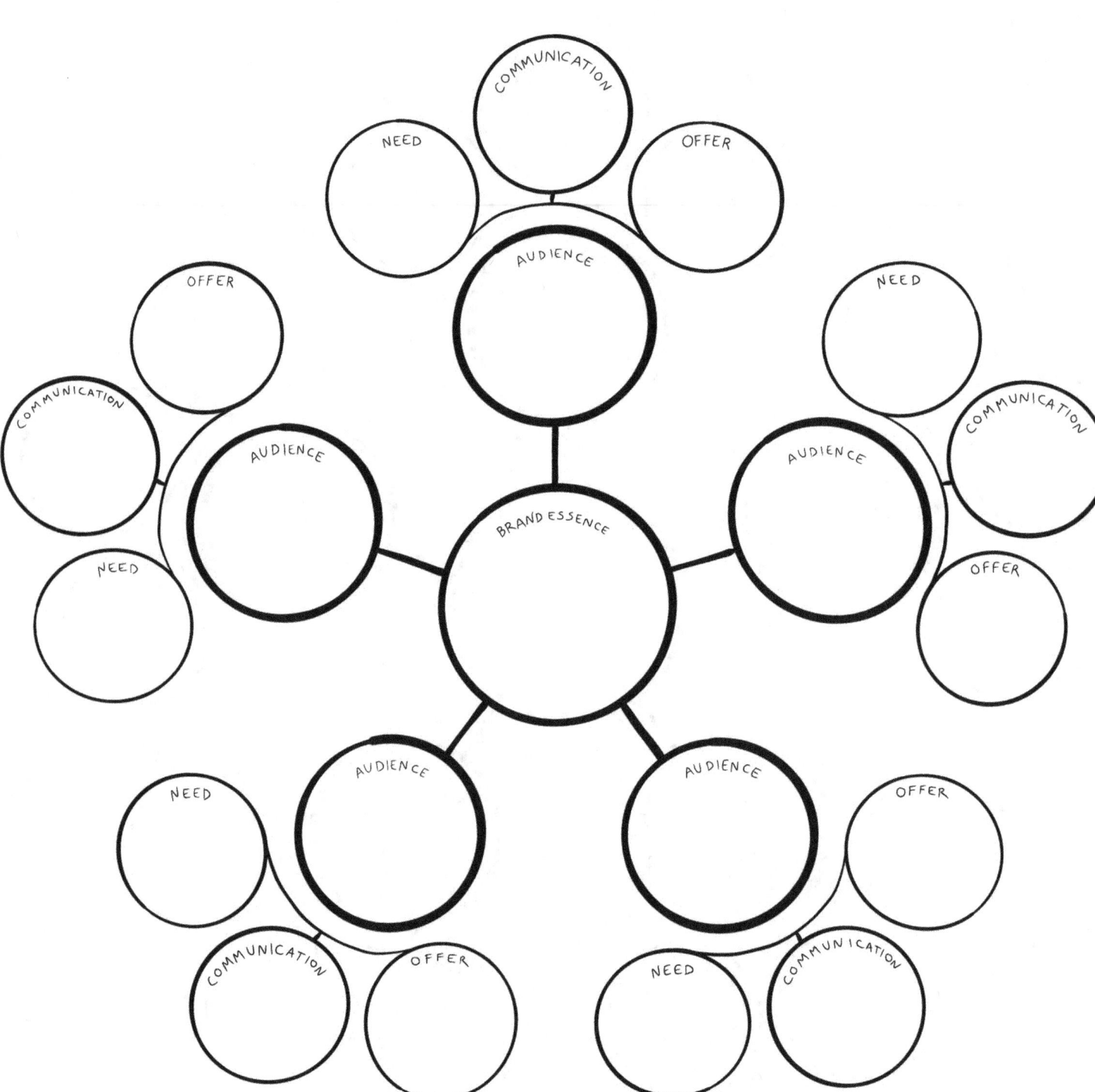

WHO IS YOUR AUDIENCE?

PROJECT:_____   DATE:_____

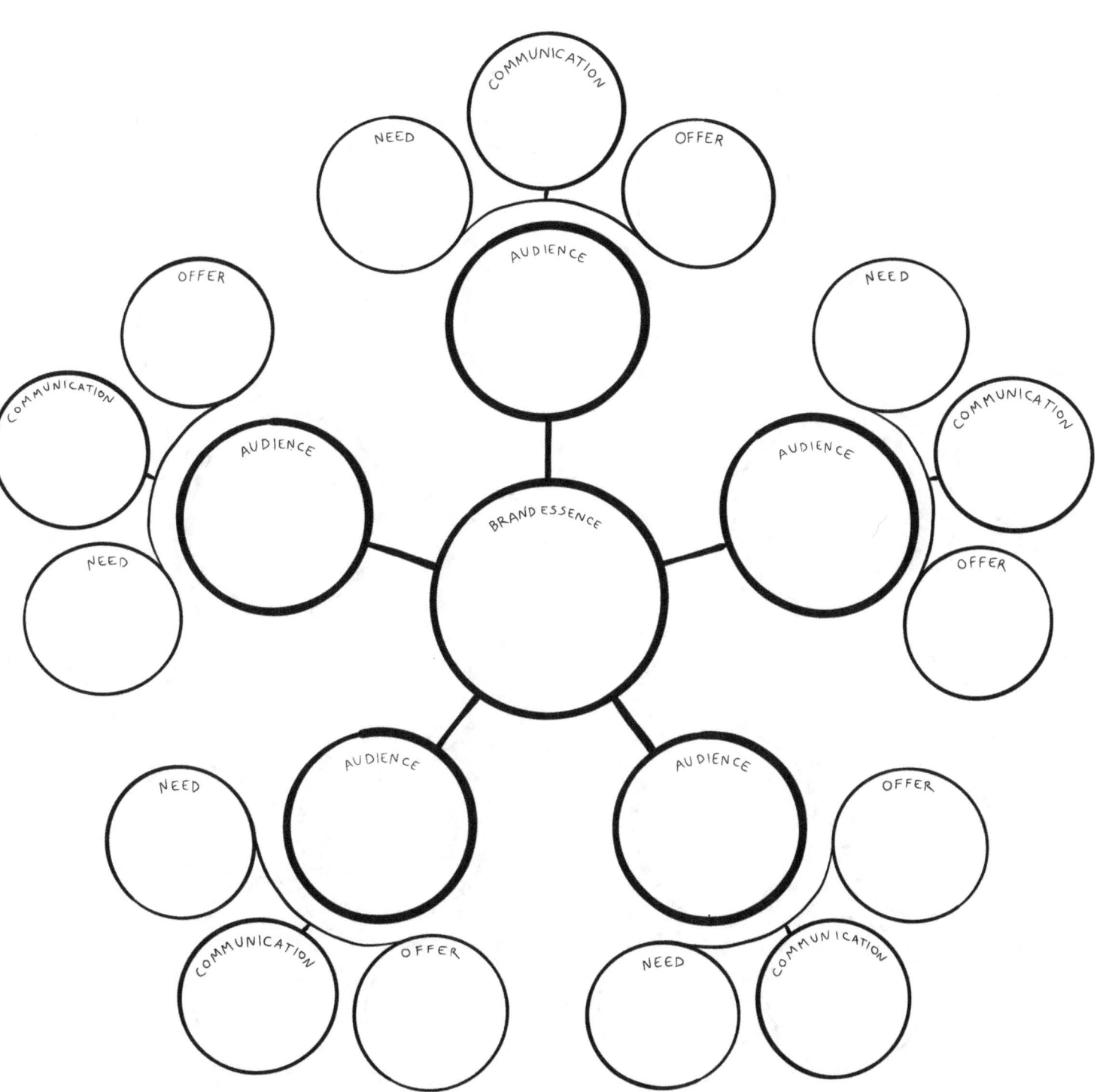

WHO IS YOUR AUDIENCE?

PROJECT:_____   DATE:_____

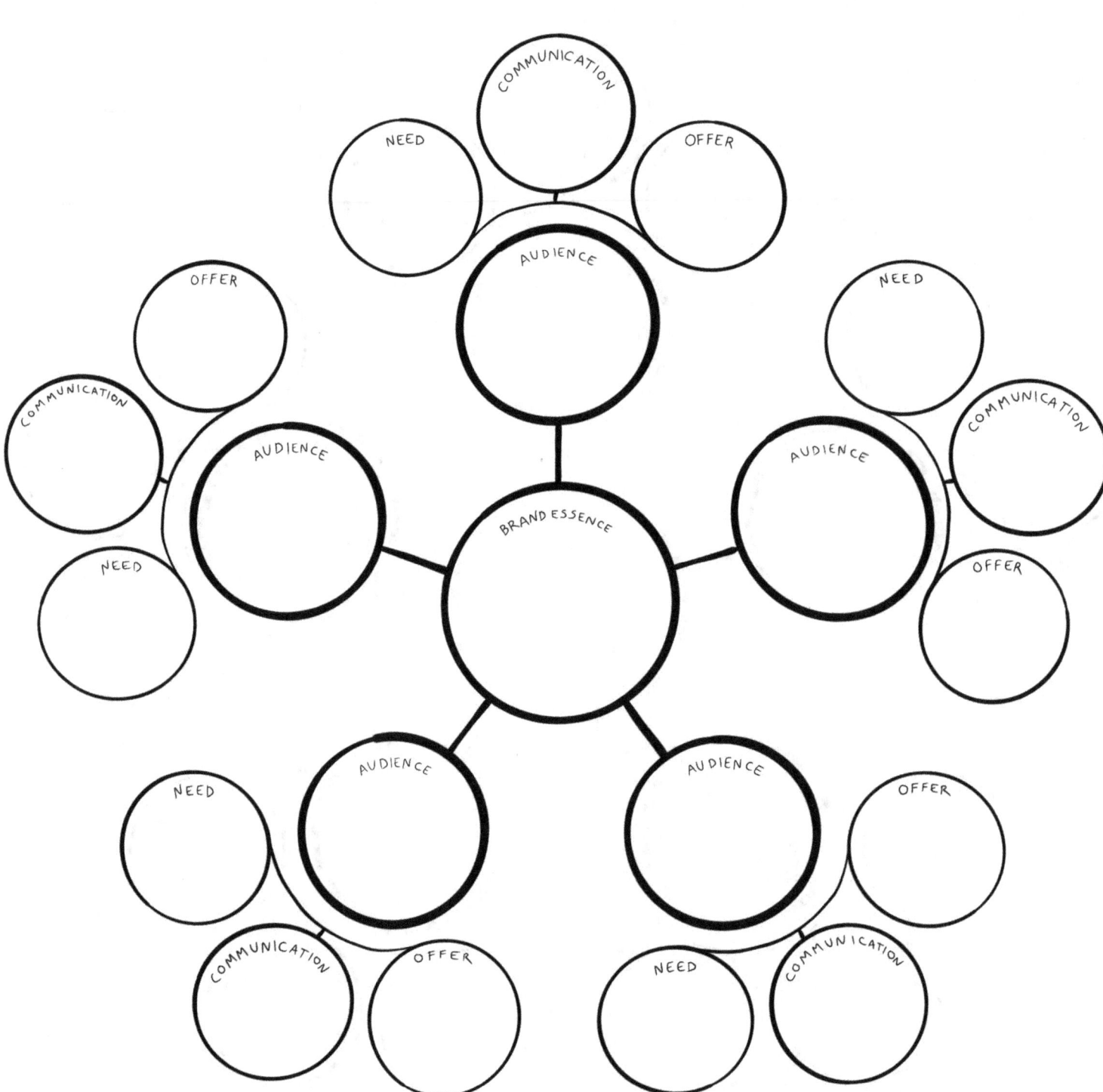

WHO IS YOUR AUDIENCE?

PROJECT:_____   DATE:_____

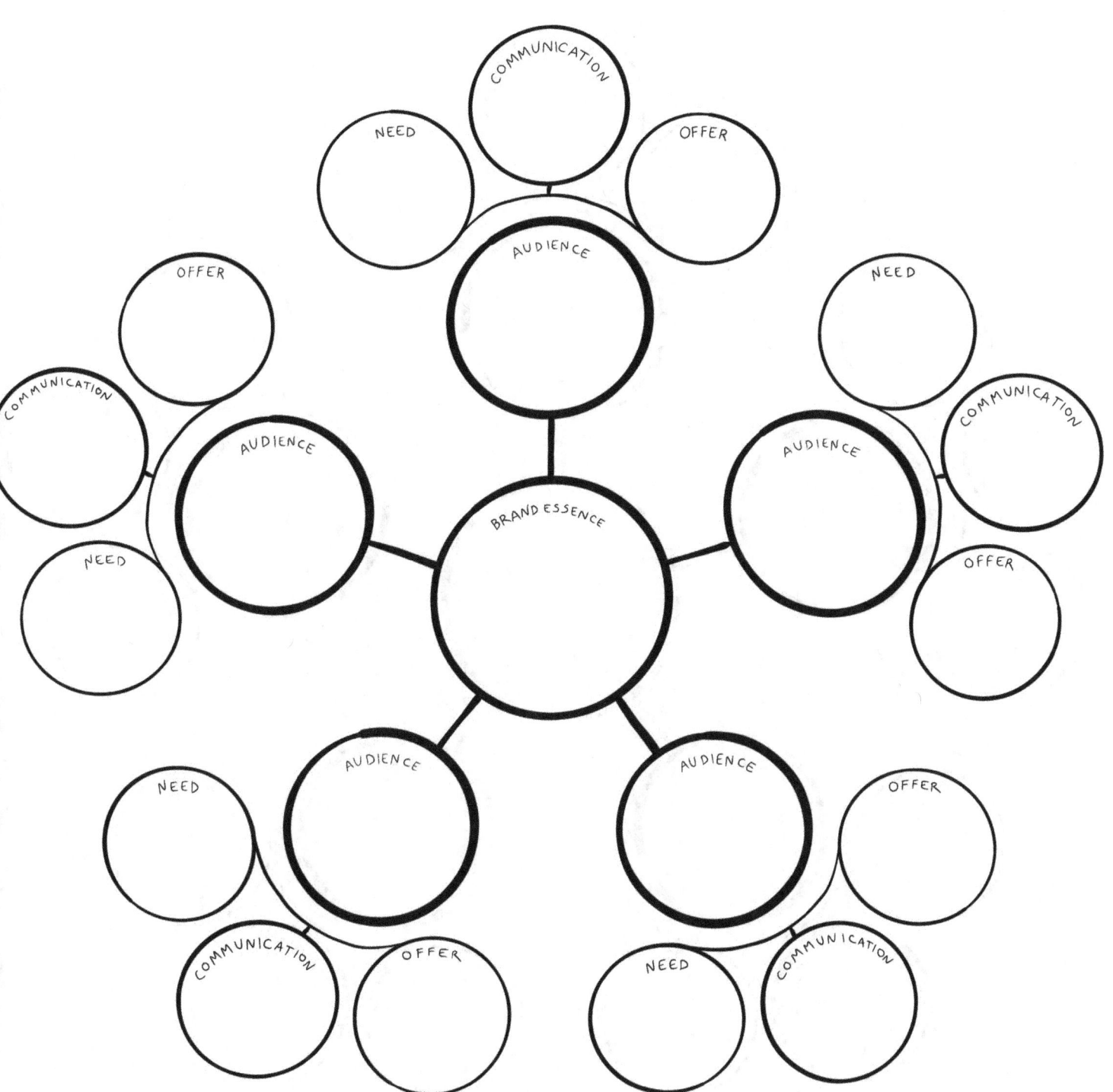

WHO IS YOUR AUDIENCE?

PROJECT:_____   DATE:_____

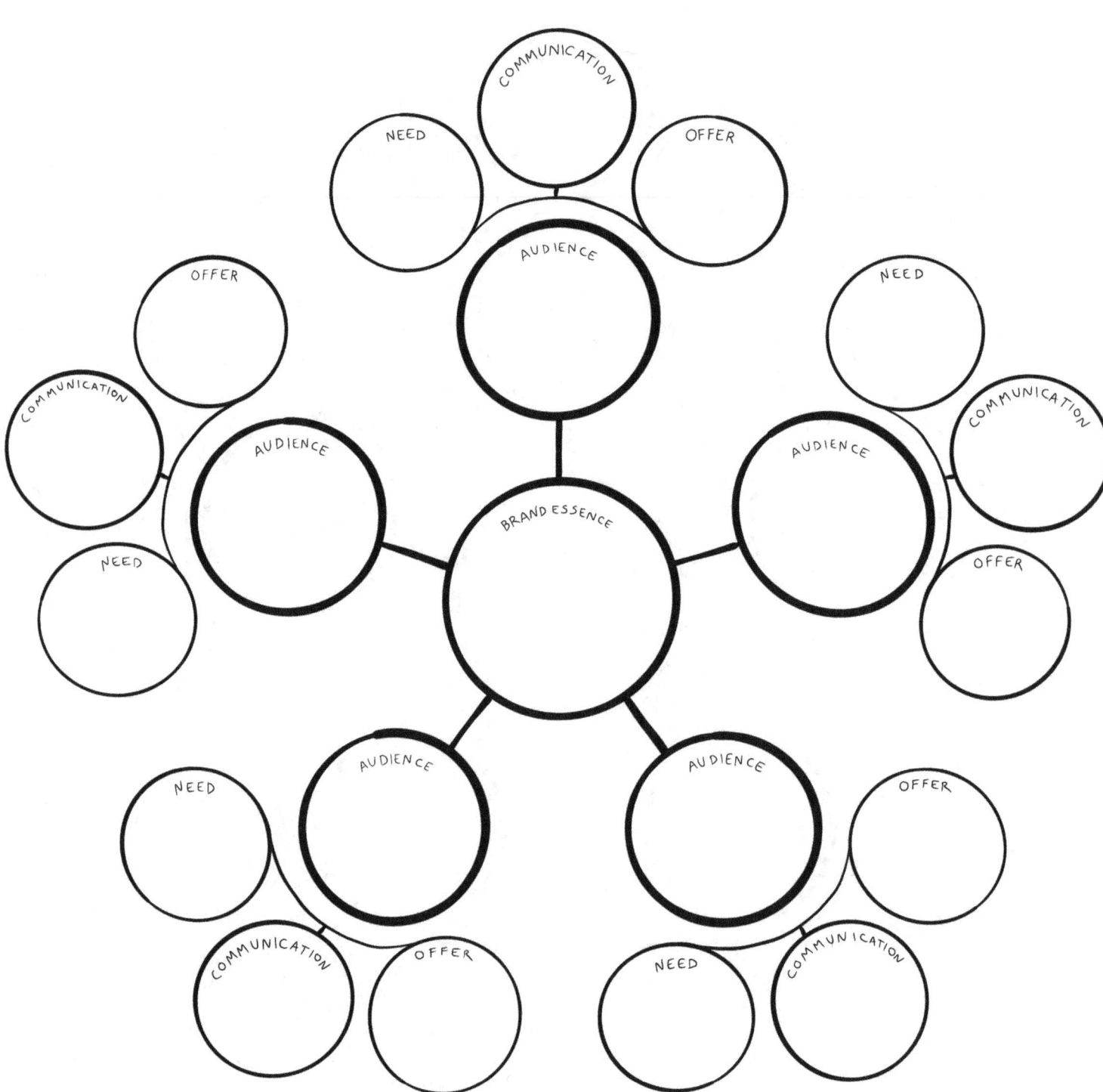

WHO IS YOUR AUDIENCE?

PROJECT:_____   DATE:_____

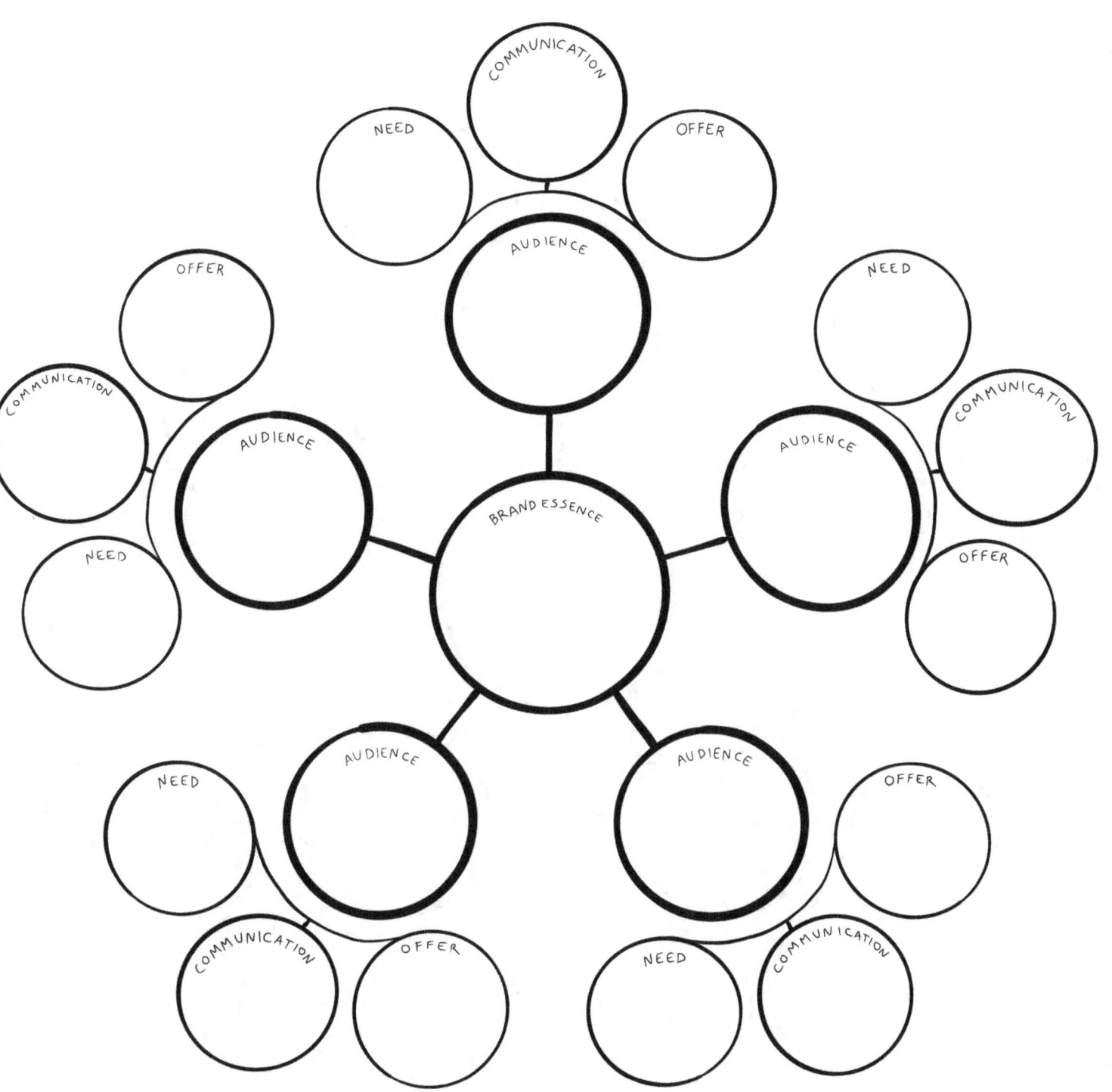

WHO IS YOUR AUDIENCE?

PROJECT:_____   DATE:_____

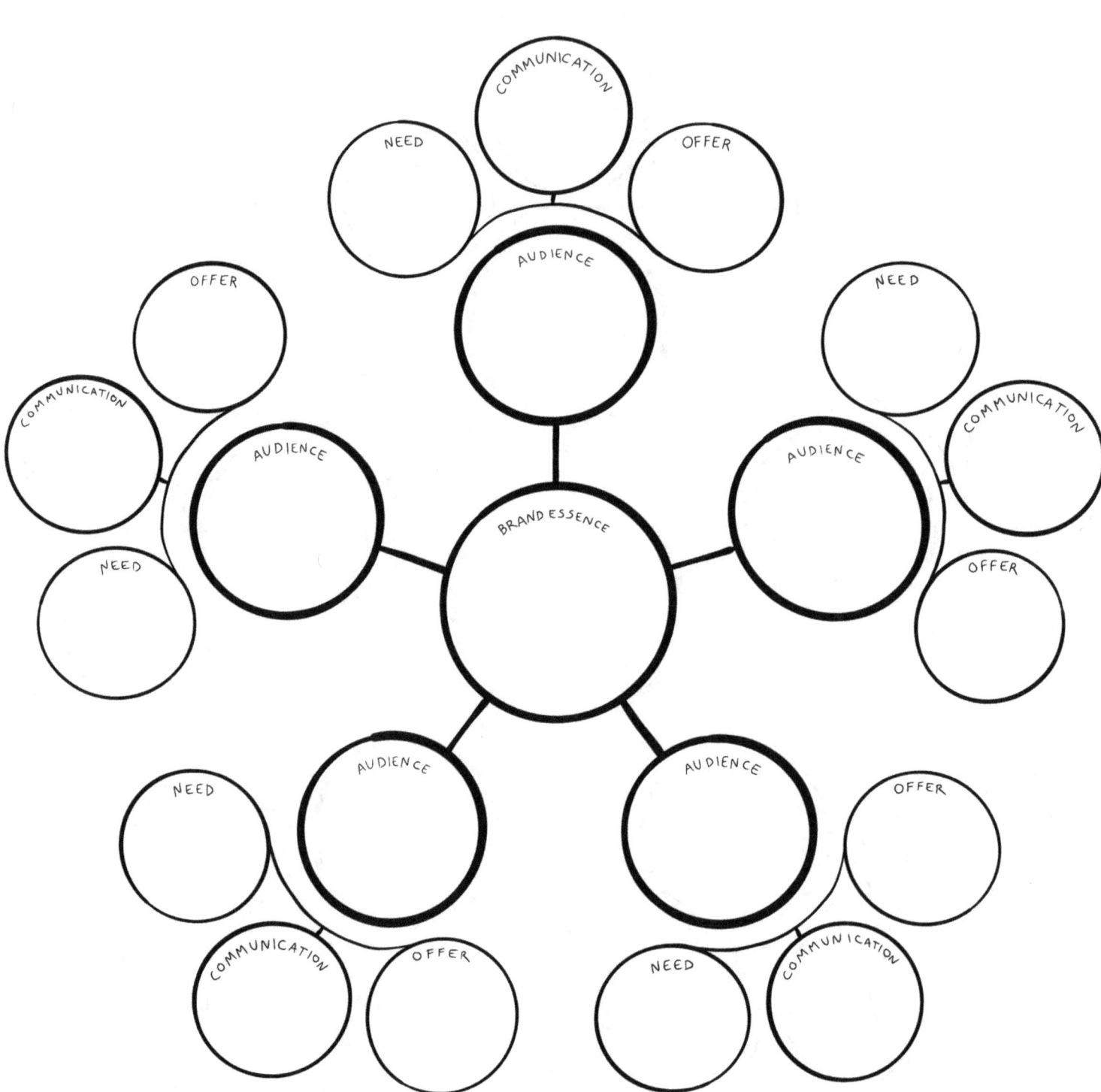

WHO IS YOUR AUDIENCE?

PROJECT:_____   DATE:_____

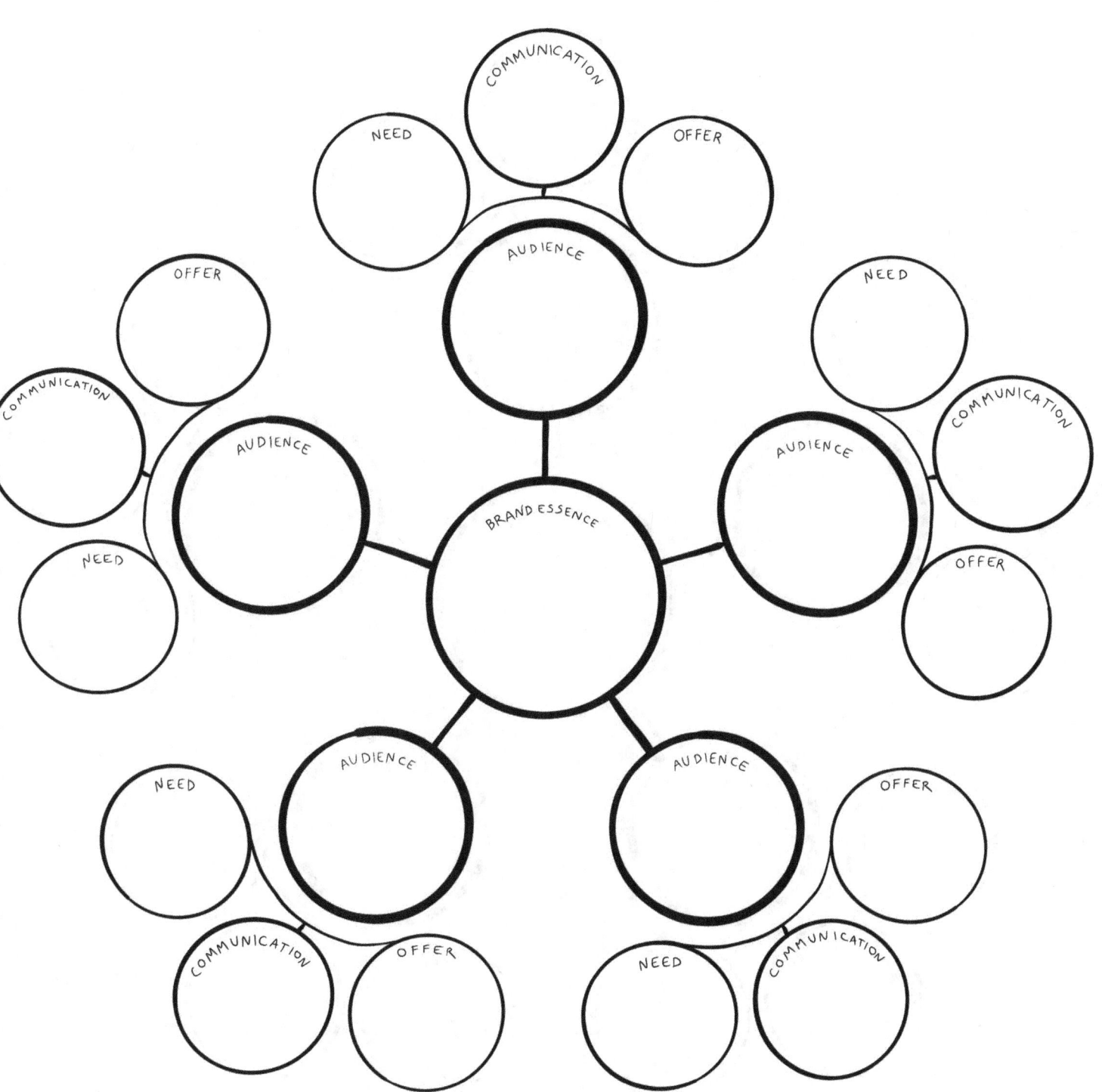

WHO IS YOUR AUDIENCE?

PROJECT:_____   DATE:_____

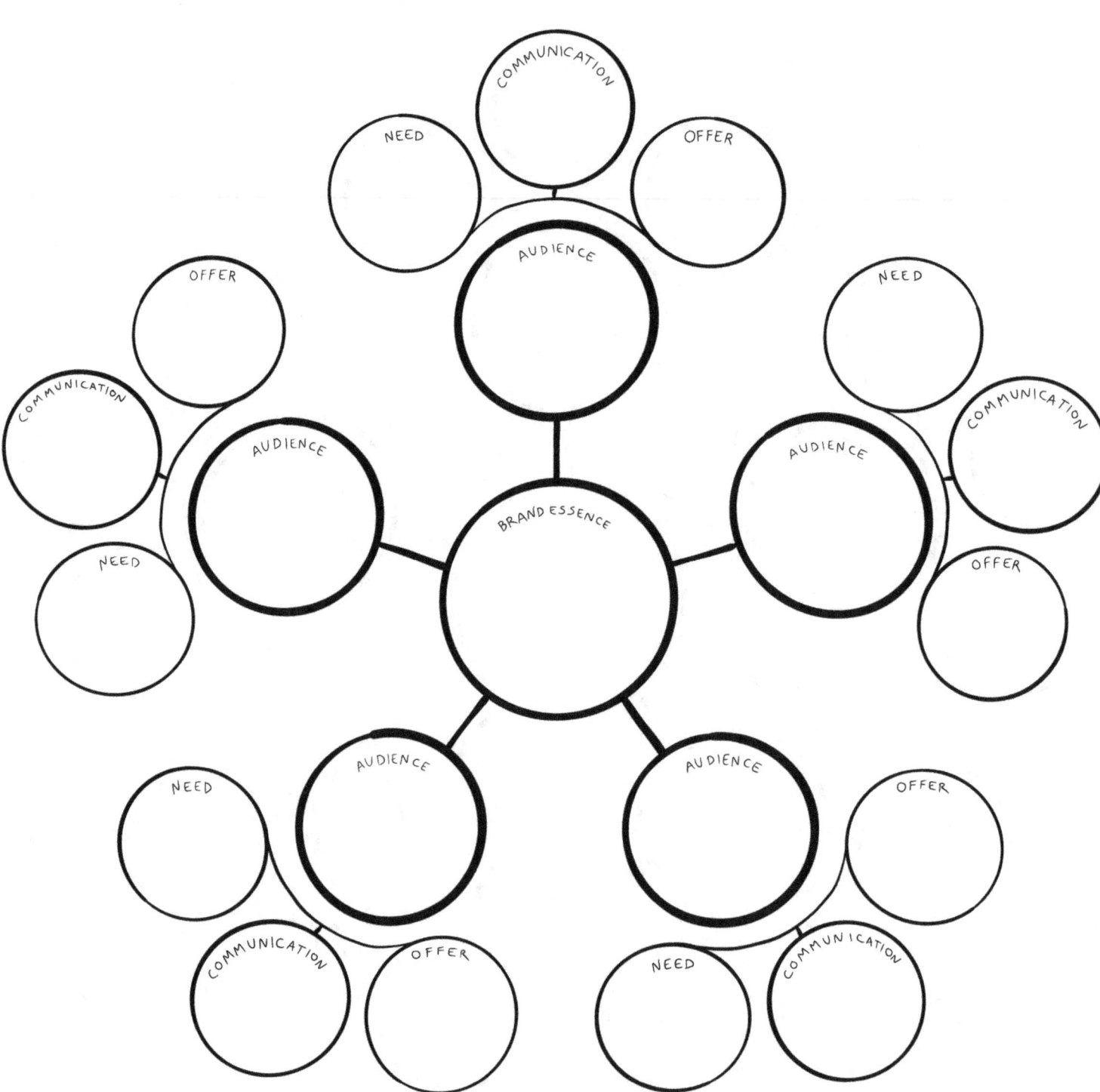

WHO IS YOUR AUDIENCE?

PROJECT:_____   DATE:_____

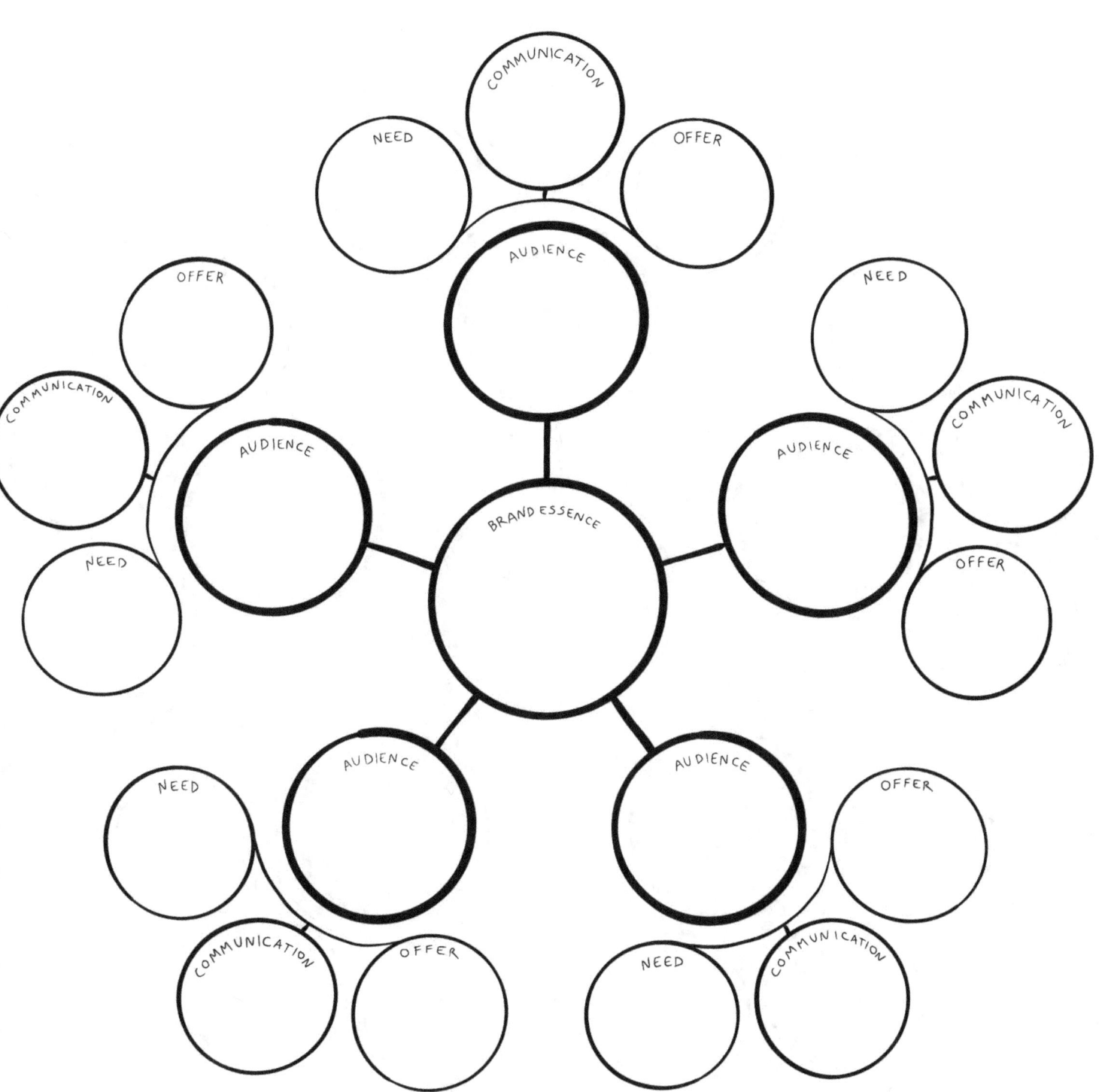

WHO IS YOUR AUDIENCE?

PROJECT:_____   DATE:_____

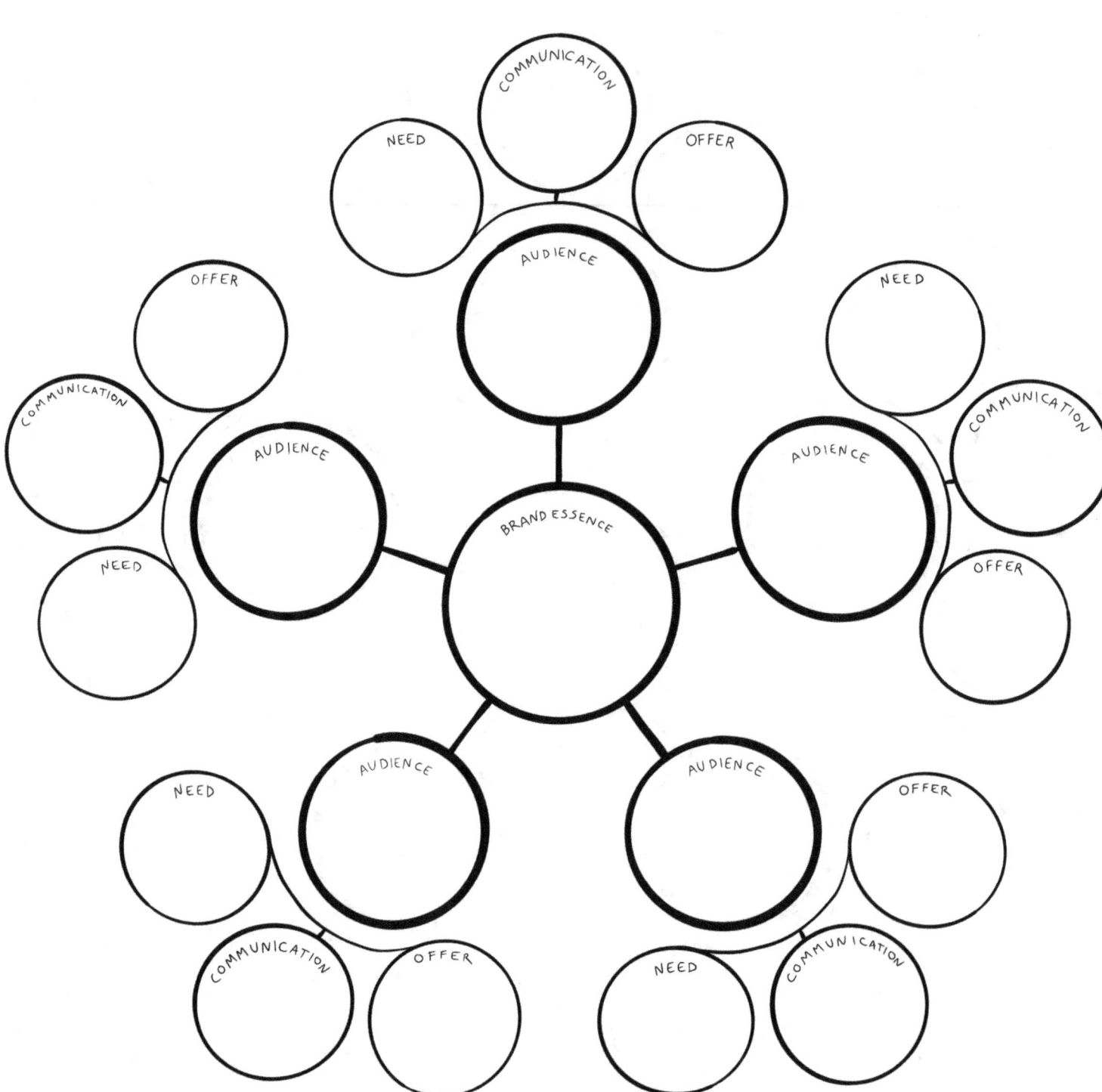

WHO IS YOUR AUDIENCE?

PROJECT:_____   DATE:_____

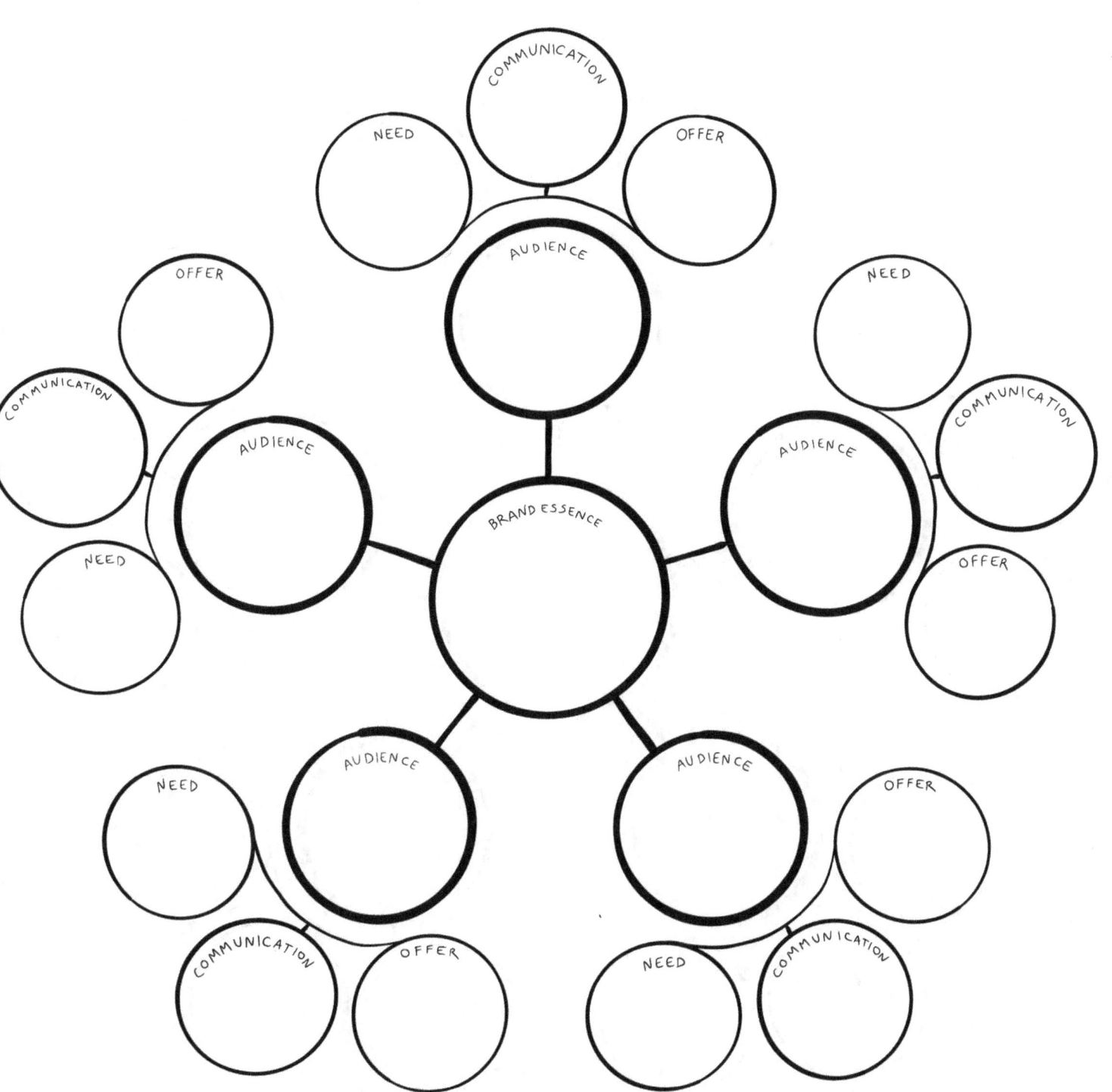

WHO IS YOUR AUDIENCE?

PROJECT: _____   DATE: _____

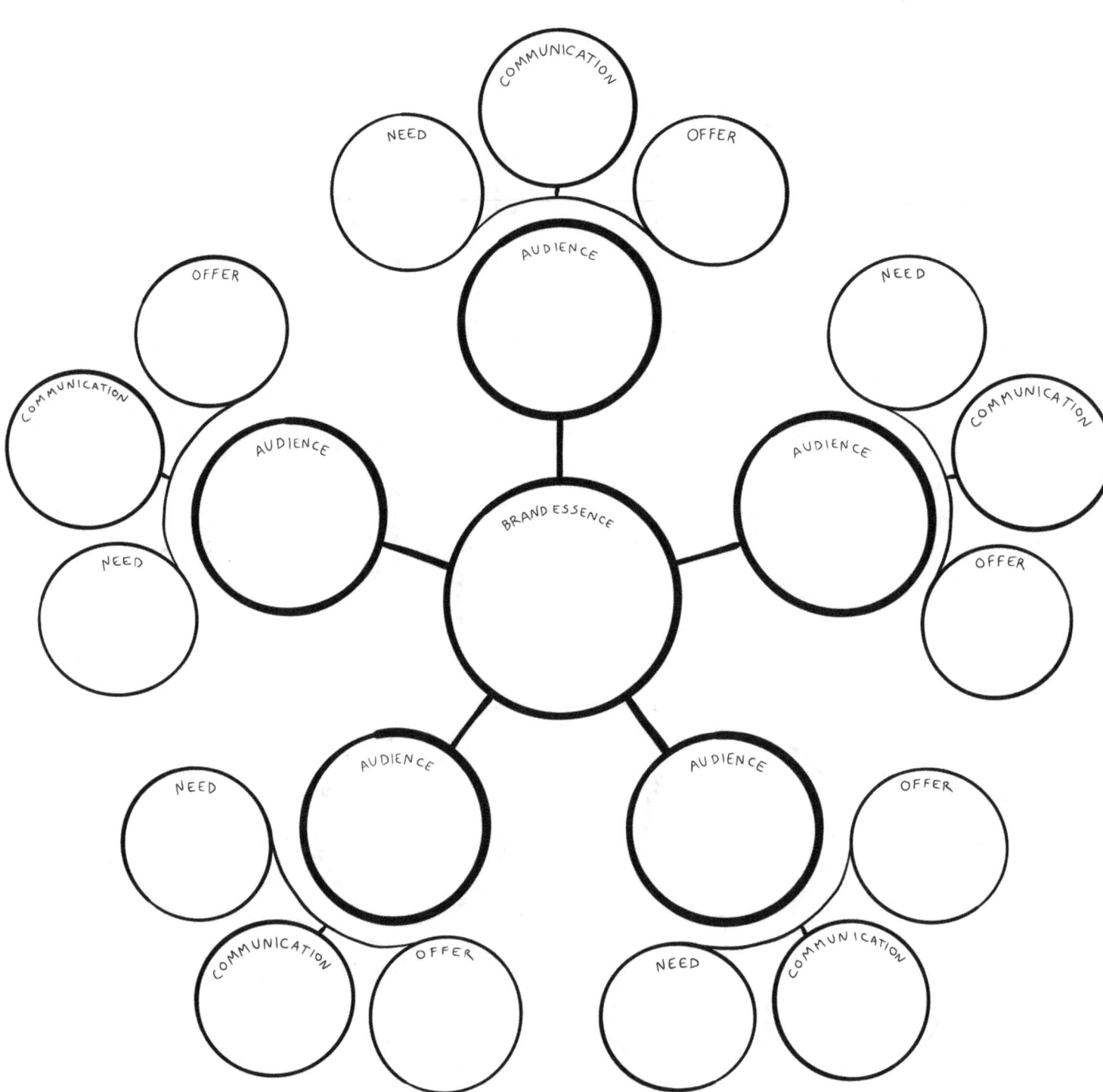

WHO IS YOUR AUDIENCE?

PROJECT:_____   DATE:_____

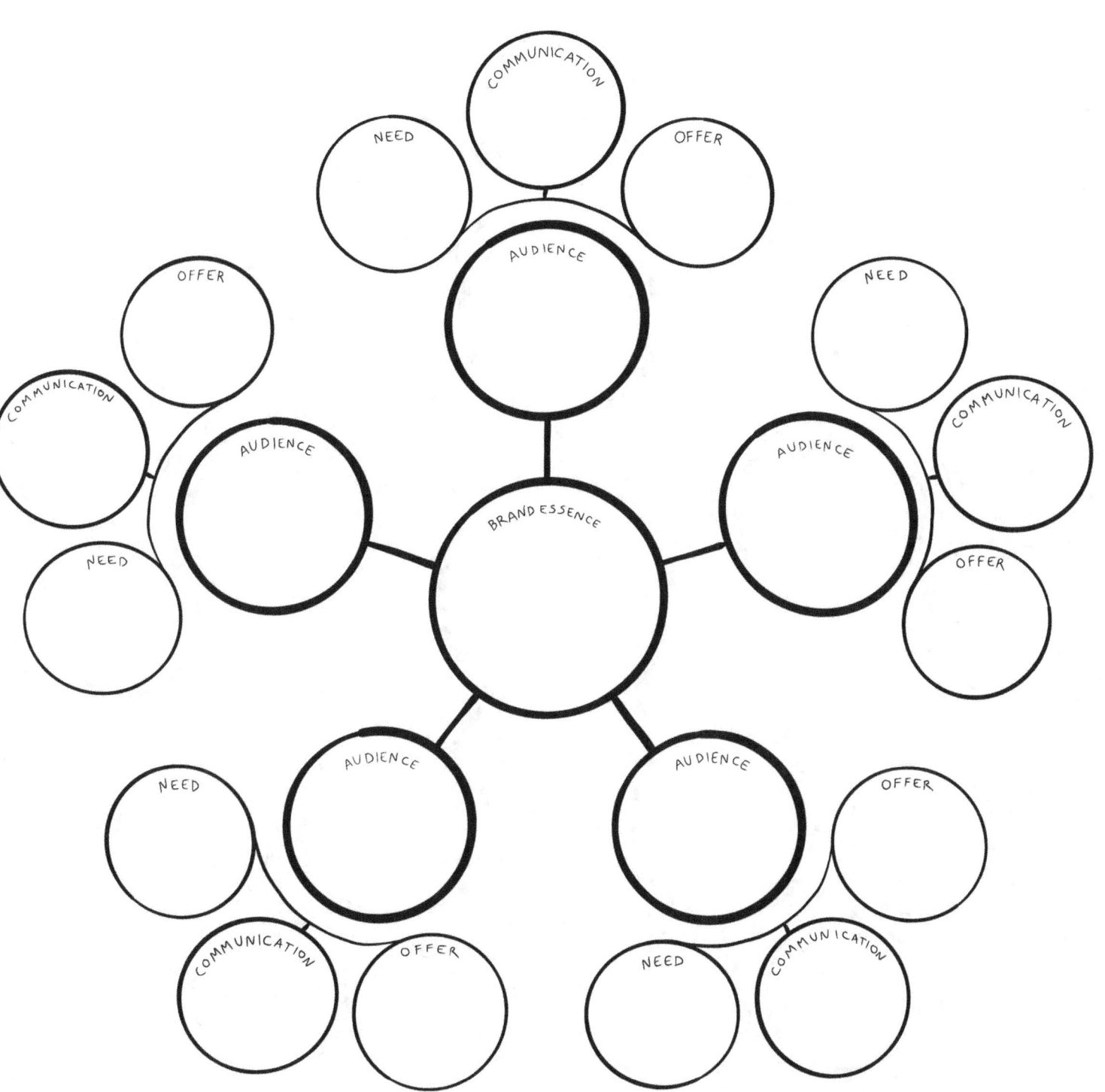

WHO IS YOUR AUDIENCE?

PROJECT:_____   DATE:_____

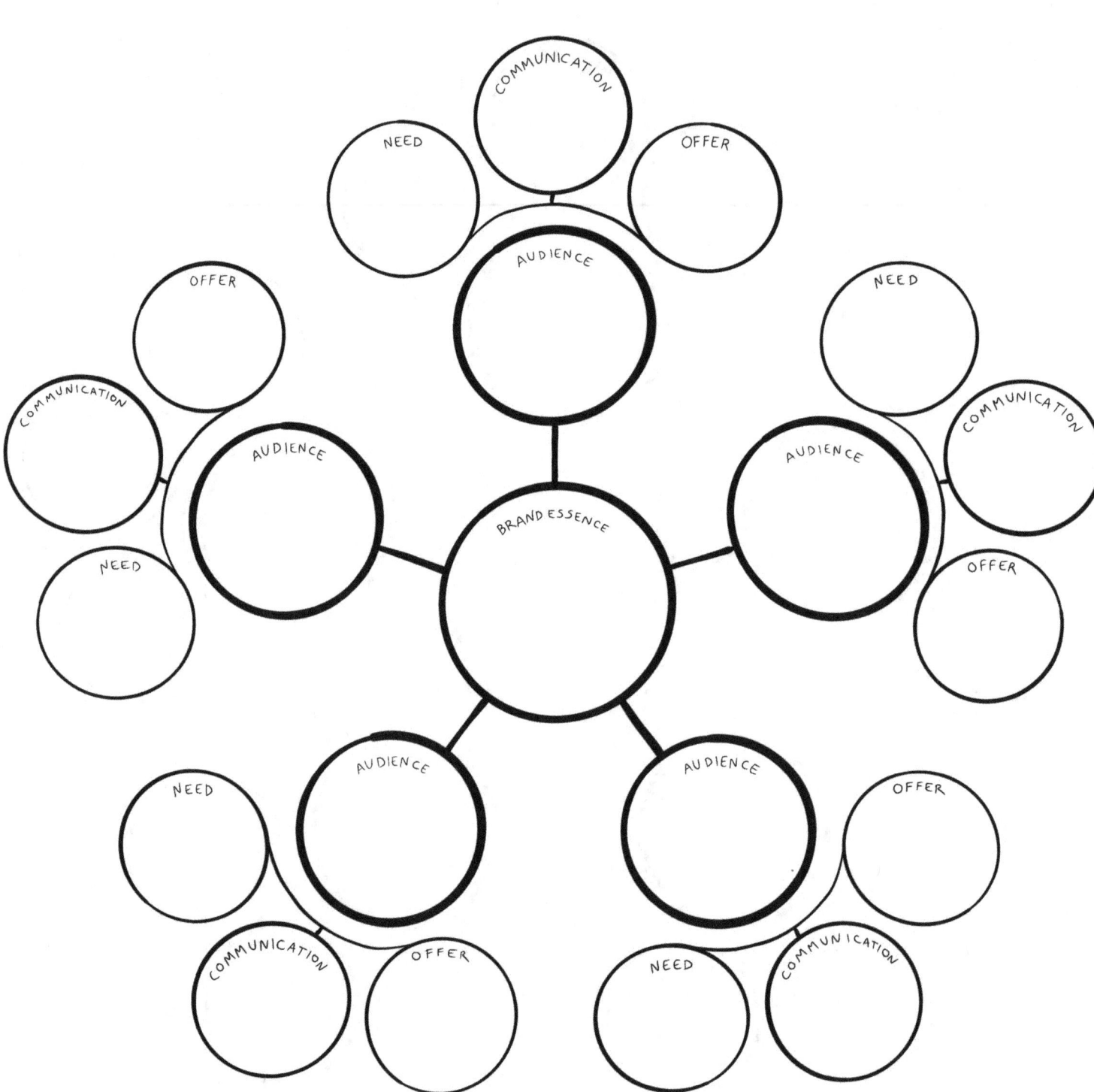

WHO IS YOUR AUDIENCE?

PROJECT:_____   DATE:_____

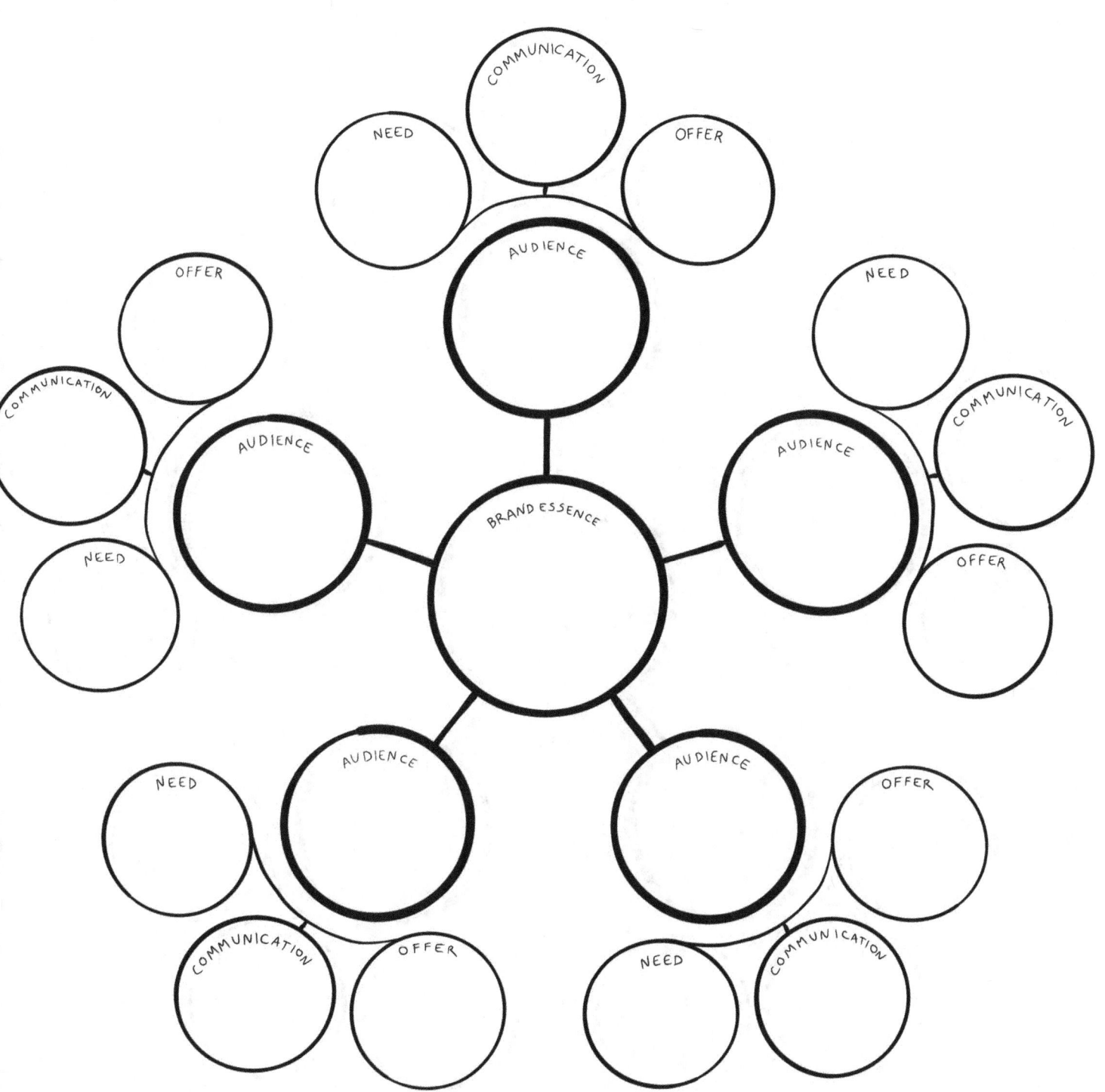

WHO IS YOUR AUDIENCE?

PROJECT:_____   DATE:_____

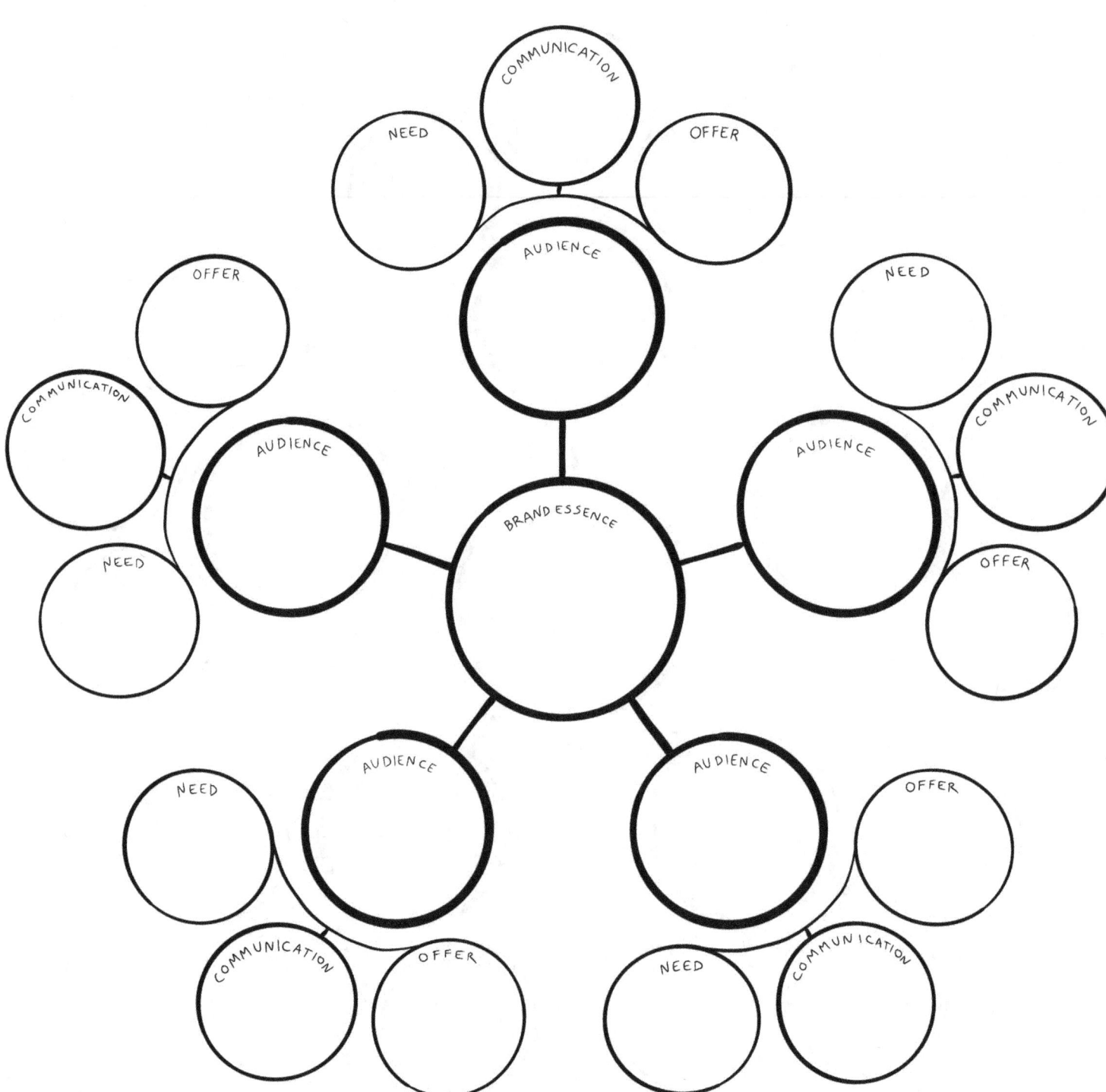

WHO IS YOUR AUDIENCE?

PROJECT:_____   DATE:_____

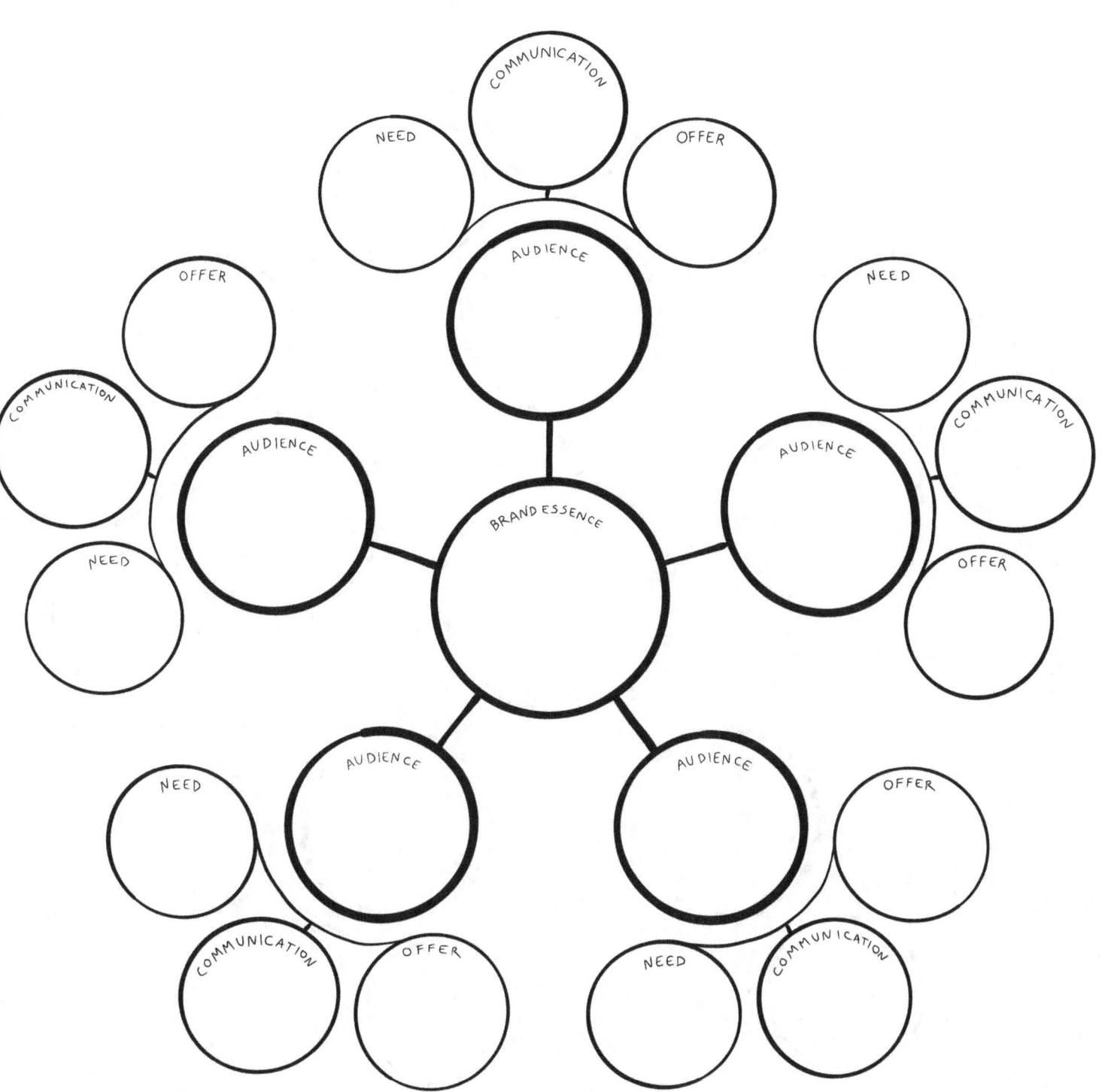

WHO IS YOUR AUDIENCE?

PROJECT: _____   DATE: _____

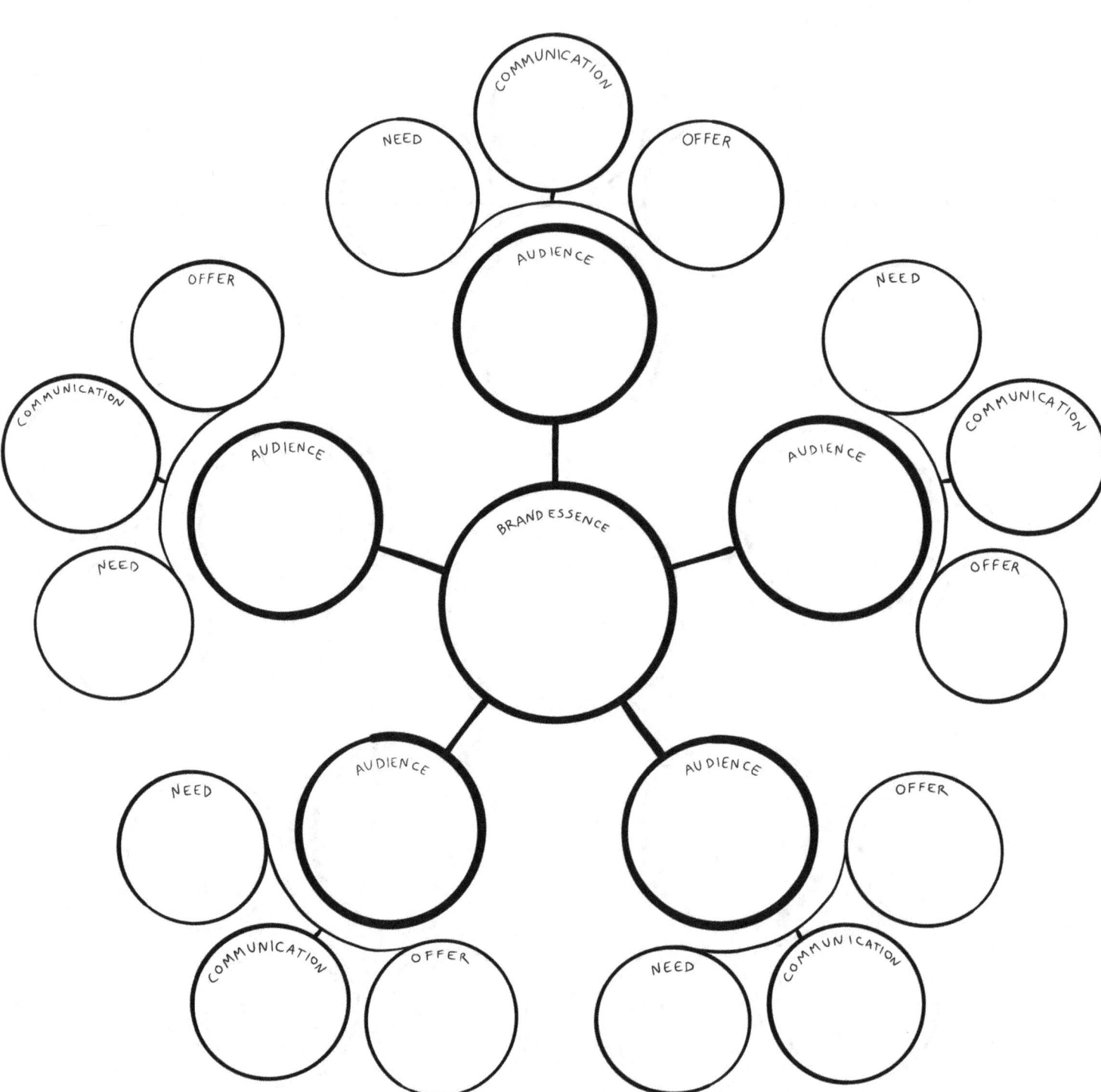

WHO IS YOUR AUDIENCE?

PROJECT:_____   DATE:_____

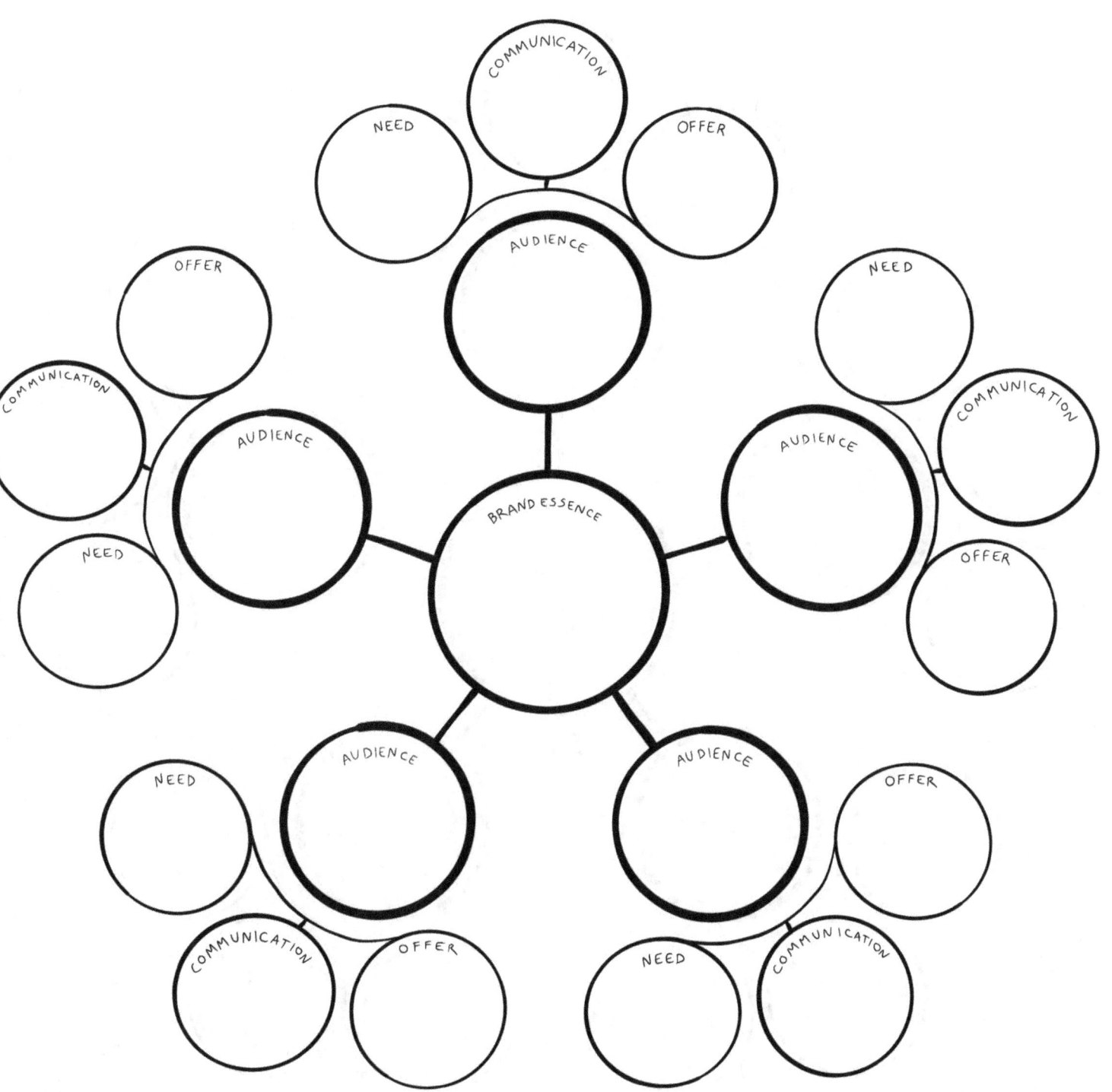

WHO IS YOUR AUDIENCE?

PROJECT:_____ DATE:_____

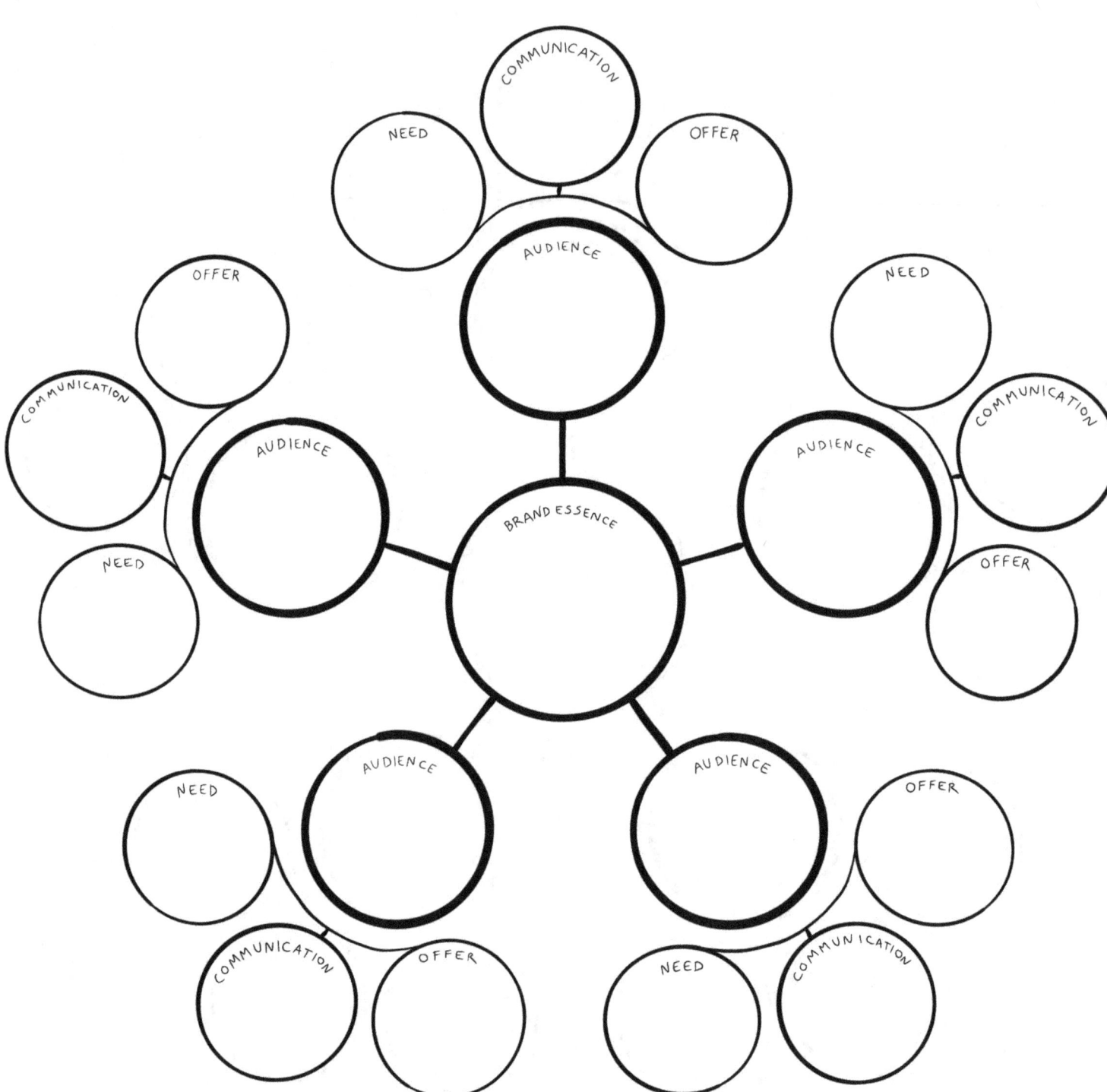

WHO IS YOUR AUDIENCE?

PROJECT: _____

DATE: _____

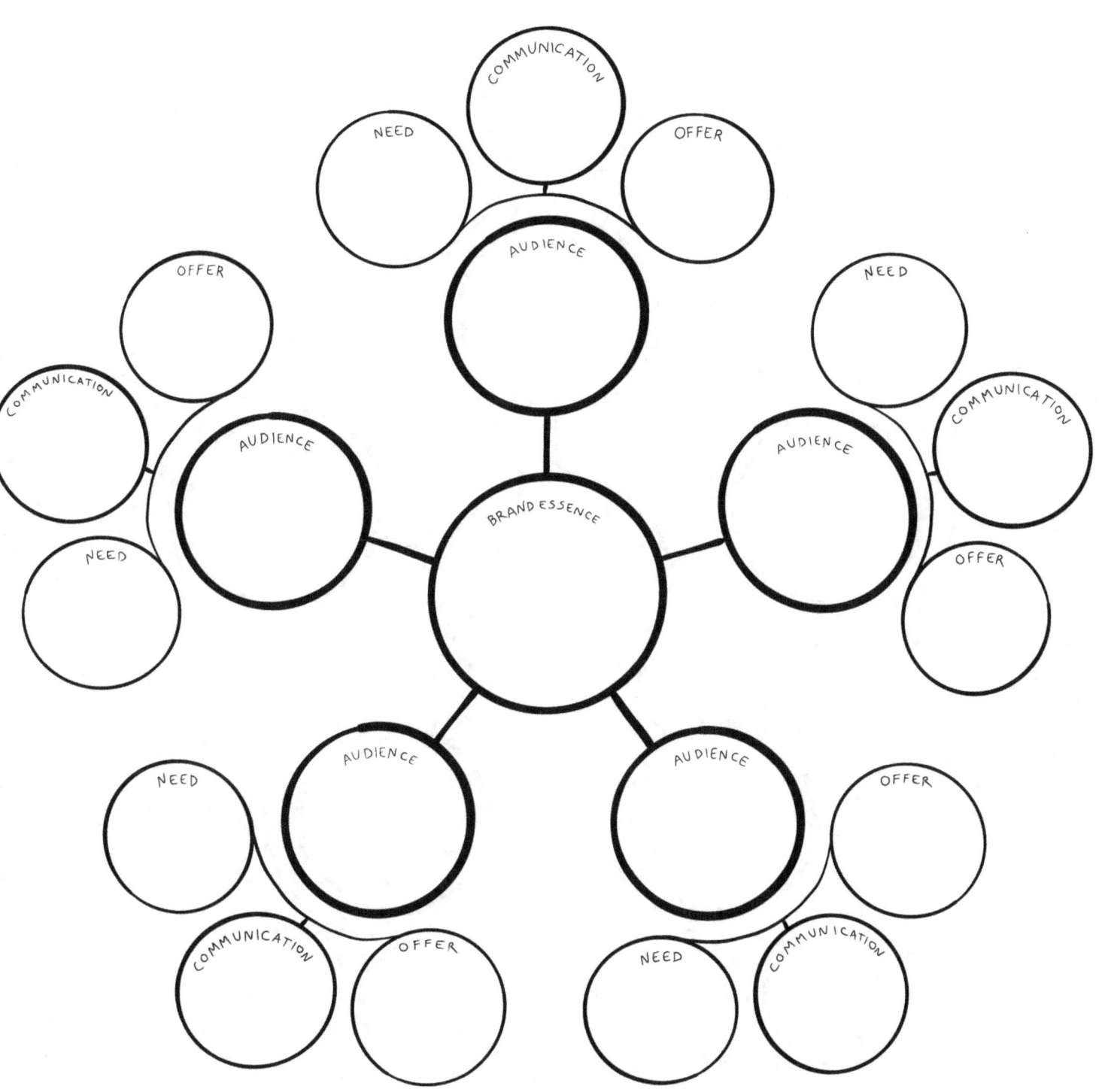

WHO IS YOUR AUDIENCE?

PROJECT:_____   DATE:_____

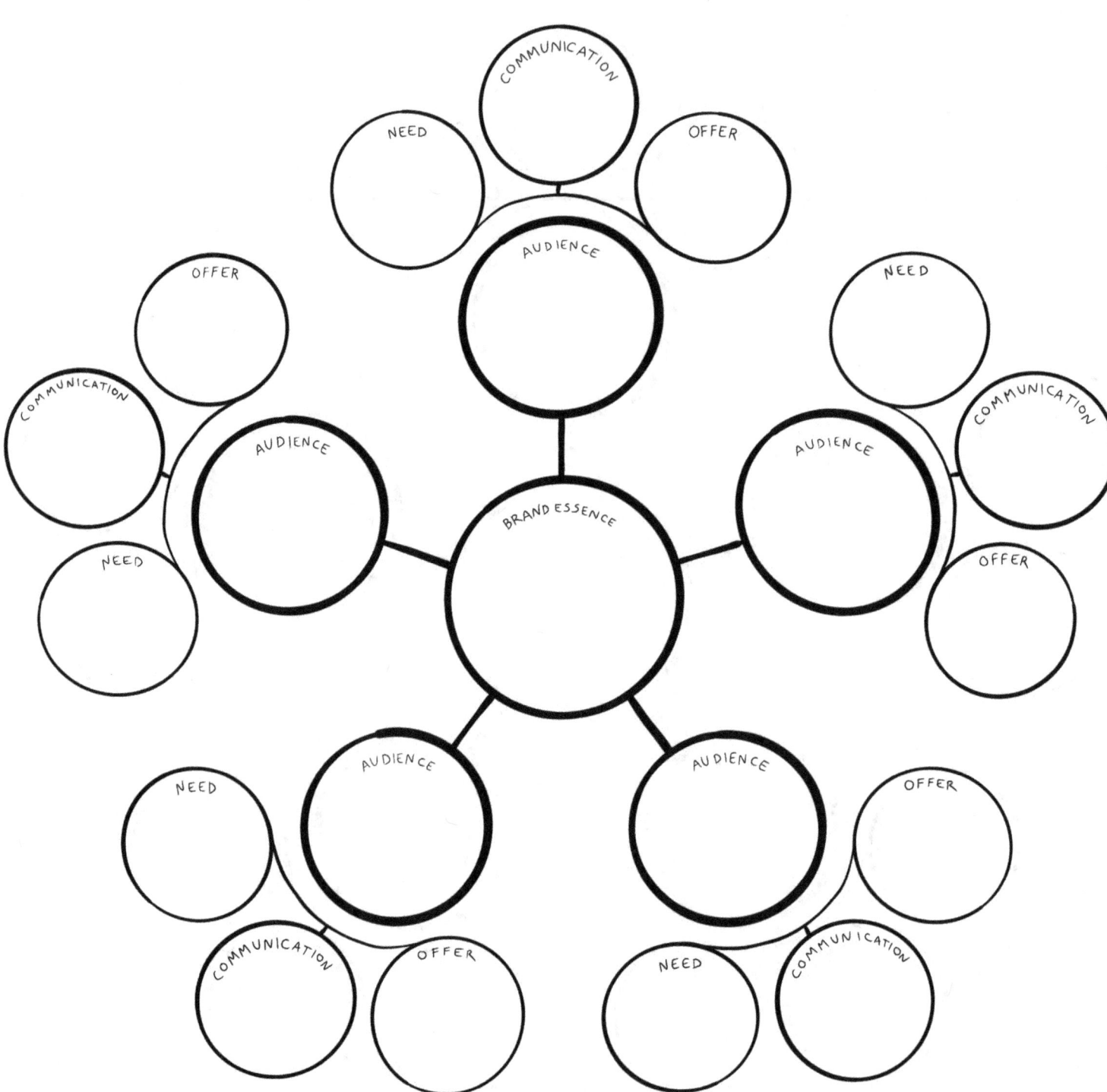

WHO IS YOUR AUDIENCE?

PROJECT:_____   DATE:_____

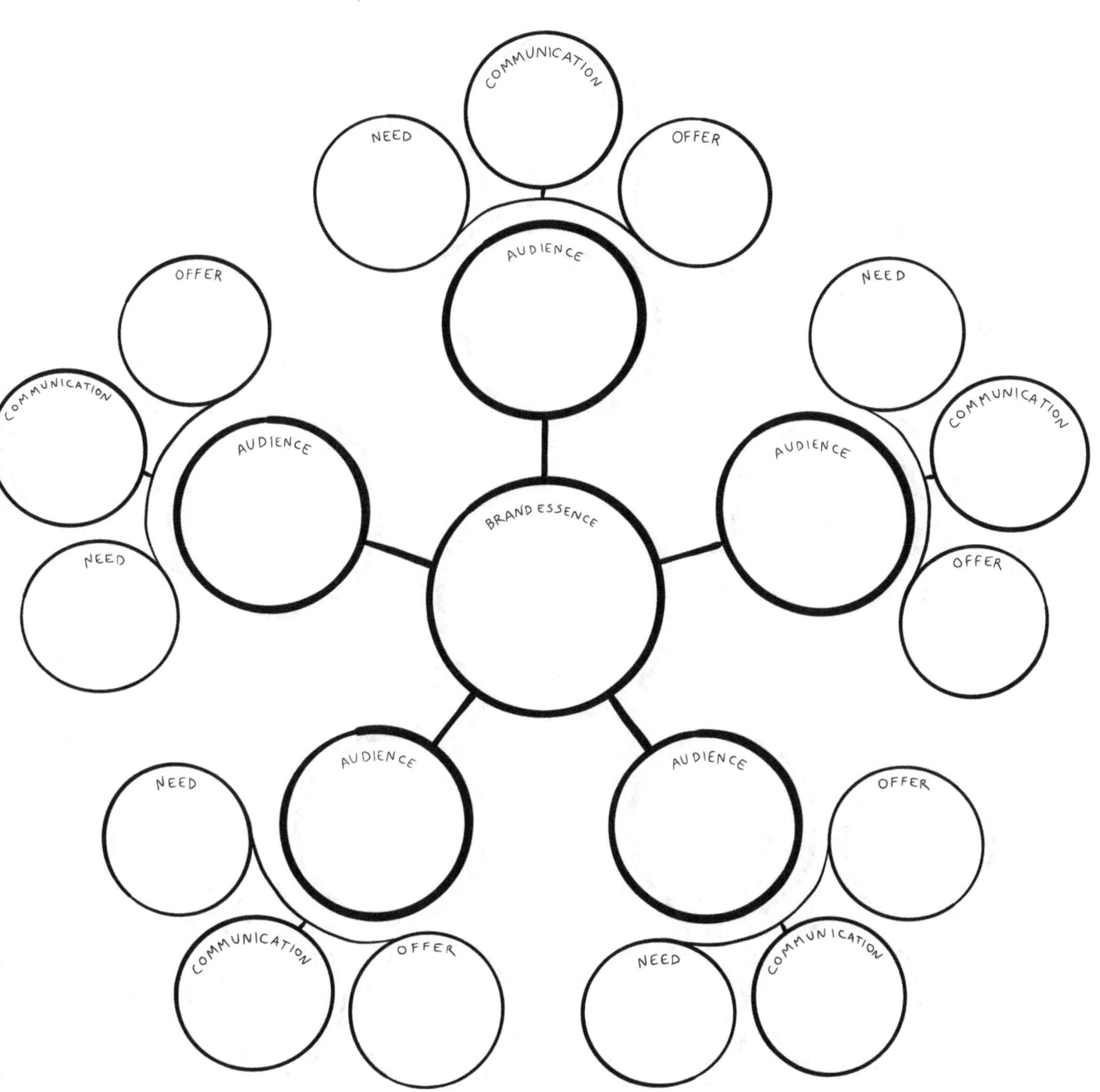

WHO IS YOUR AUDIENCE?

PROJECT: _____   DATE: _____

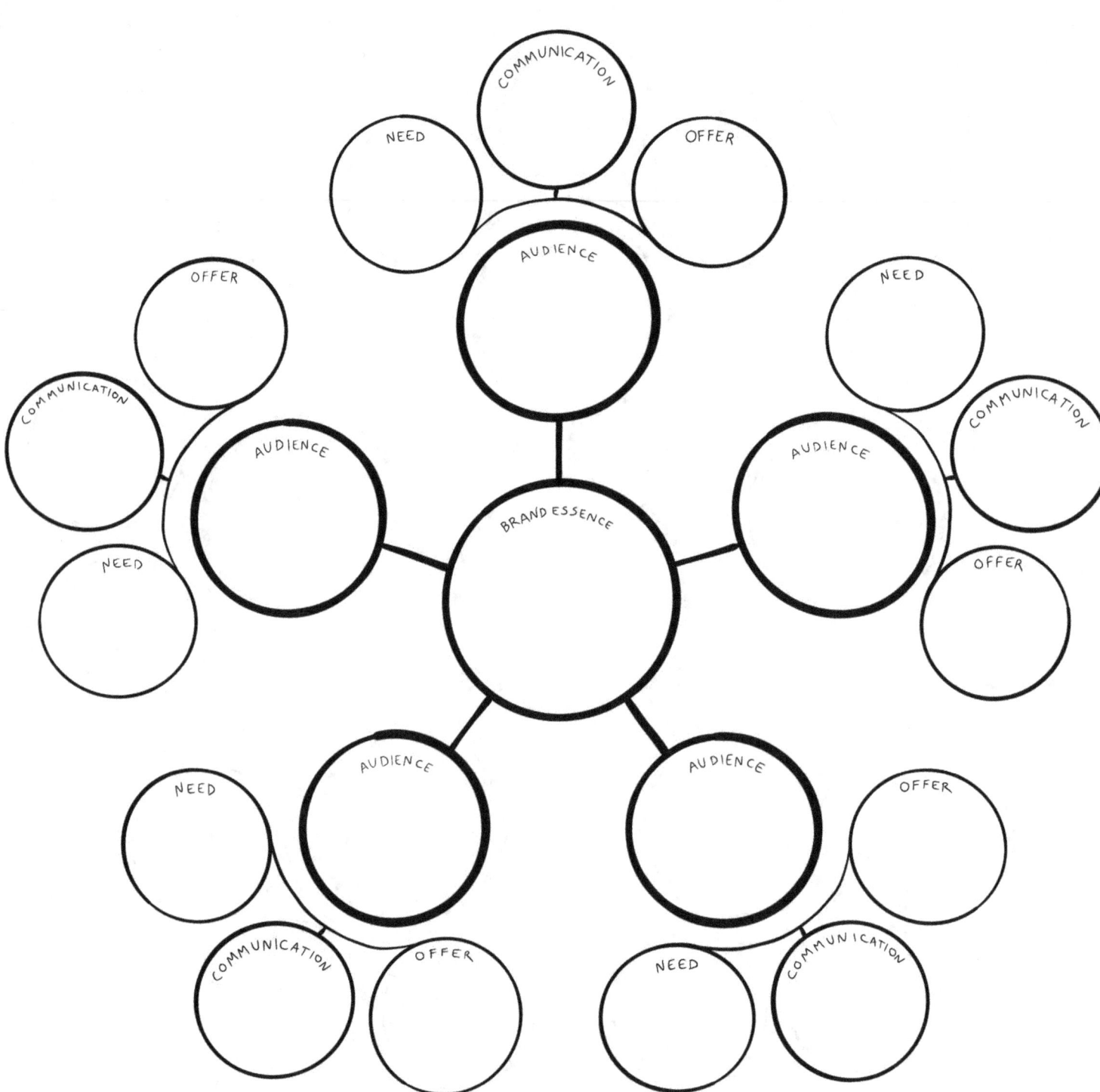

WHO IS YOUR AUDIENCE?

PROJECT:_____   DATE:_____

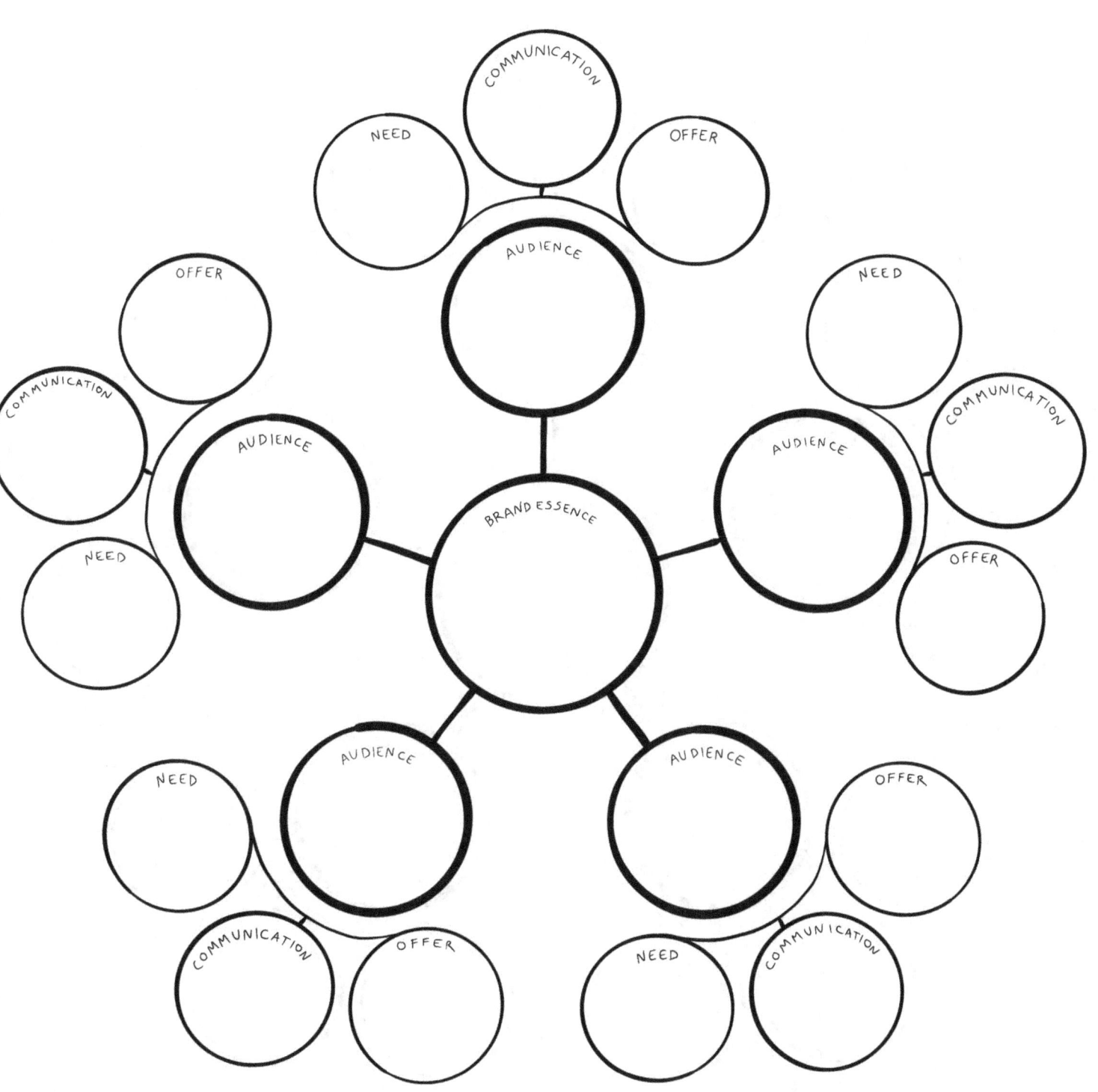

WHO IS YOUR AUDIENCE?

PROJECT:_____

DATE:_____

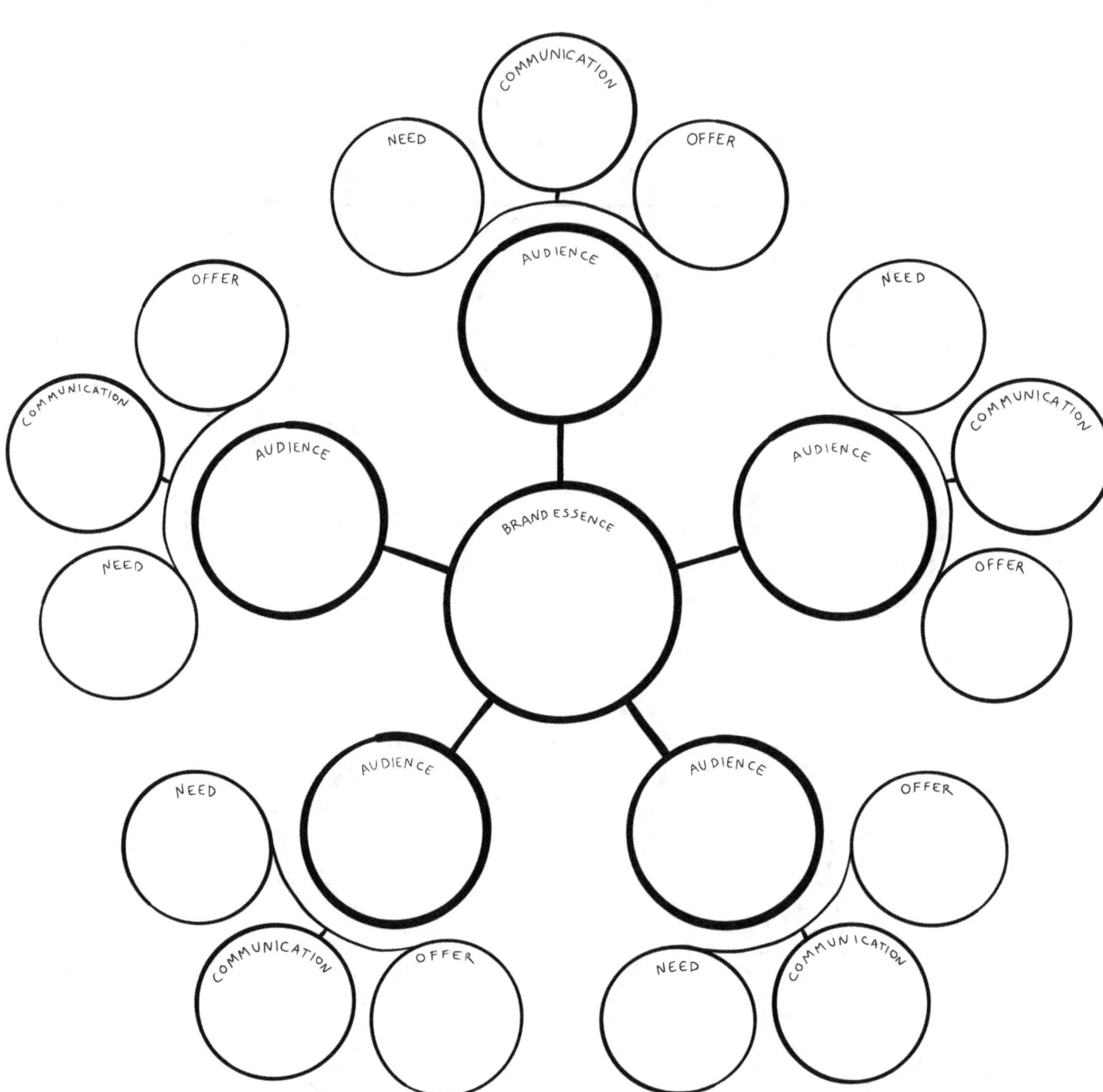

WHO IS YOUR AUDIENCE?

PROJECT:_____   DATE:_____

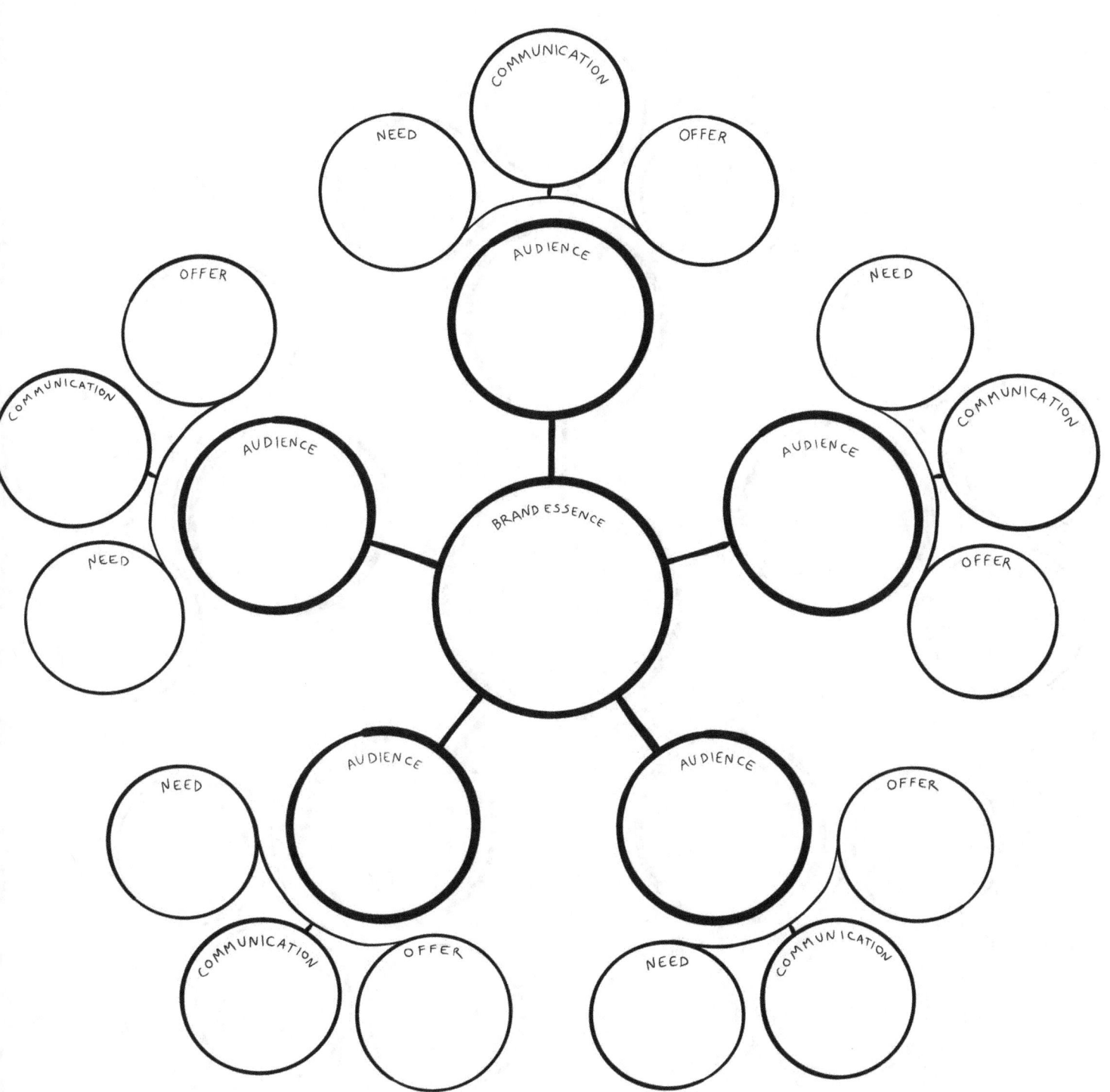

WHO IS YOUR AUDIENCE?

PROJECT:_____   DATE:_____

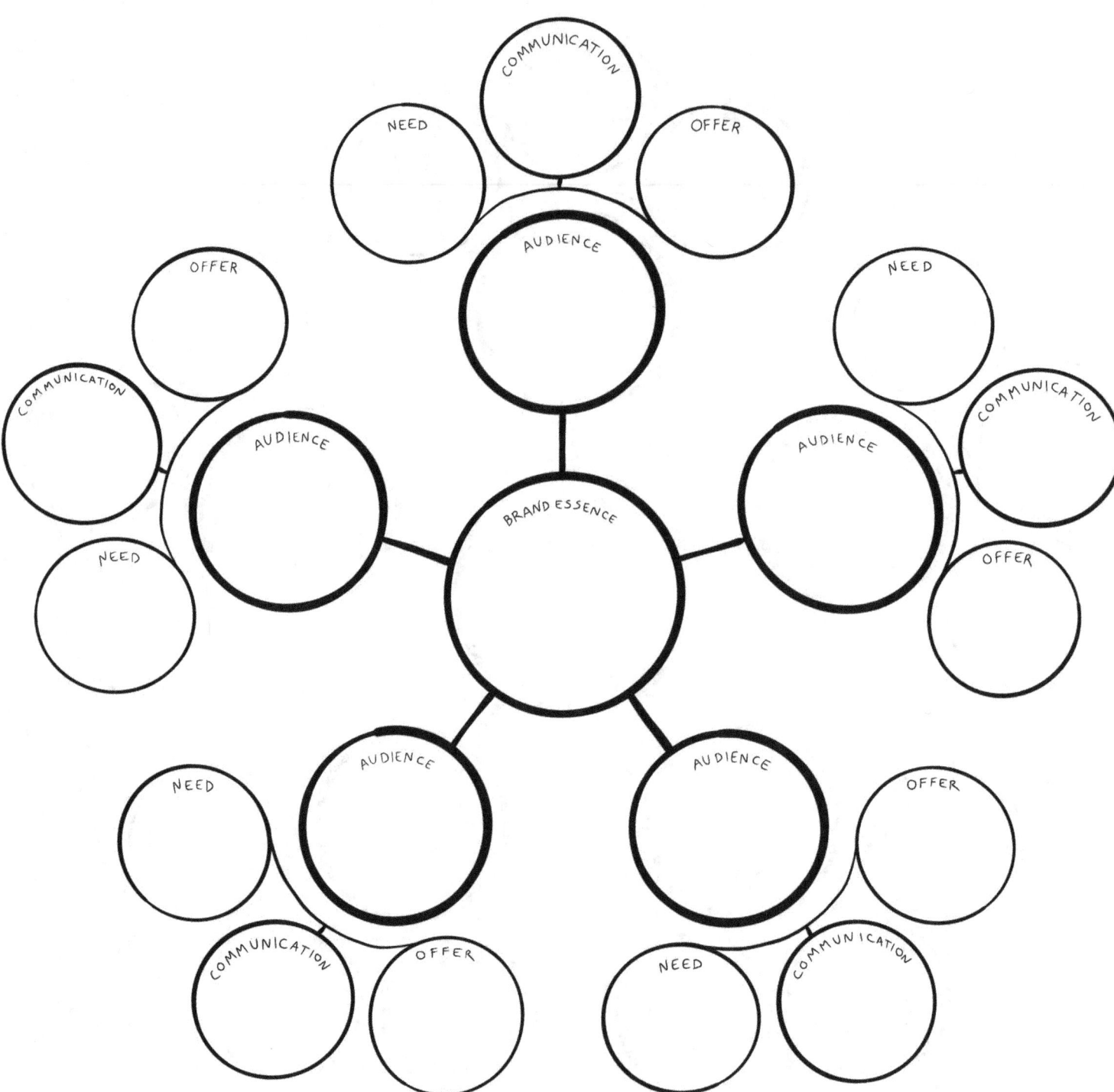

WHO IS YOUR AUDIENCE?

PROJECT:_____   DATE:_____

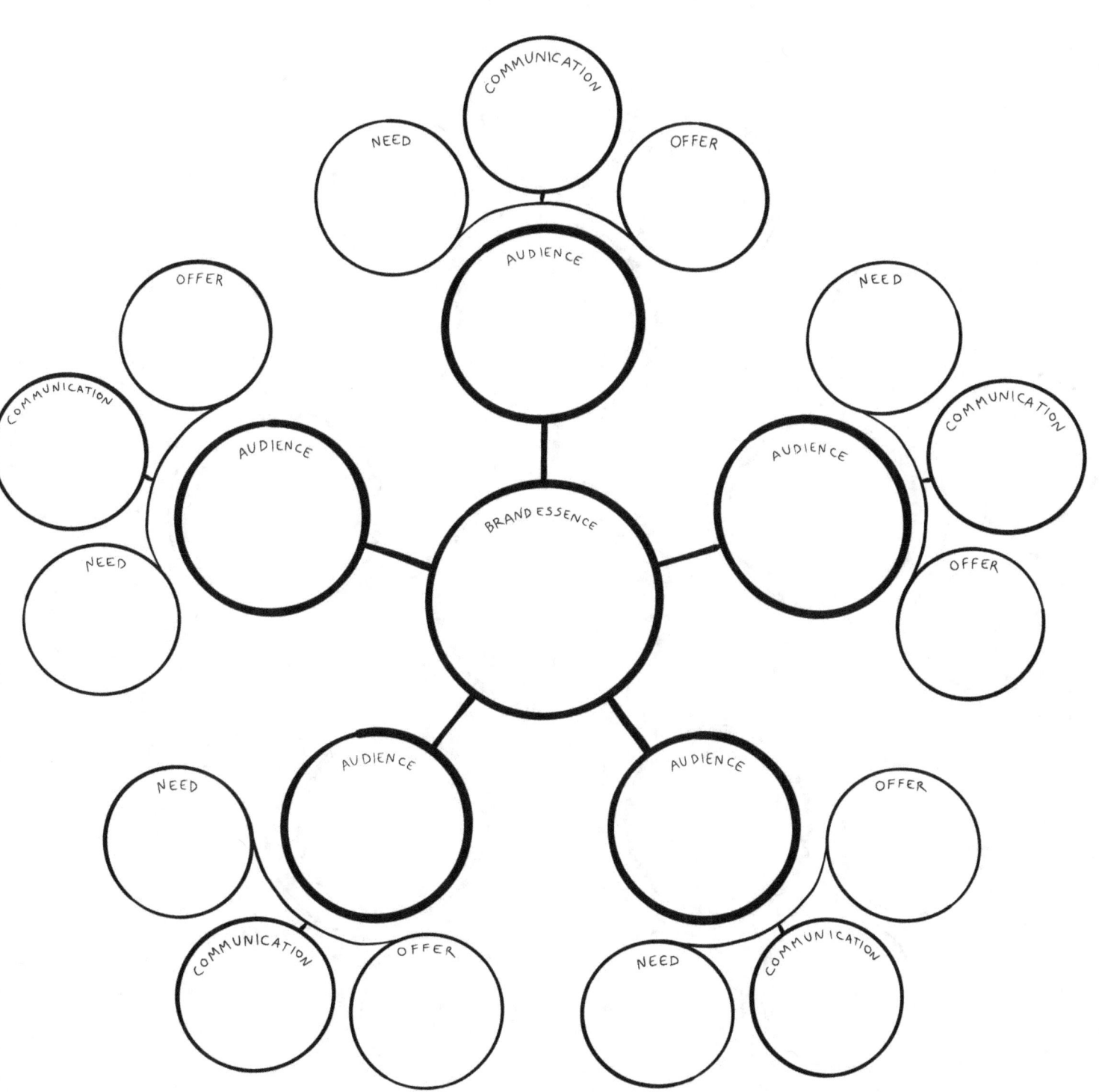

WHO IS YOUR AUDIENCE?

PROJECT:_____   DATE:_____

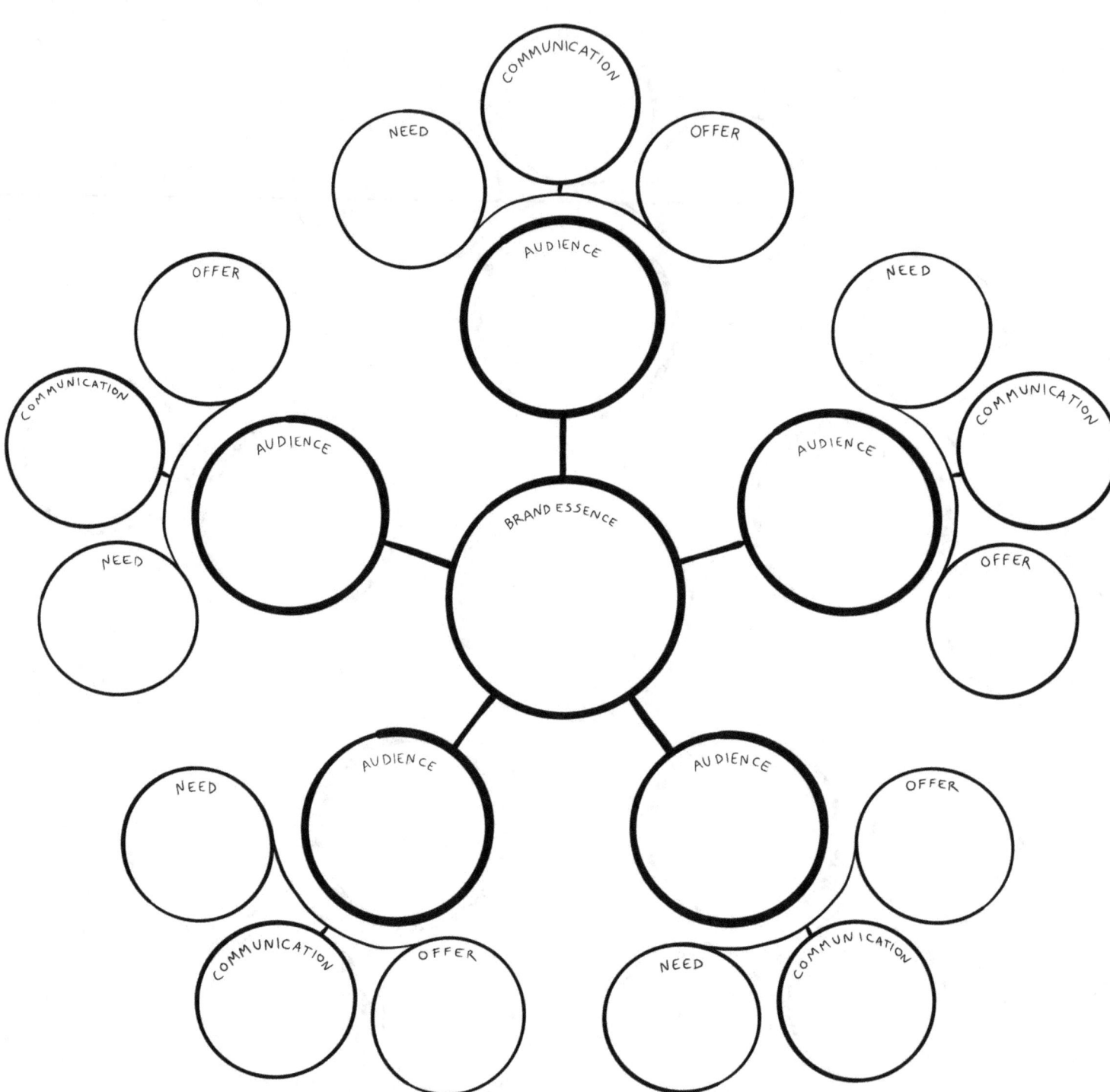

WHO IS YOUR AUDIENCE?

PROJECT:_____

DATE:_____

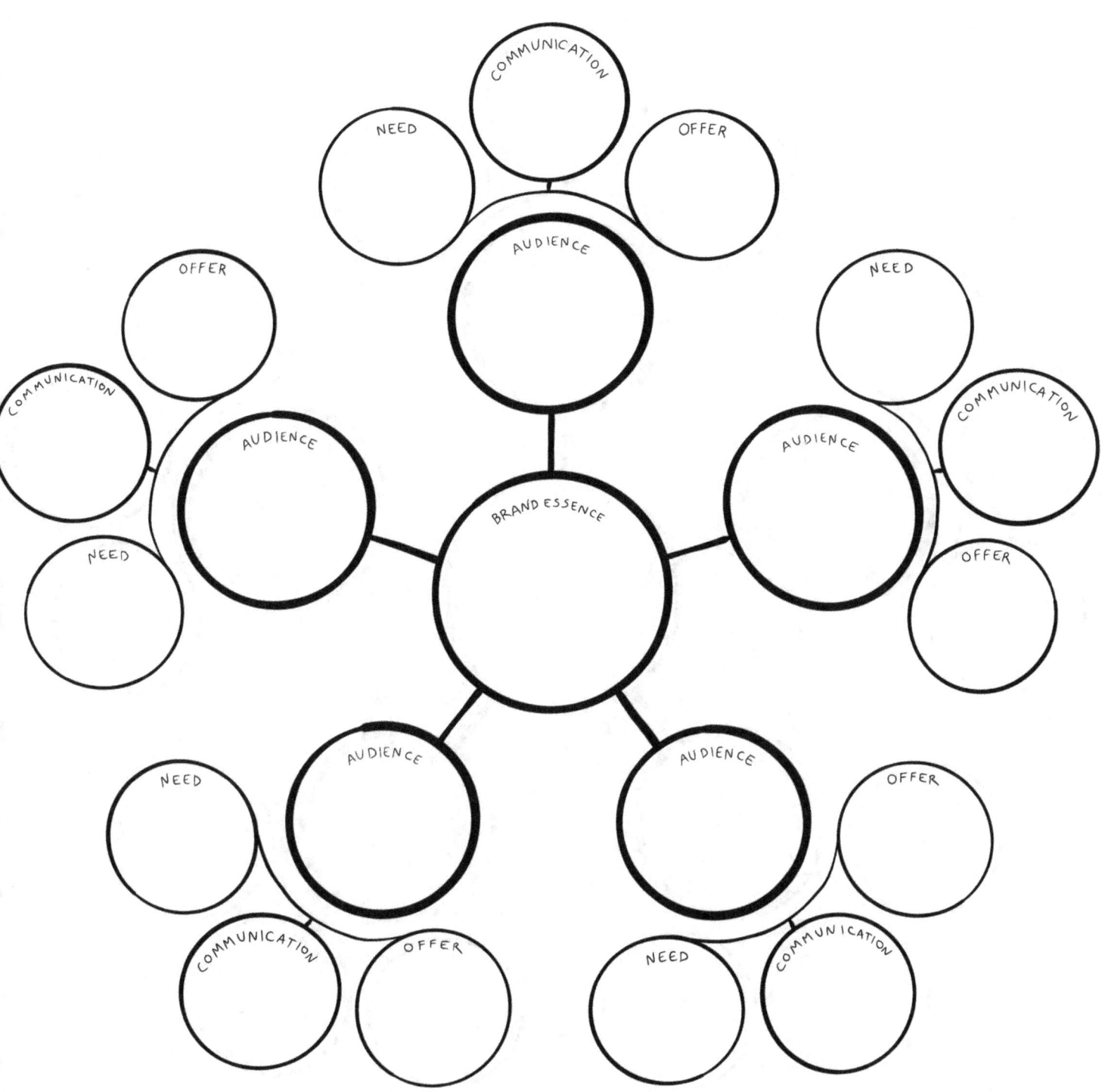

WHO IS YOUR AUDIENCE?

PROJECT:_____   DATE:_____

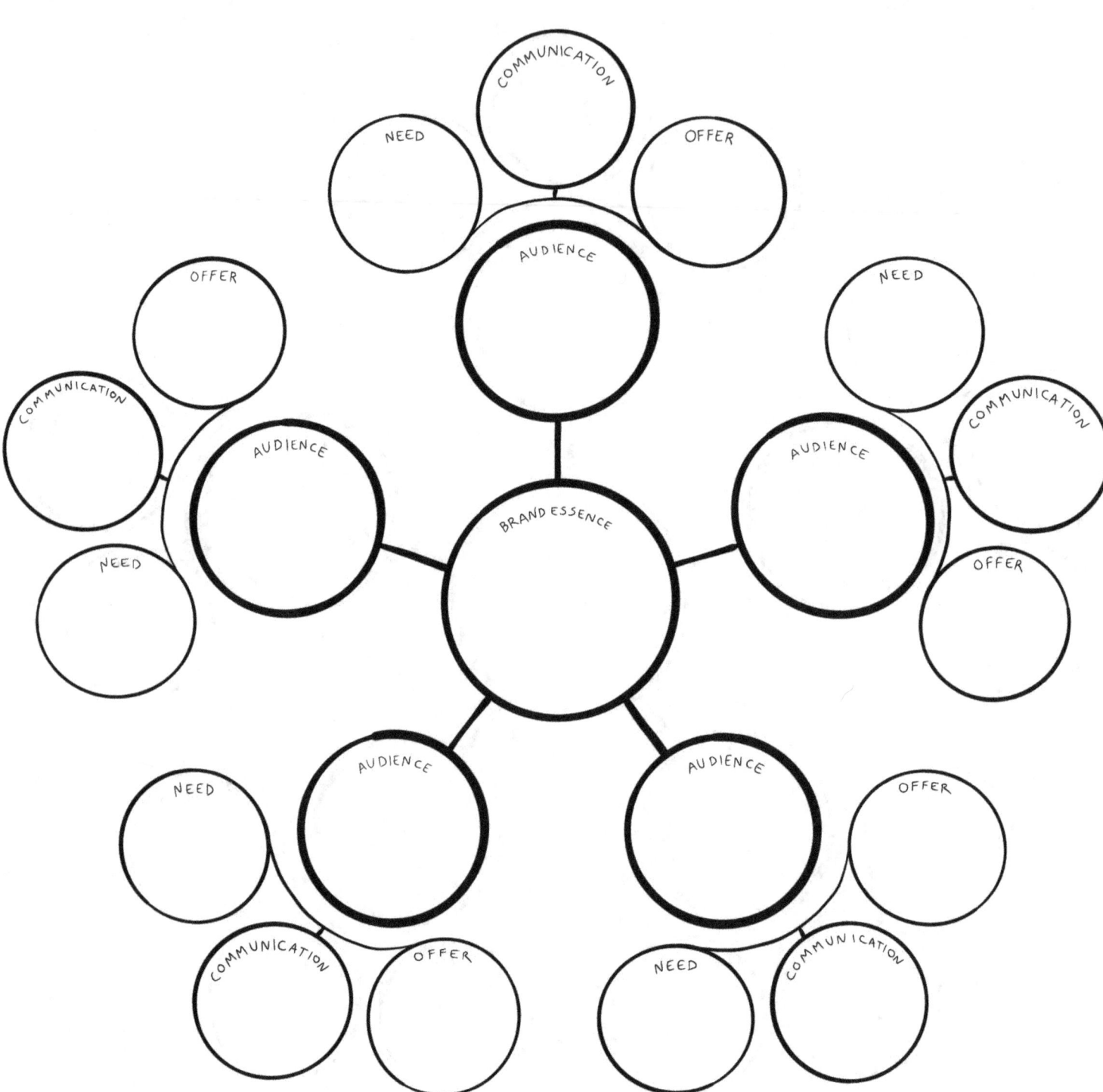

WHO IS YOUR AUDIENCE?

PROJECT:_____   DATE:_____

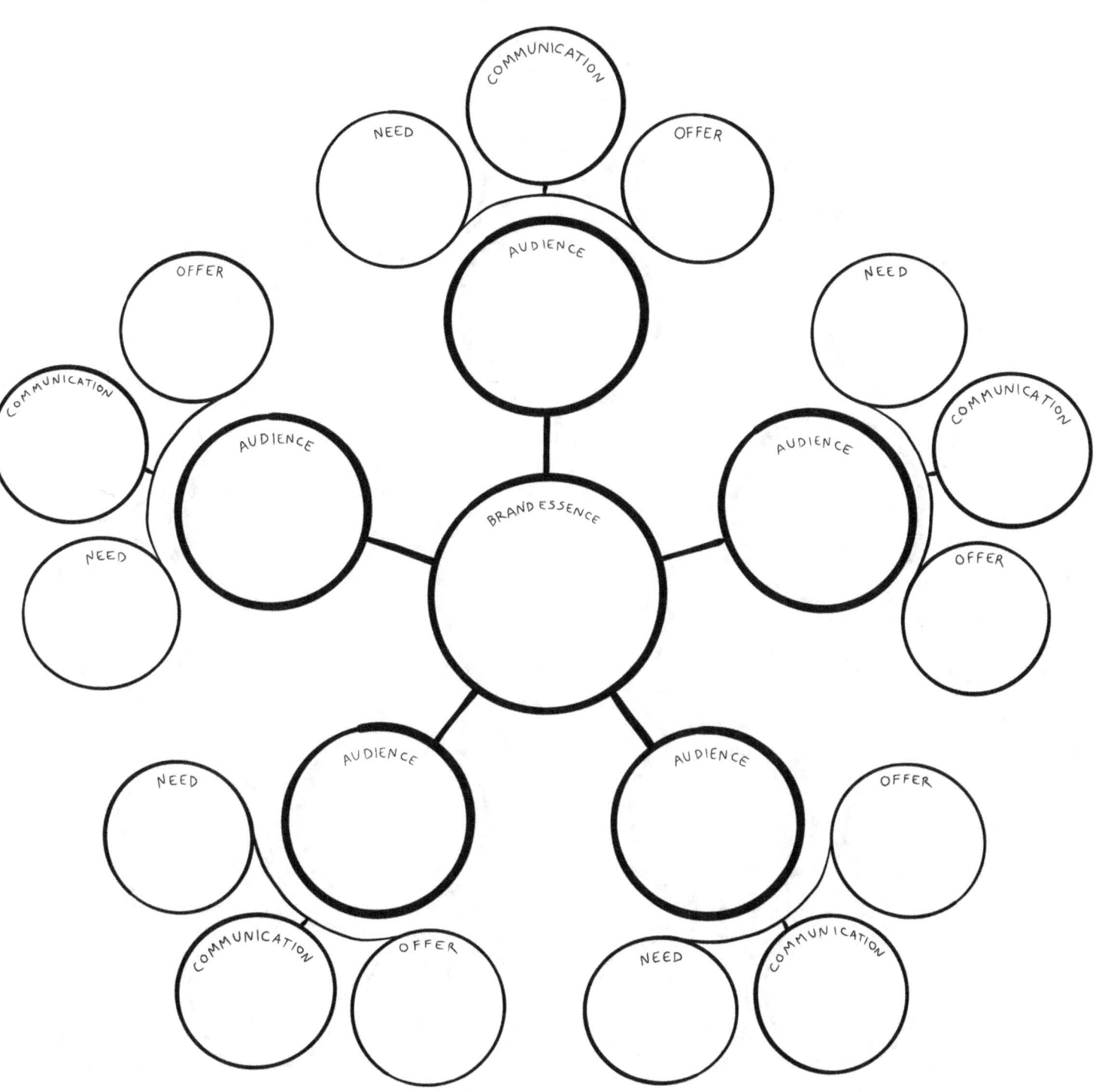

WHO IS YOUR AUDIENCE?

PROJECT:_____   DATE:_____

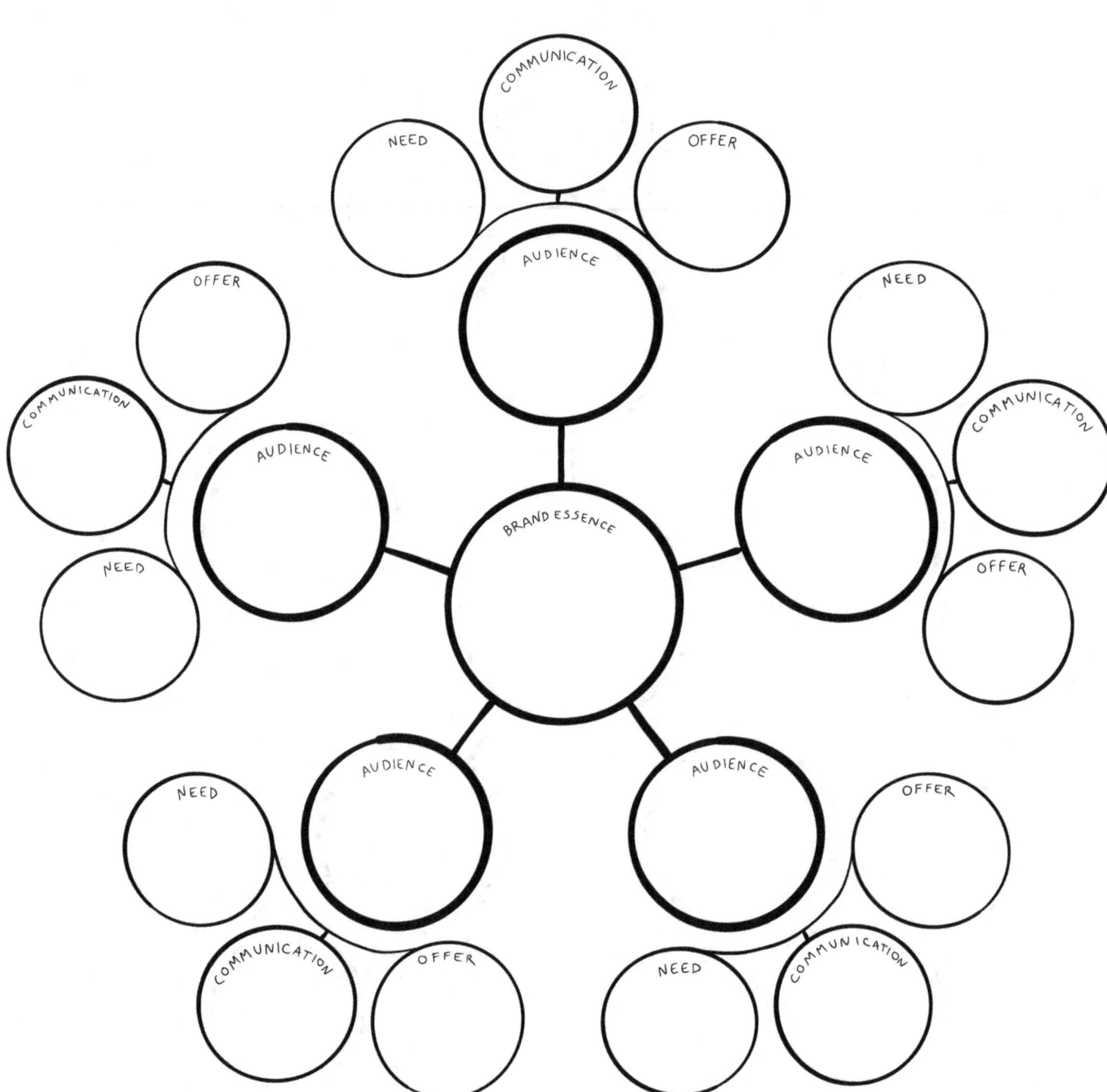

WHO IS YOUR AUDIENCE?

PROJECT:_____

DATE:_____

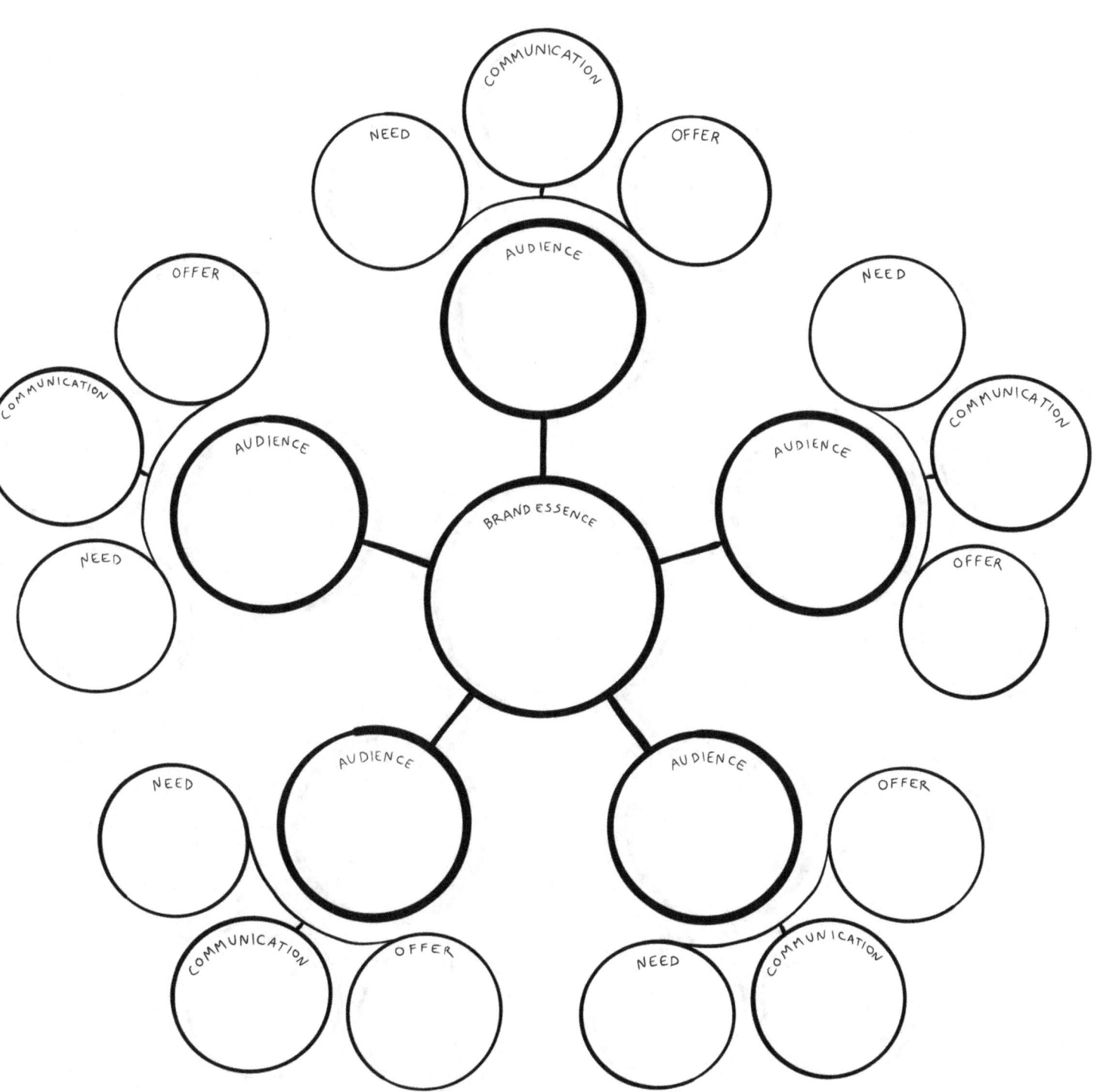

WHO IS YOUR AUDIENCE?

PROJECT:_____   DATE:_____

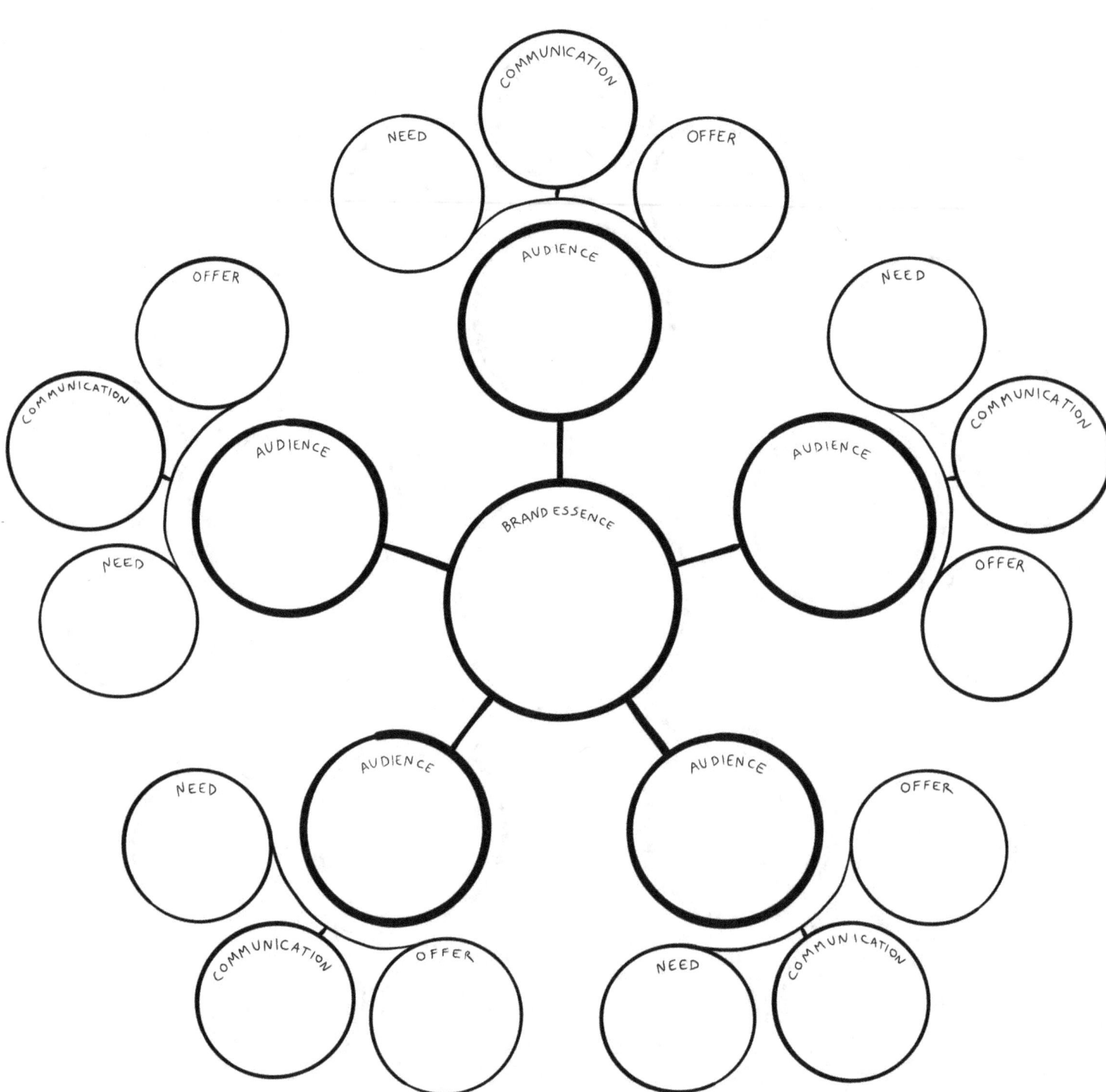

WHO IS YOUR AUDIENCE?

PROJECT:_____   DATE:_____

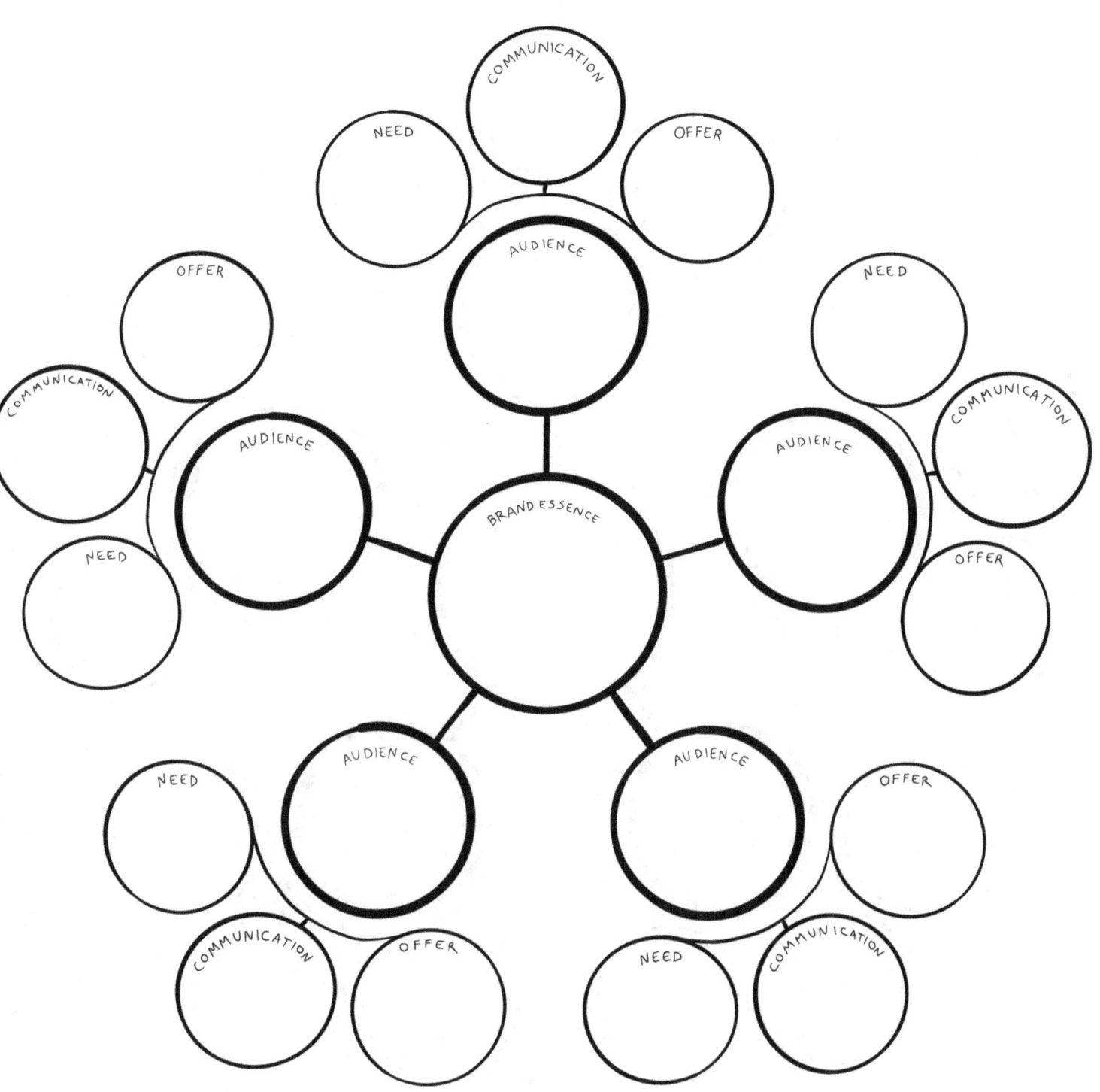

WHO IS YOUR AUDIENCE?

PROJECT:_____   DATE:_____

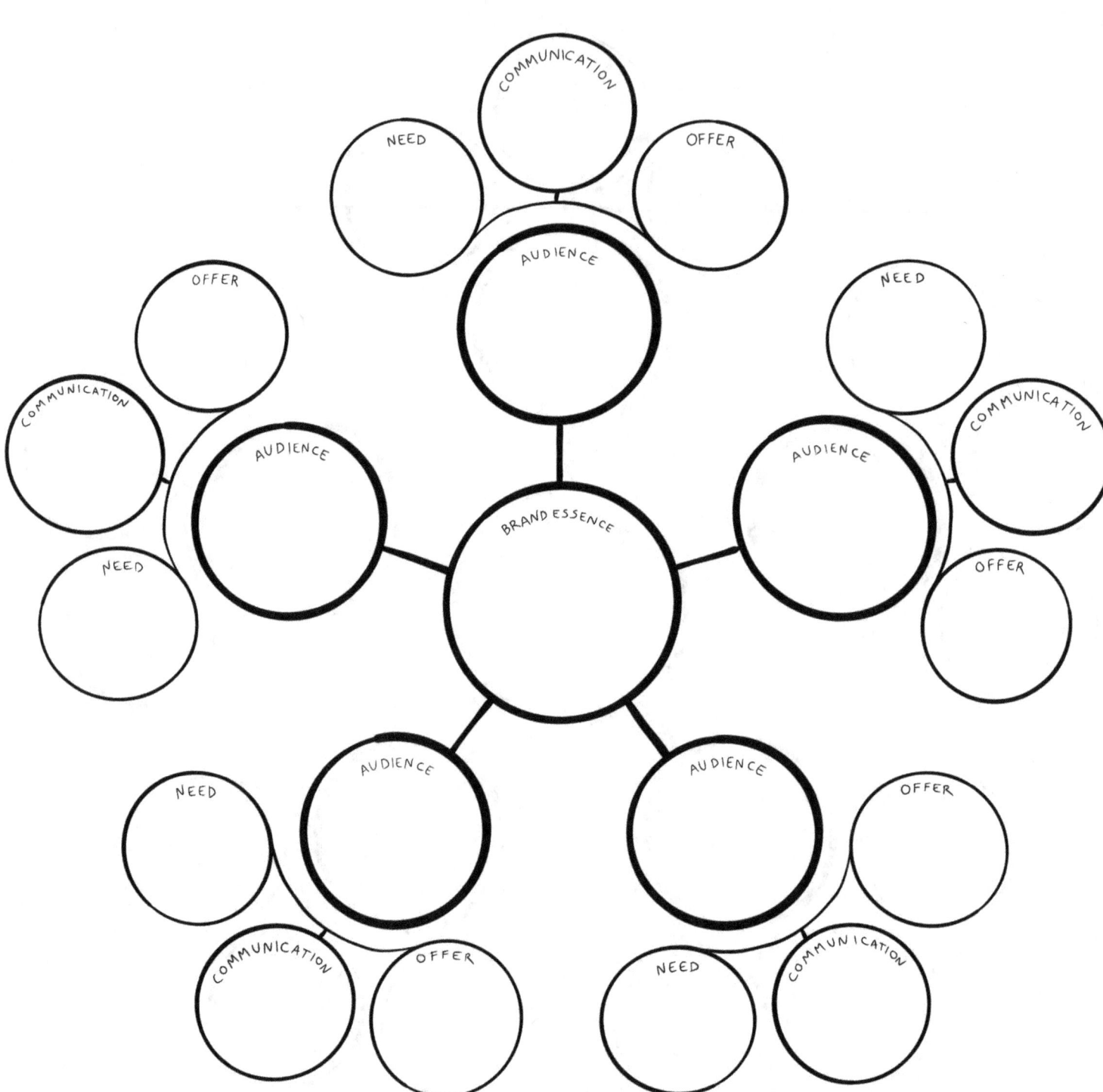

WHO IS YOUR AUDIENCE?

PROJECT:_____   DATE:_____

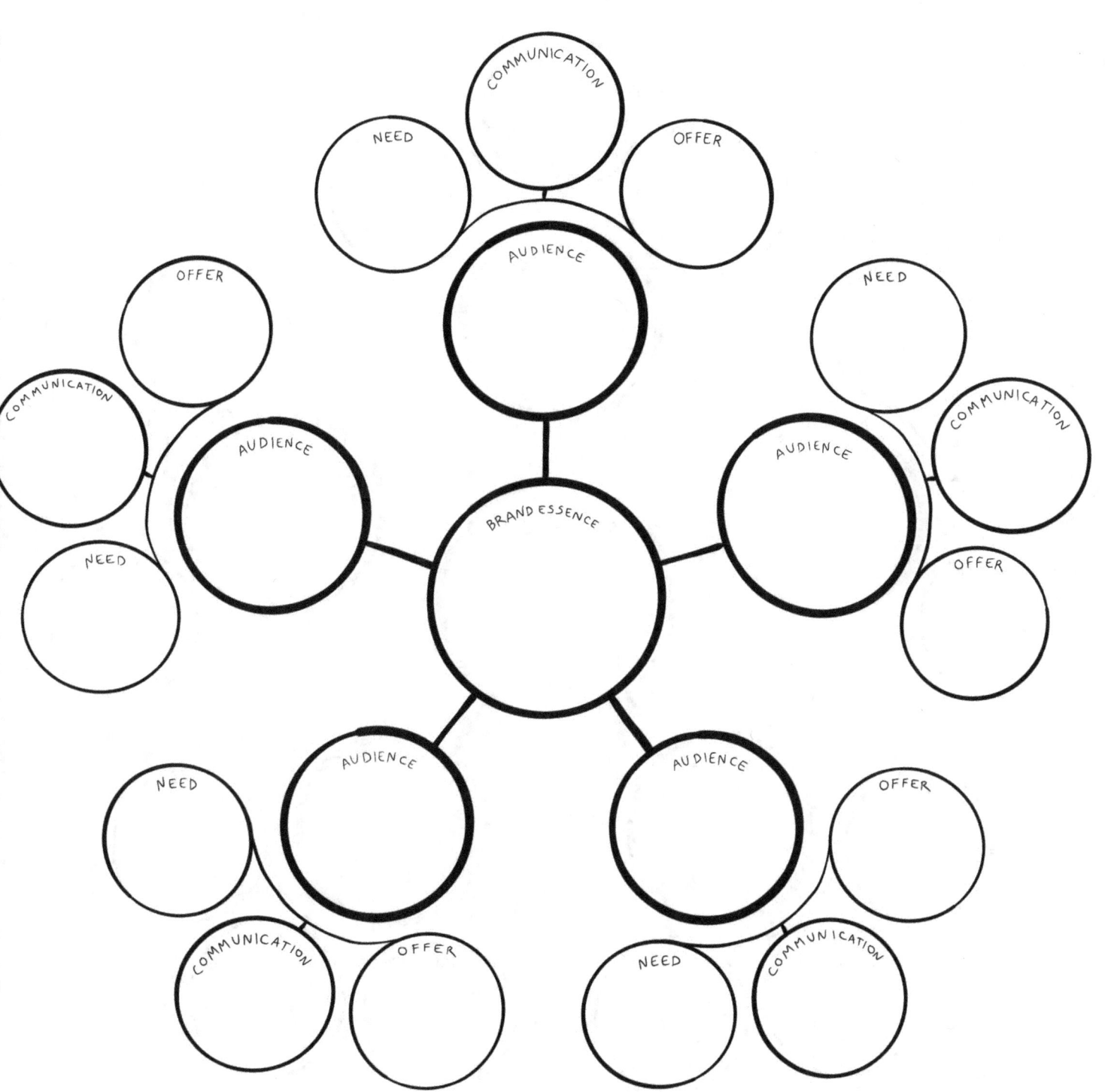

WHO IS YOUR AUDIENCE?

PROJECT:_____   DATE:_____

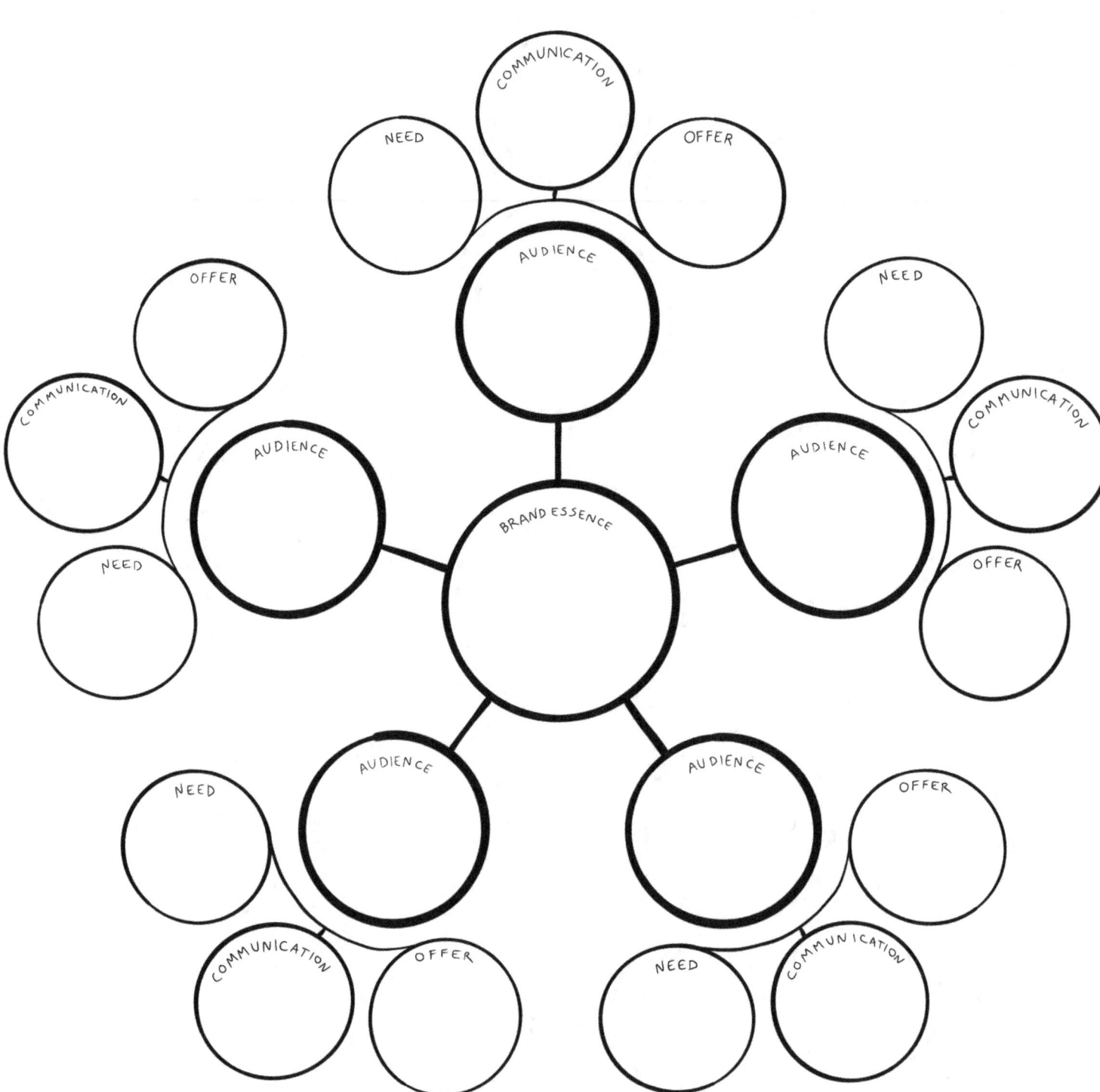

WHO IS YOUR AUDIENCE?

PROJECT:_____   DATE:_____

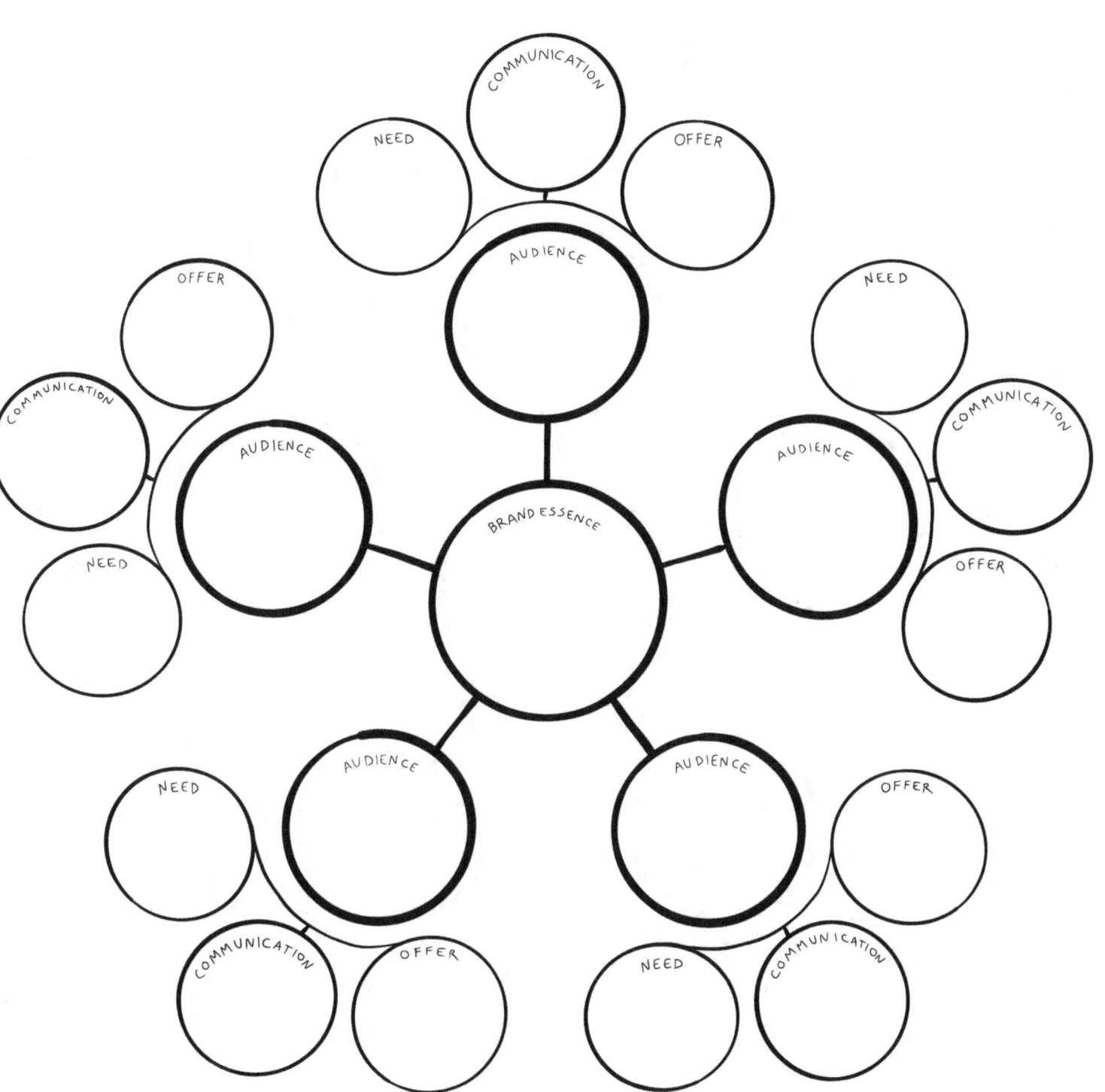

WHO IS YOUR AUDIENCE?

PROJECT:_____   DATE:_____

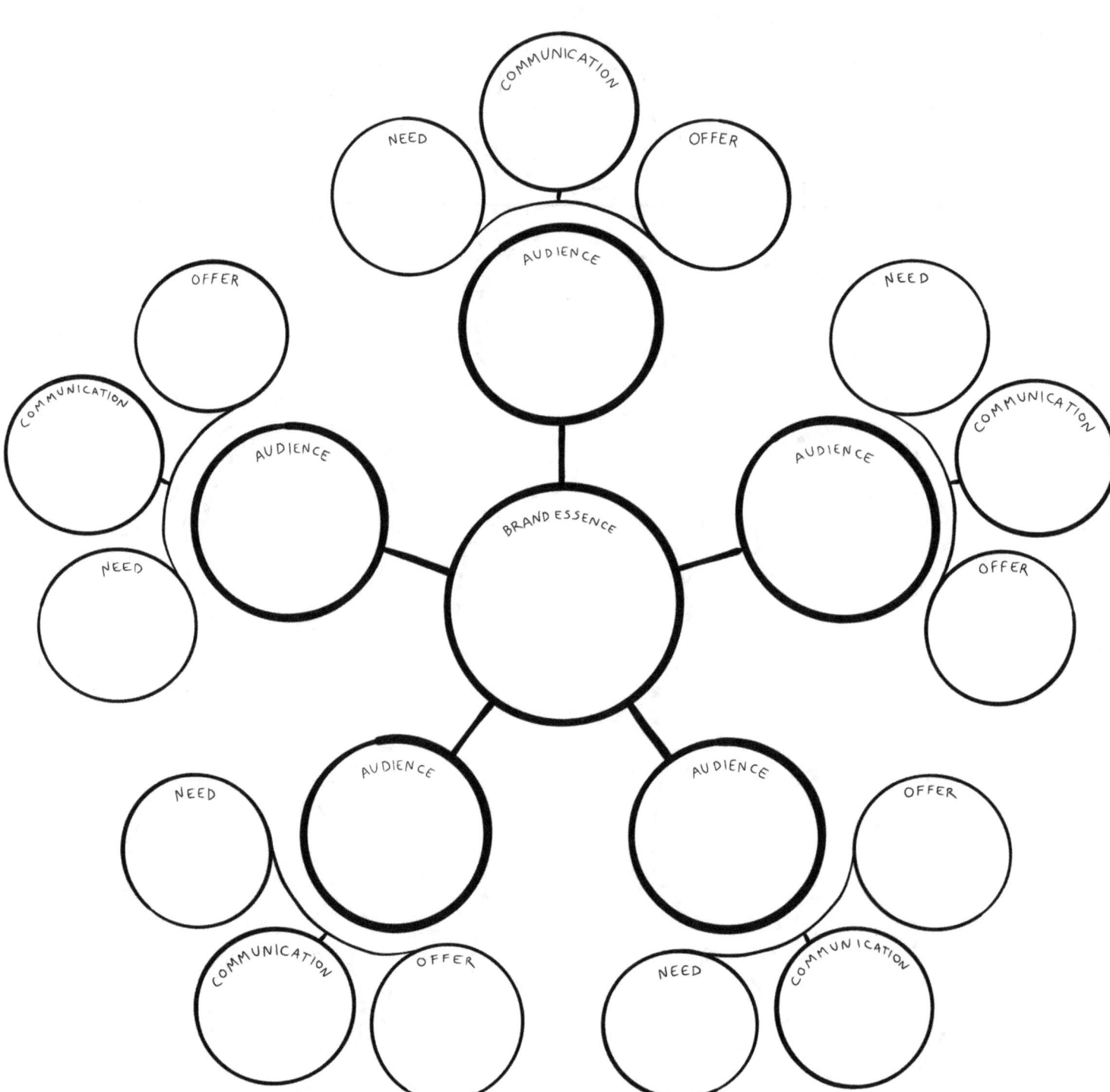

WHO IS YOUR AUDIENCE?

PROJECT:_____   DATE:_____

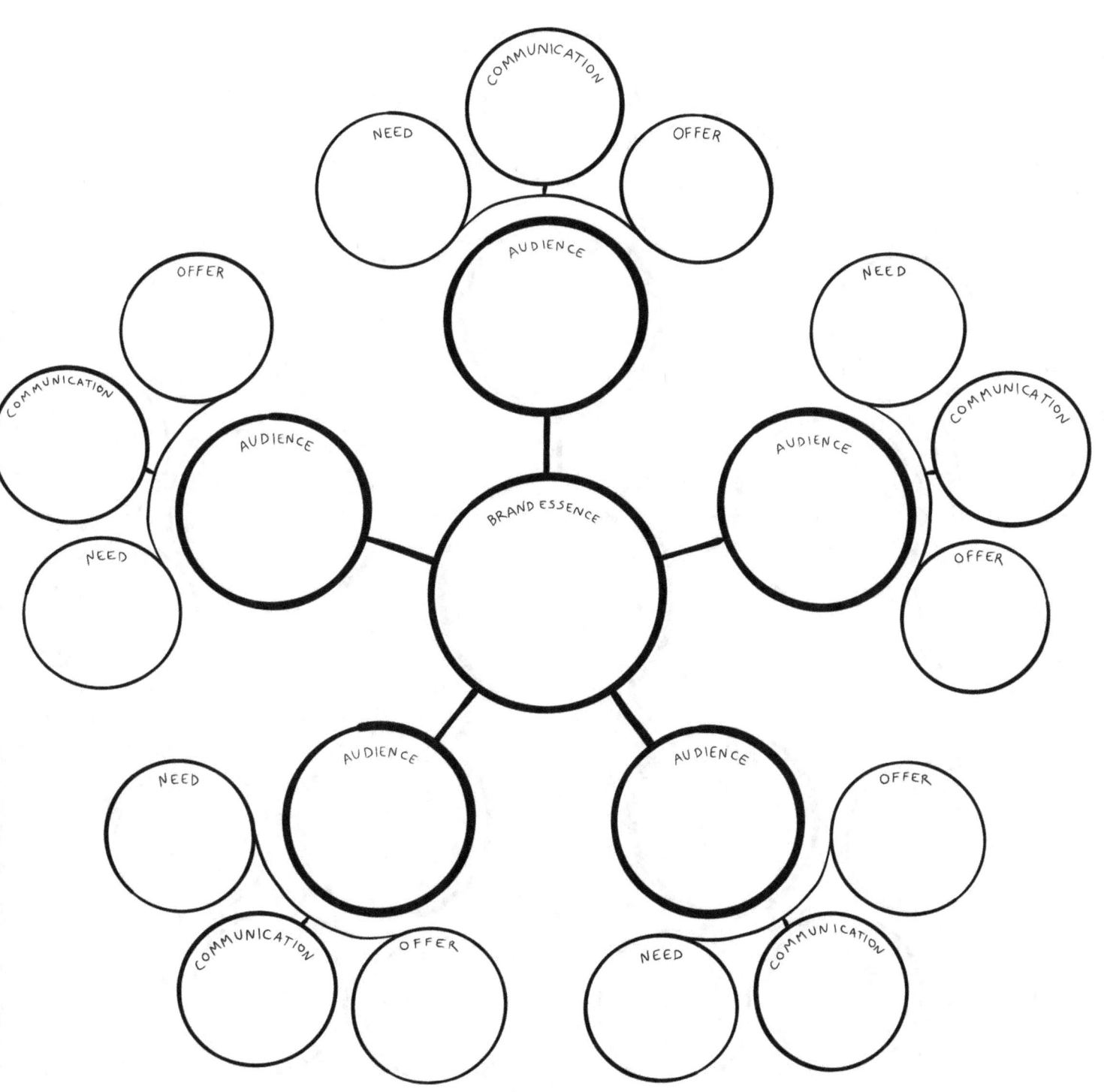

WHO IS YOUR AUDIENCE?

PROJECT:_____   DATE:_____

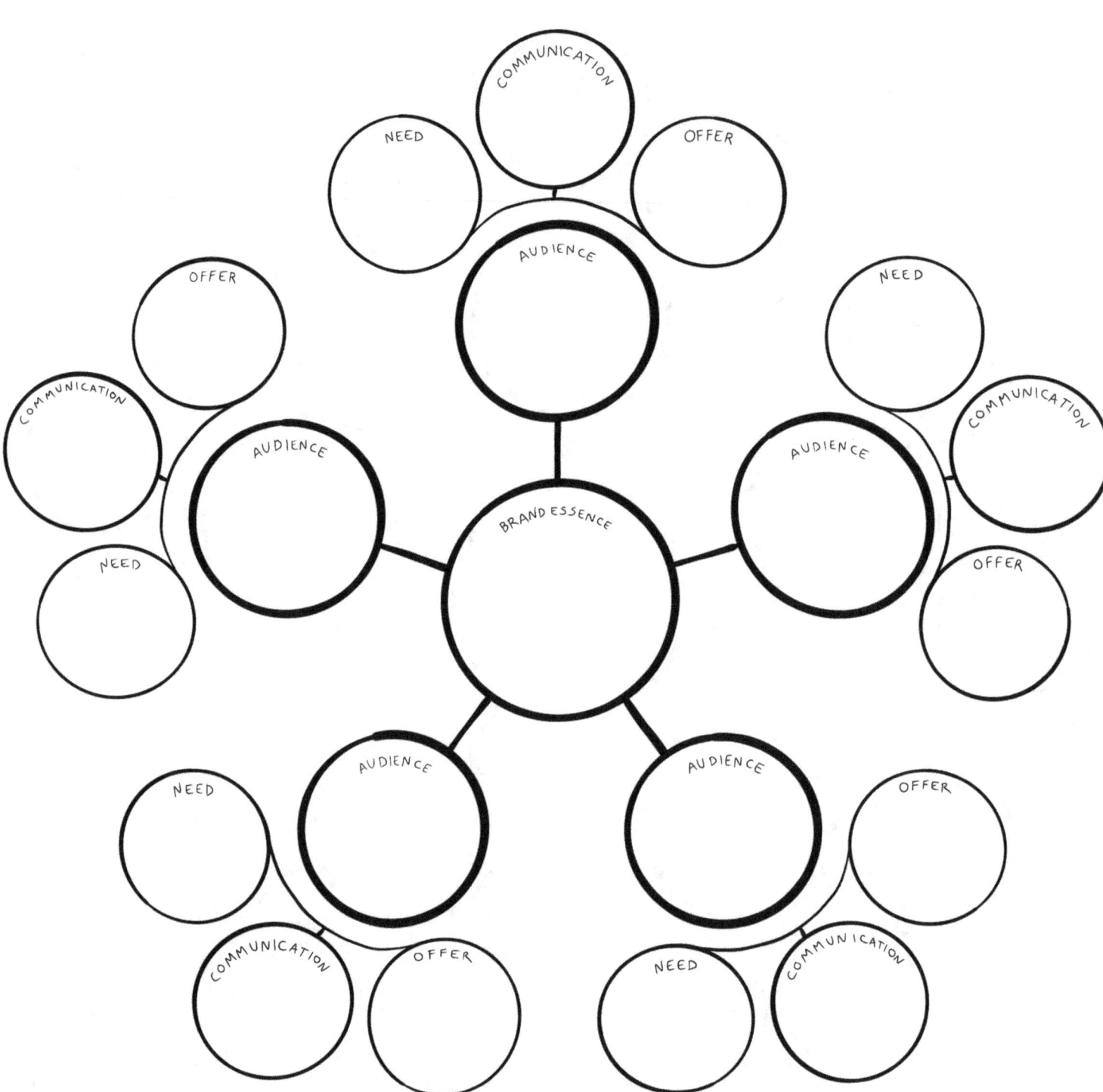

WHO IS YOUR AUDIENCE?

PROJECT:_____   DATE:_____

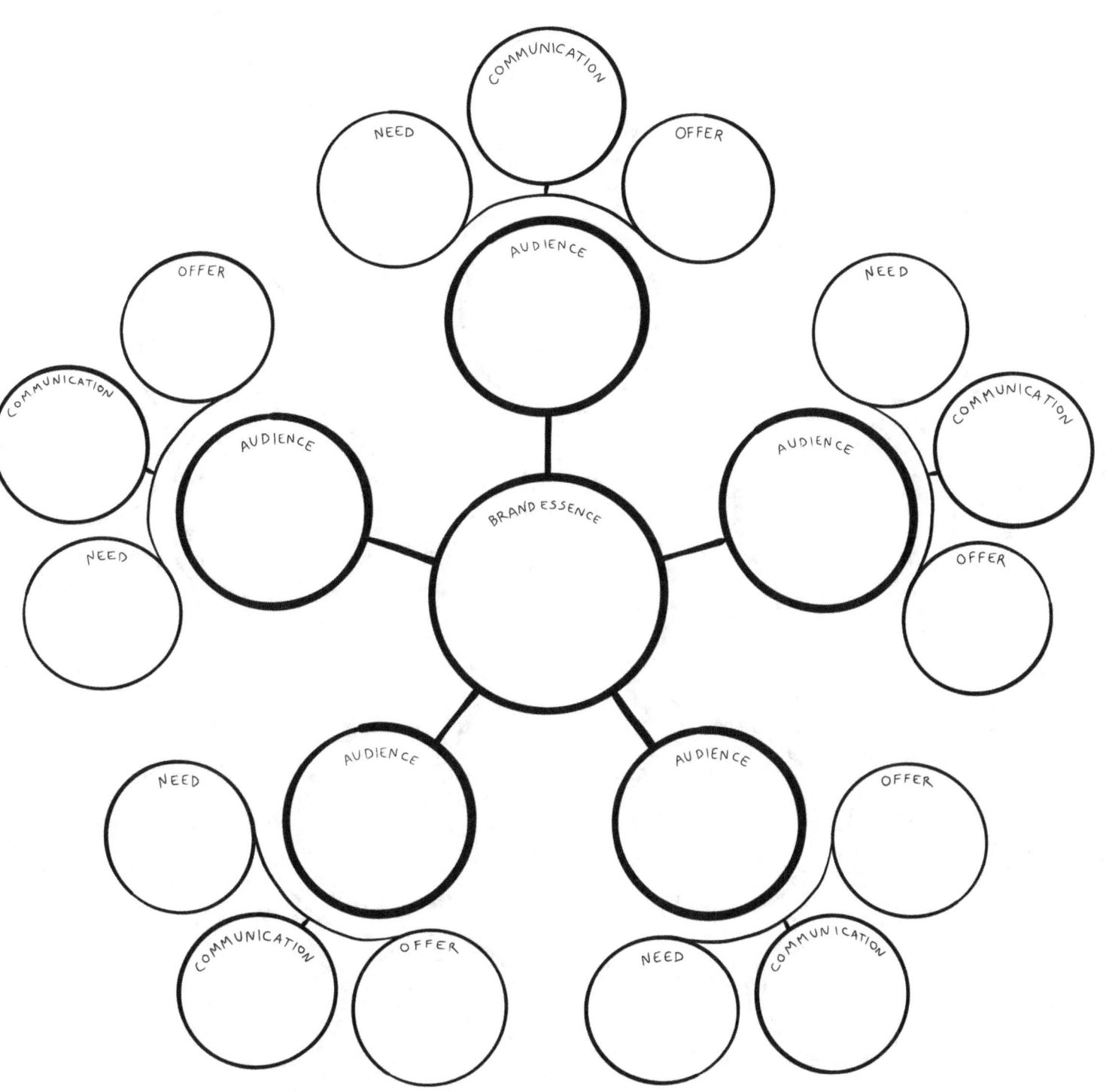

WHO IS YOUR AUDIENCE?

PROJECT:_____   DATE:_____

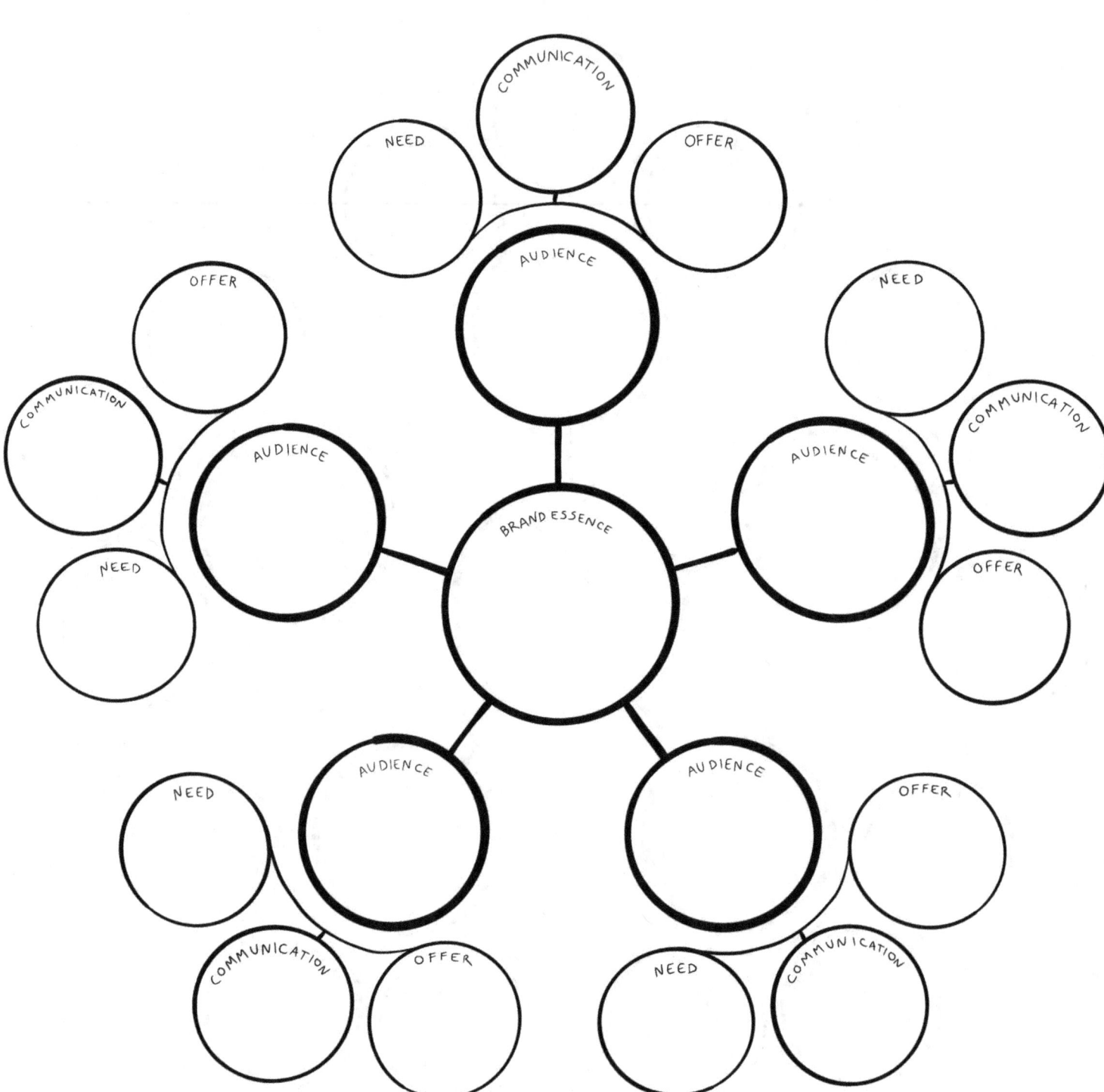

WHO IS YOUR AUDIENCE?

PROJECT:_____   DATE:_____

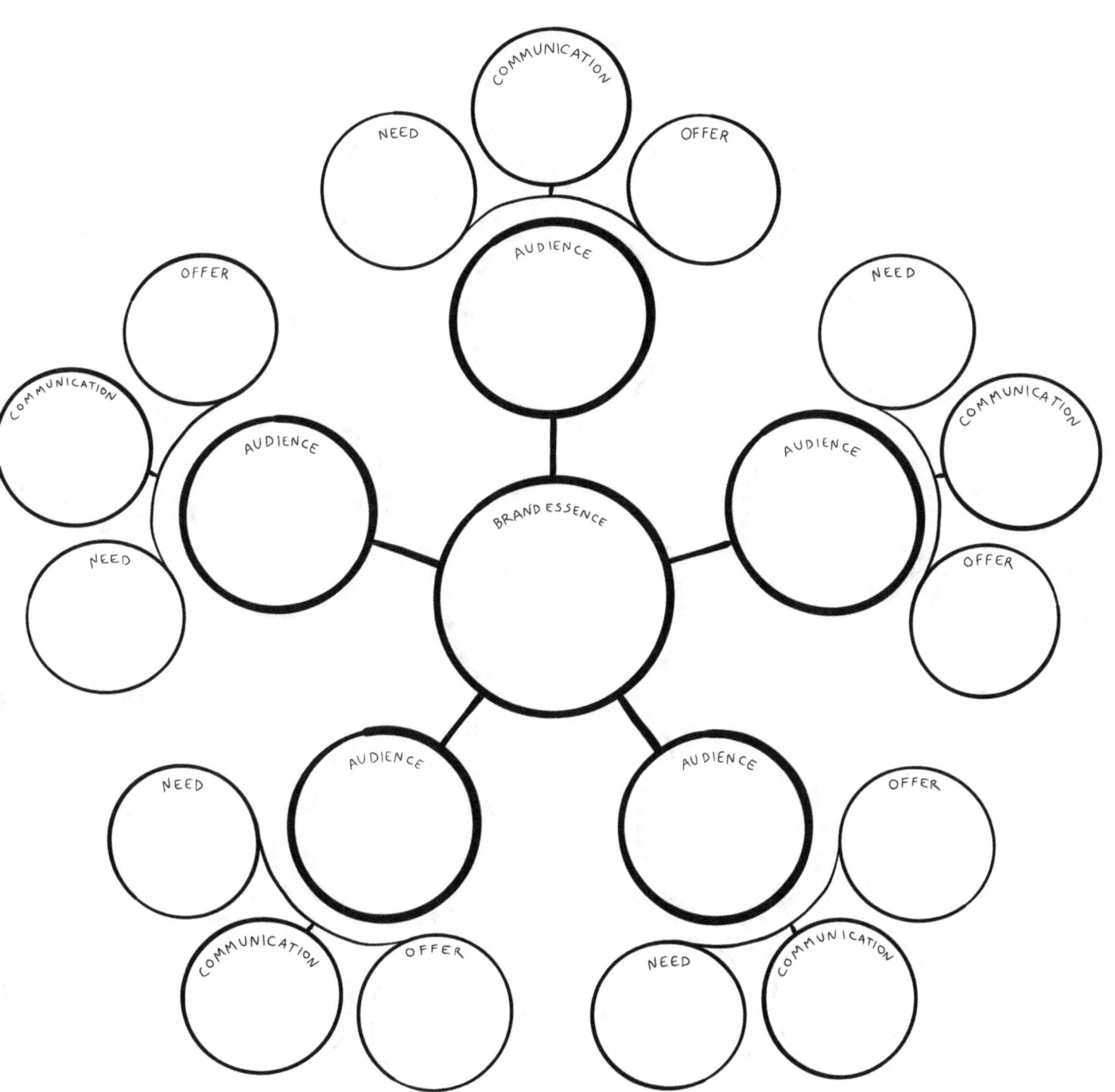

WHO IS YOUR AUDIENCE?

PROJECT:_____   DATE:_____

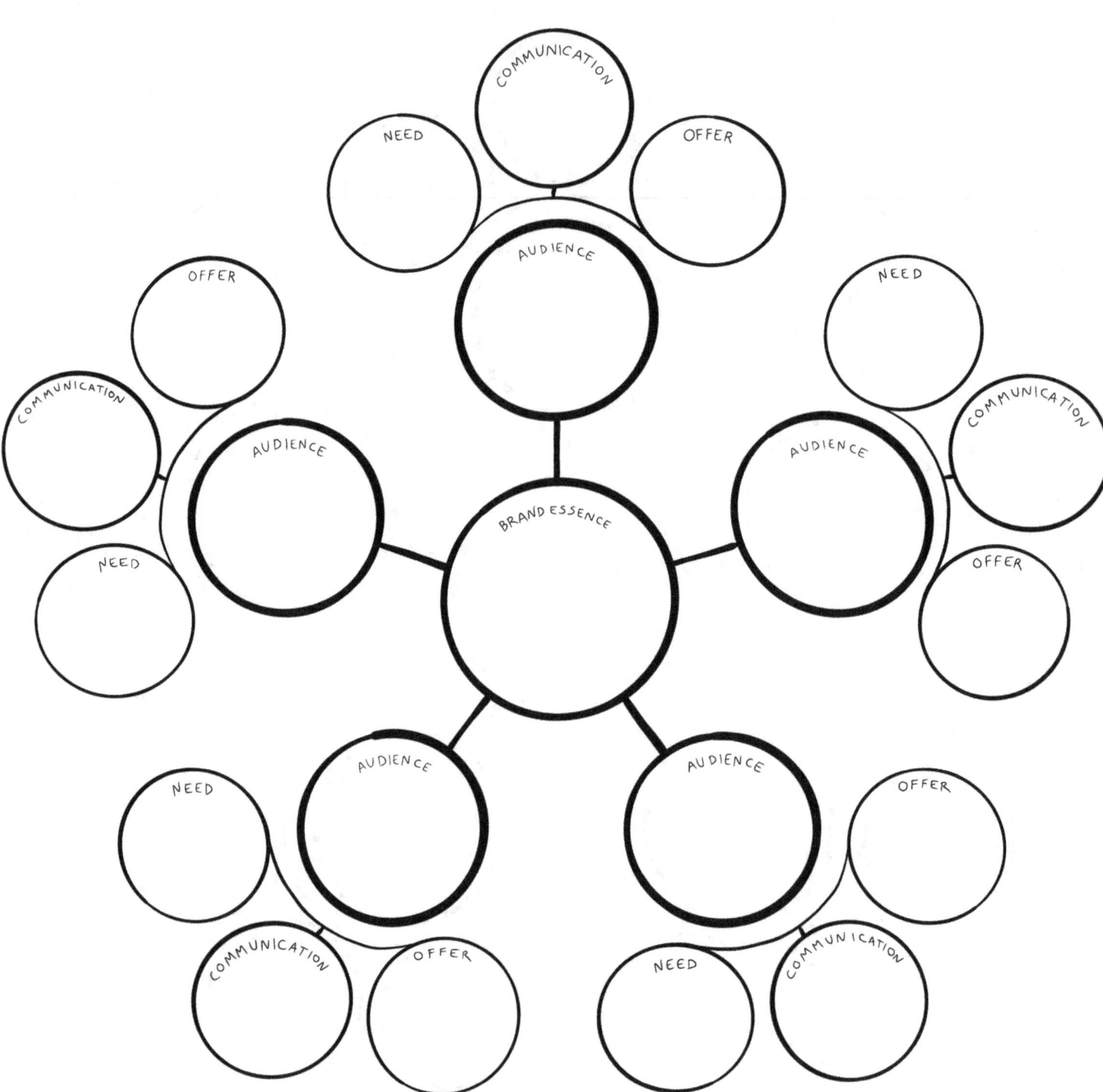

WHO IS YOUR AUDIENCE?

PROJECT:_____   DATE:_____

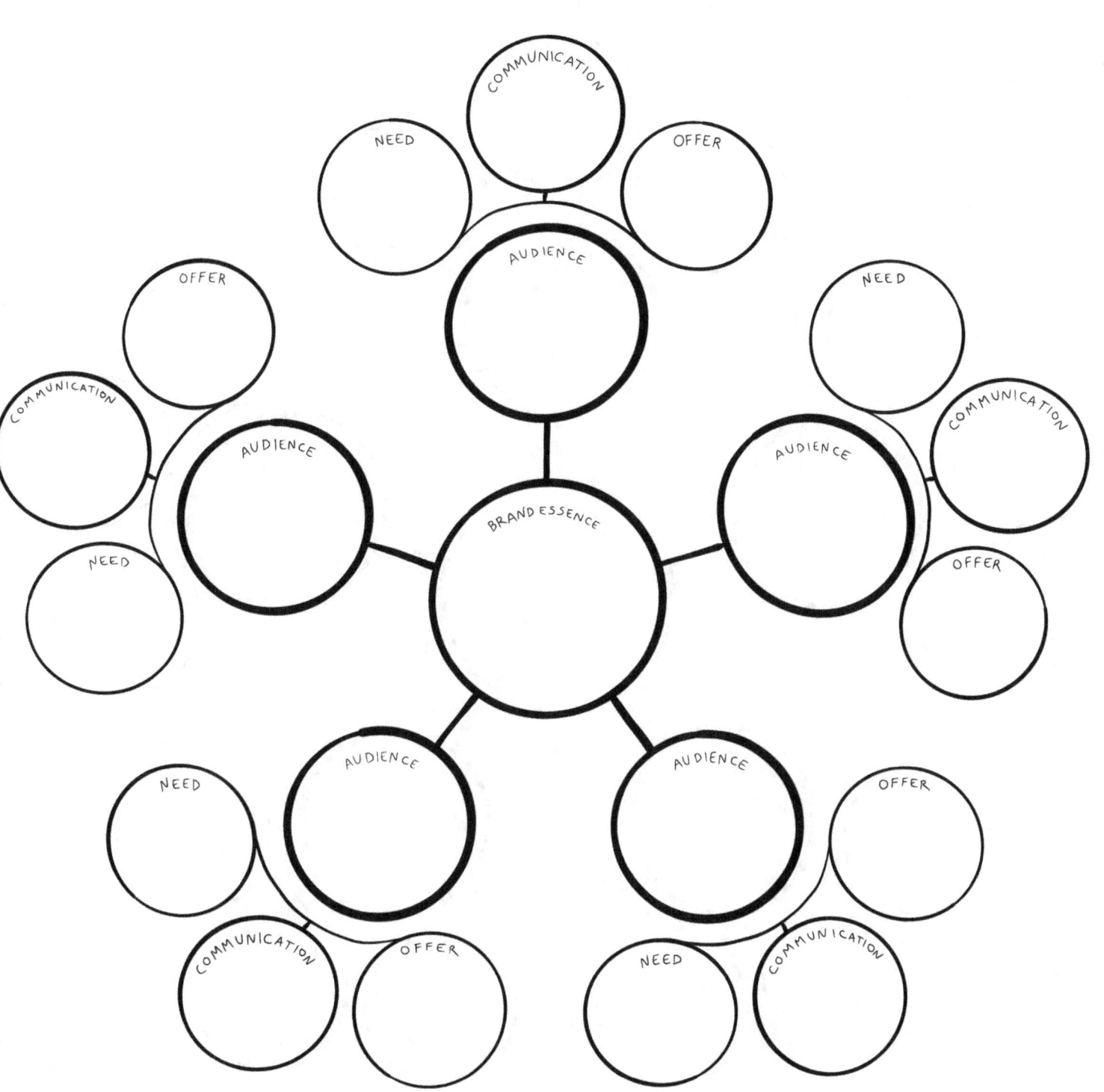

WHO IS YOUR AUDIENCE?

PROJECT:_____   DATE:_____

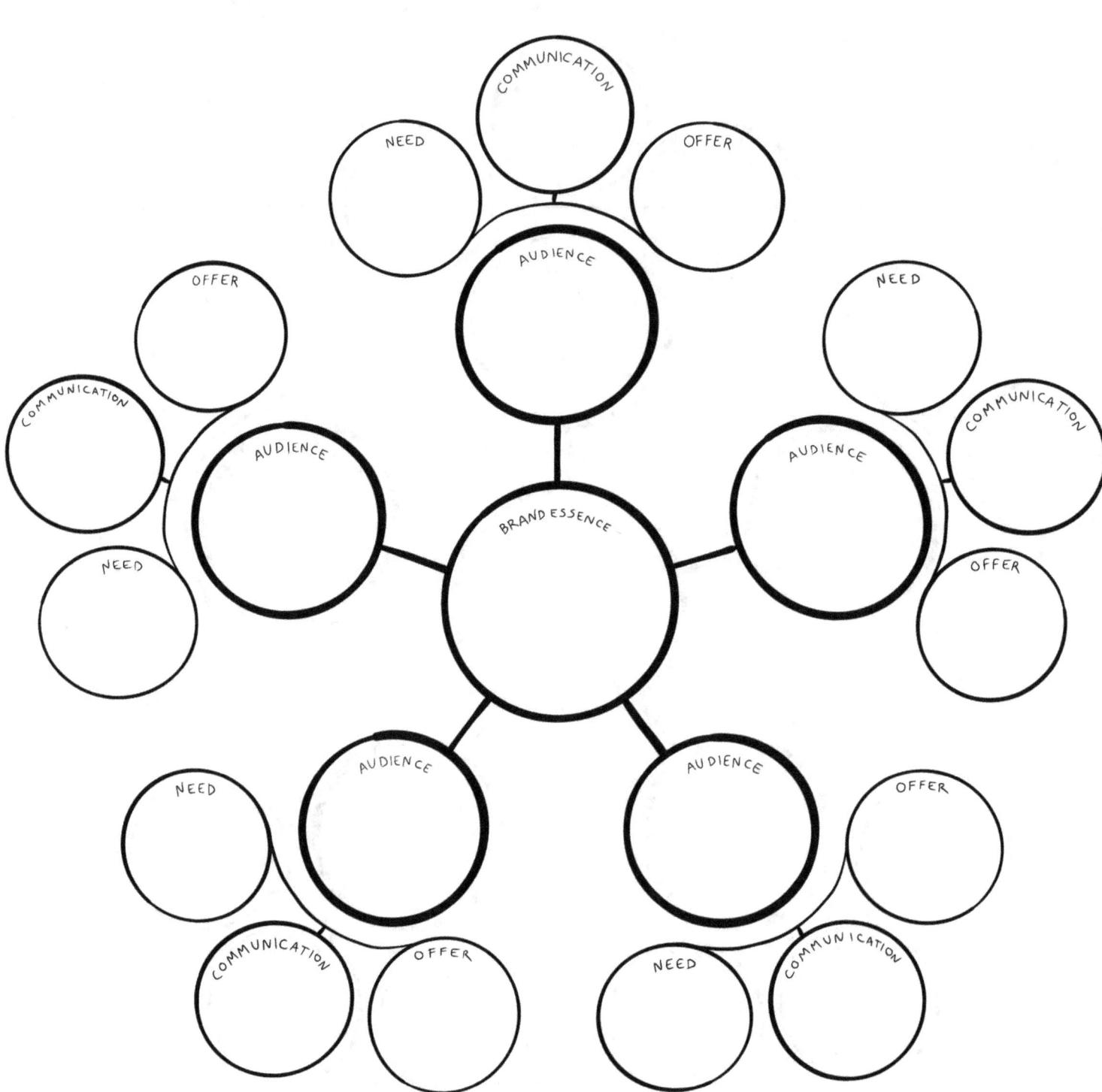

WHO IS YOUR AUDIENCE?

PROJECT:_____   DATE:_____

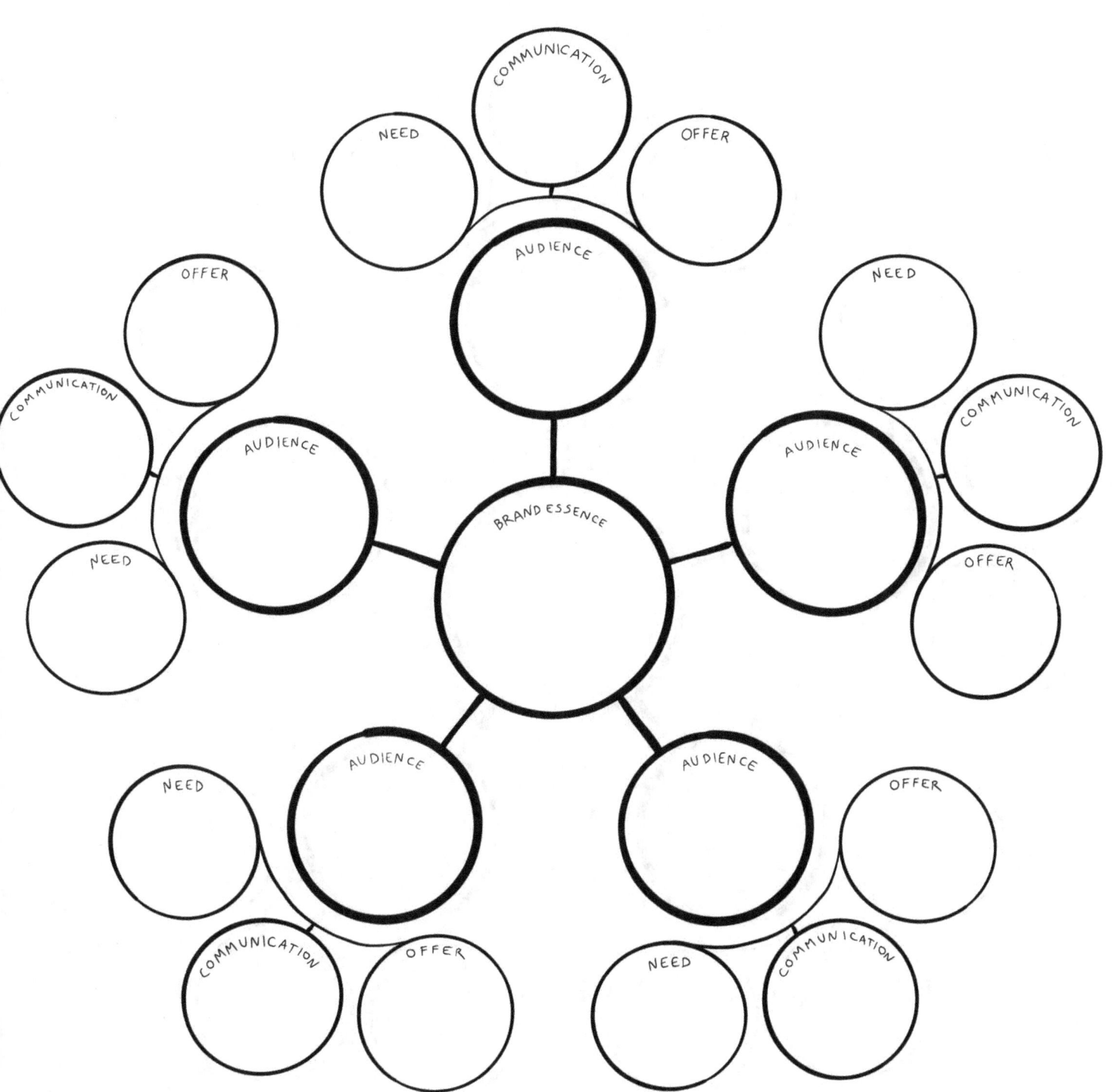

WHO IS YOUR AUDIENCE?

PROJECT:_____   DATE:_____

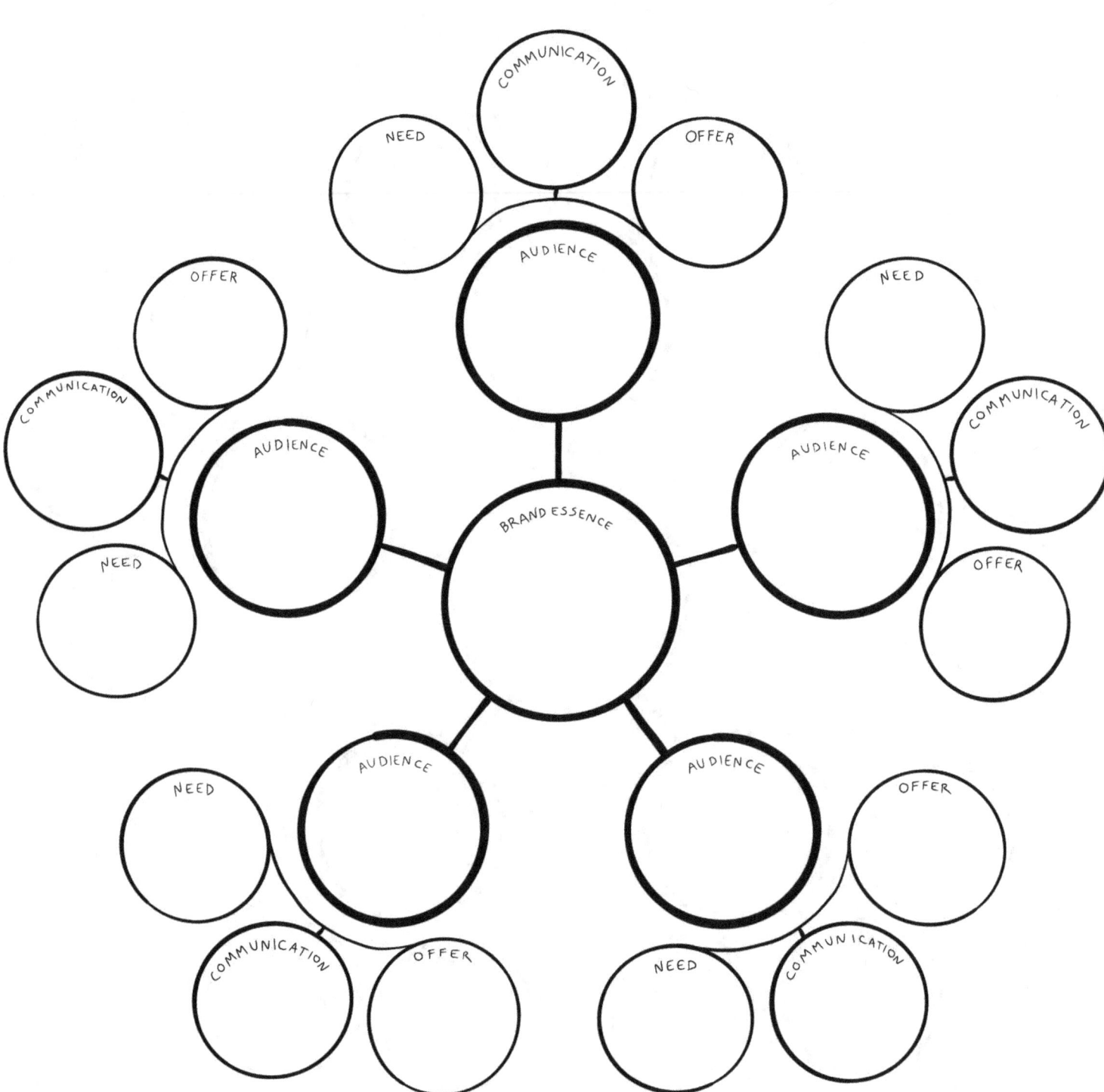

WHO IS YOUR AUDIENCE?

PROJECT: _____   DATE: _____

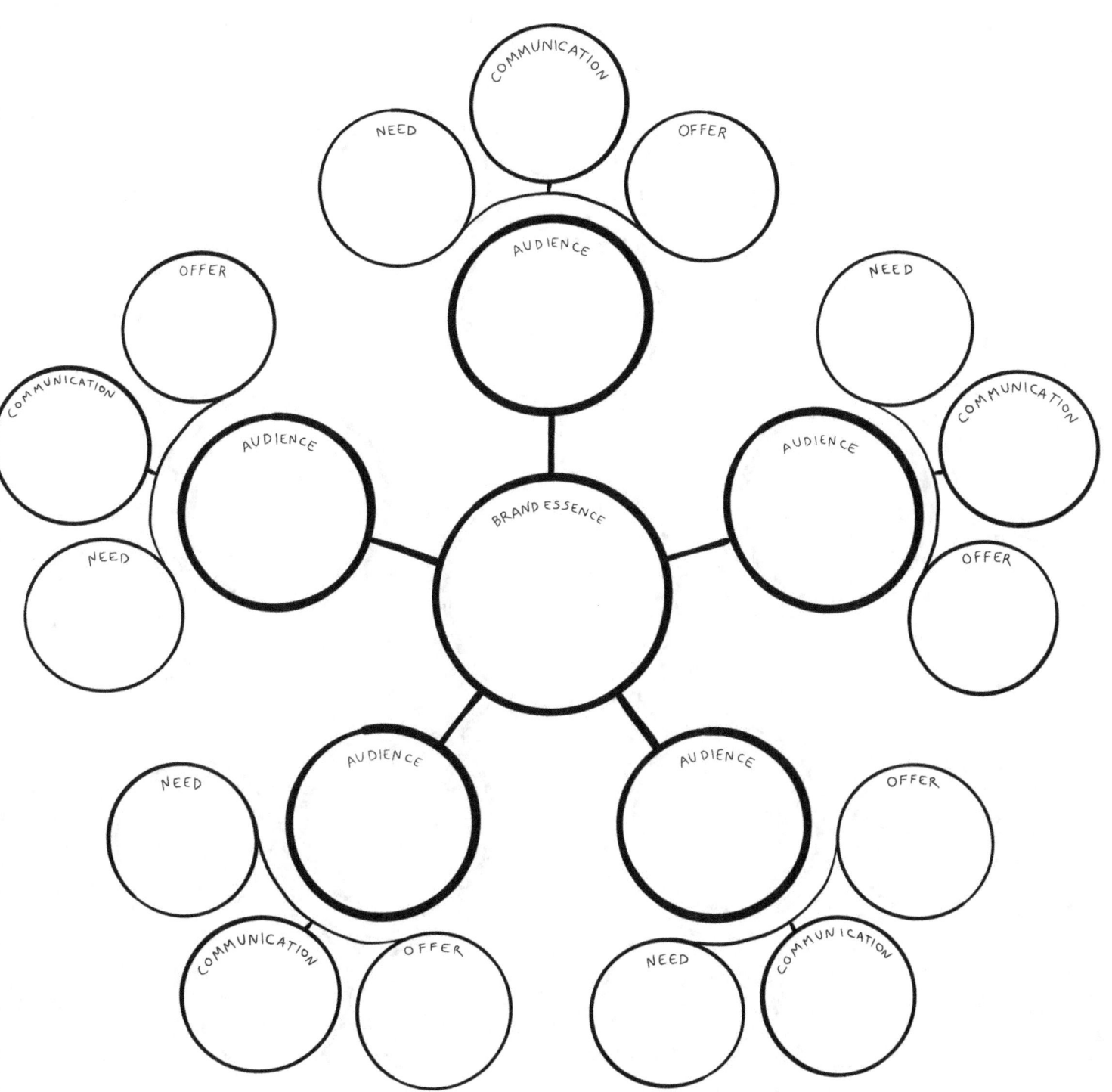

WHO IS YOUR AUDIENCE?

PROJECT:_____   DATE:_____

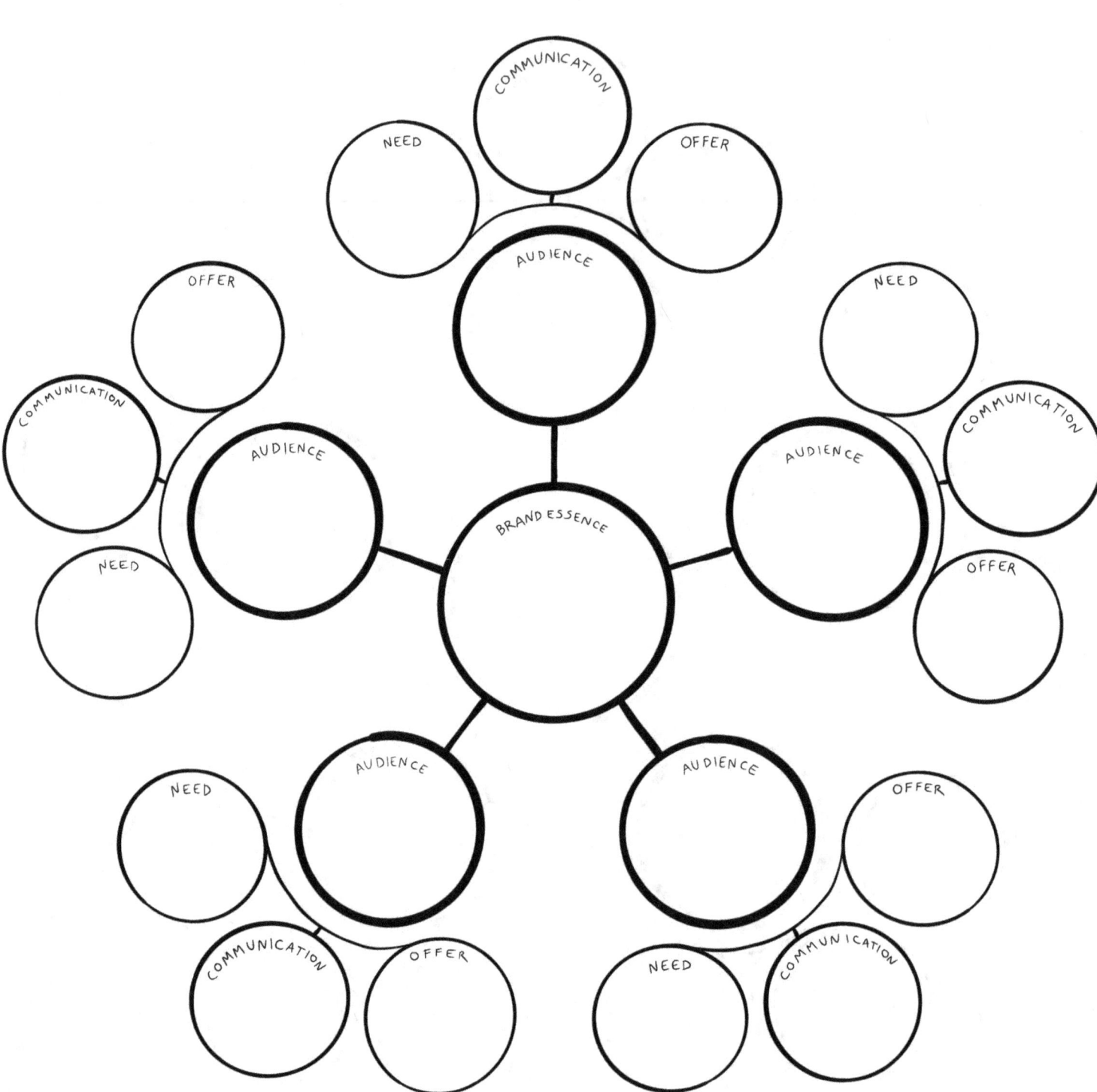

WHO IS YOUR AUDIENCE?

PROJECT:_____   DATE:_____

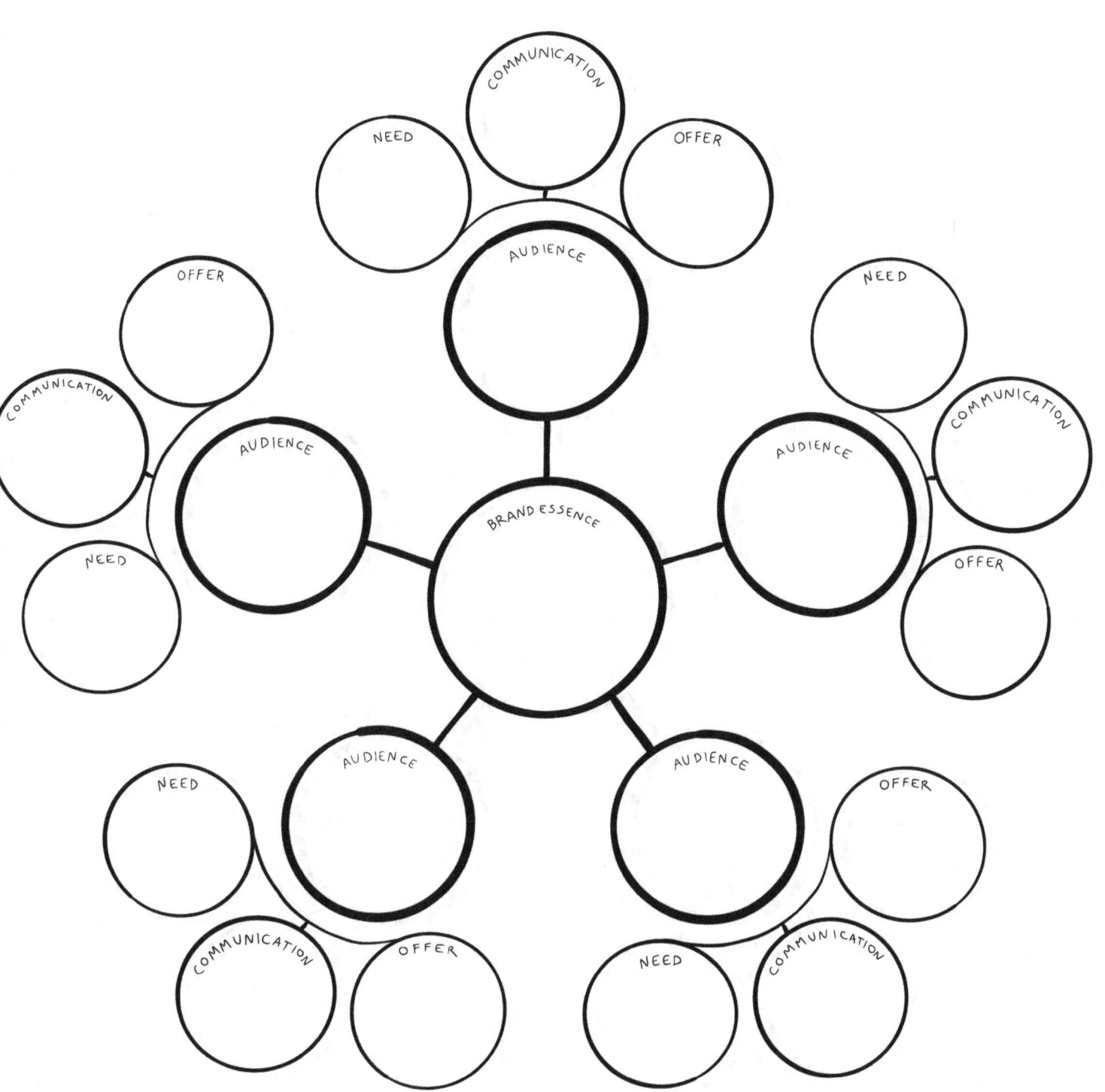

WHO IS YOUR AUDIENCE?

PROJECT:_____   DATE:_____

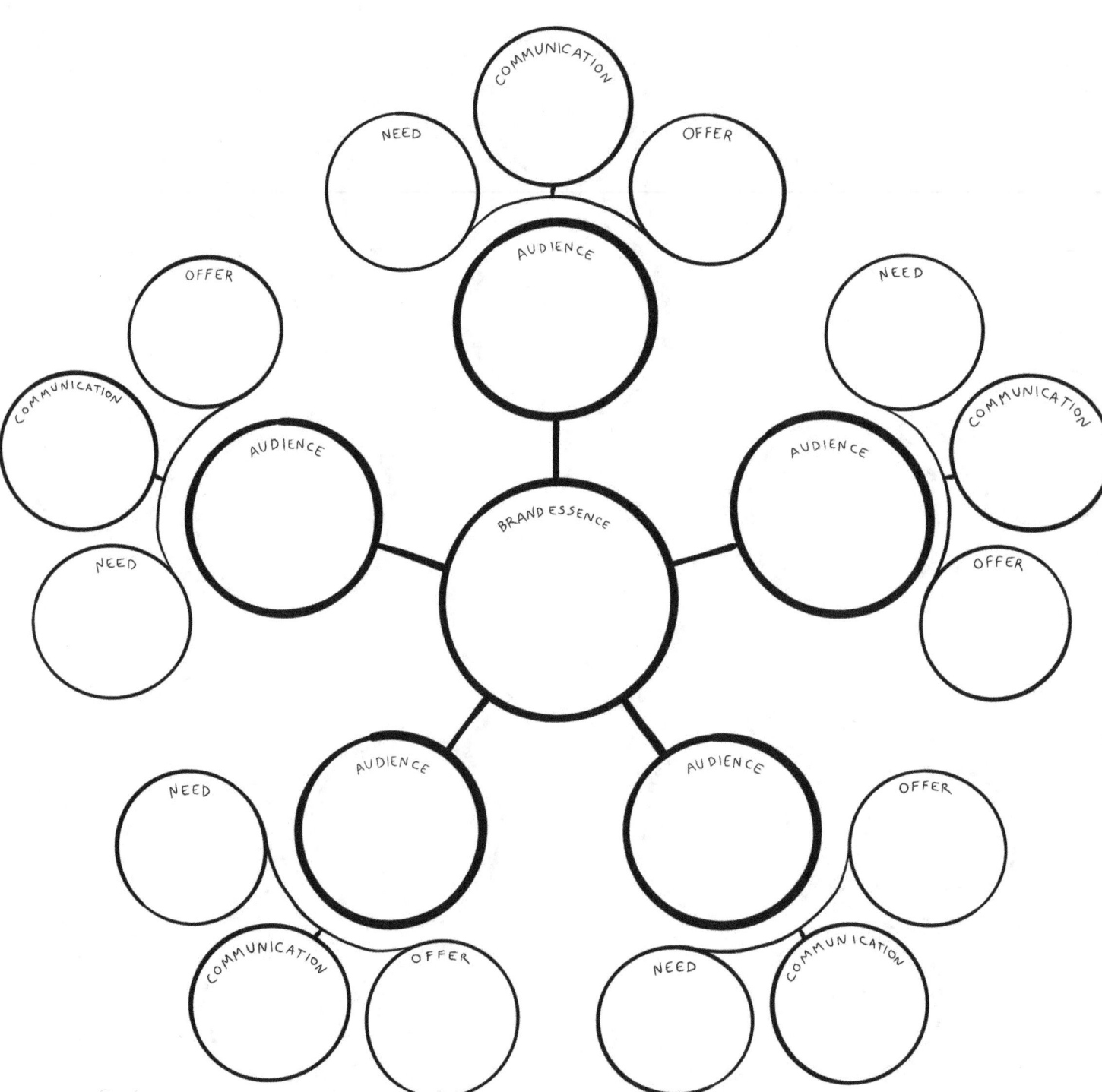

WHO IS YOUR AUDIENCE?

PROJECT:_____   DATE:_____

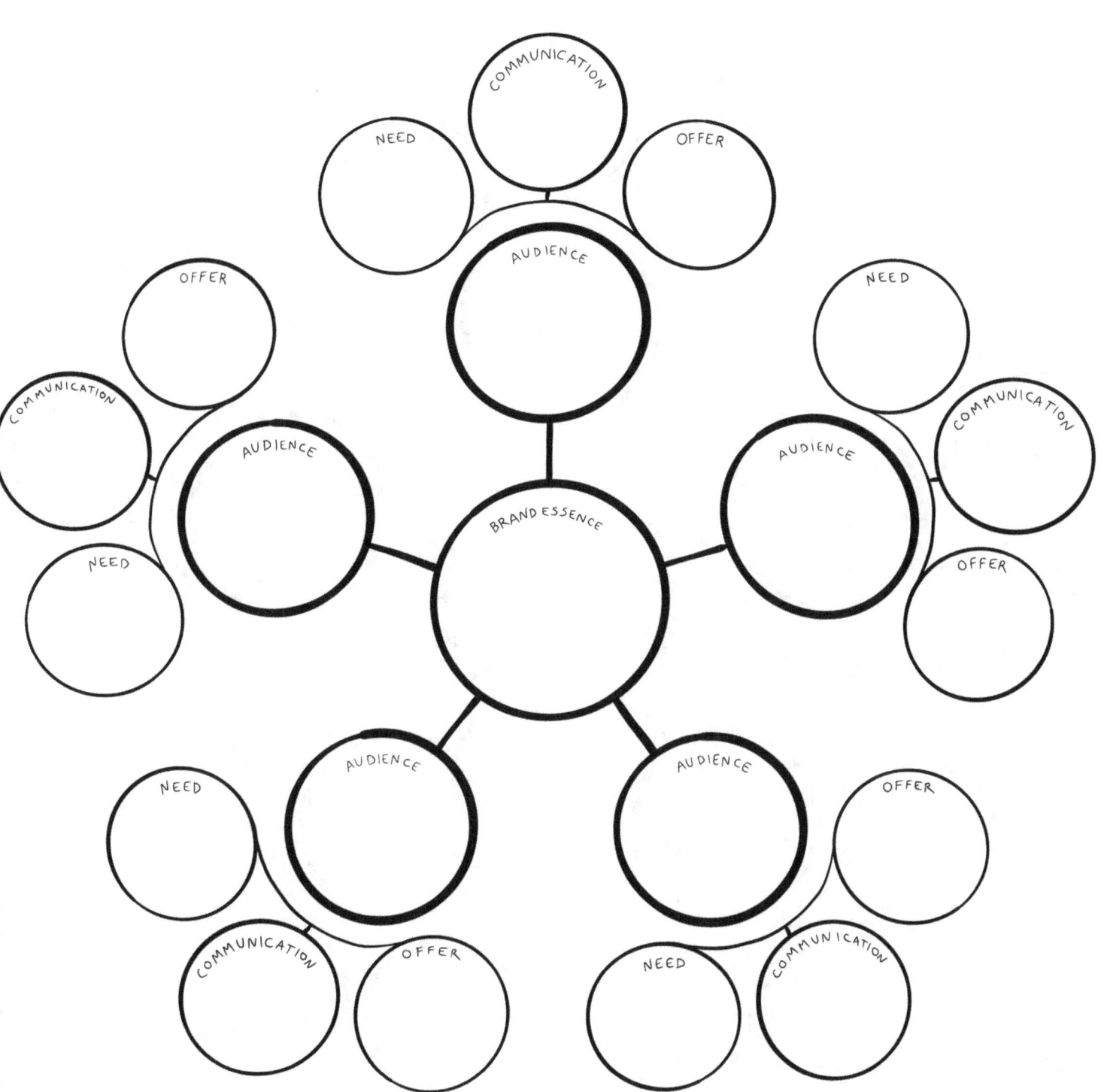

WHO IS YOUR AUDIENCE?

PROJECT:_____   DATE:_____

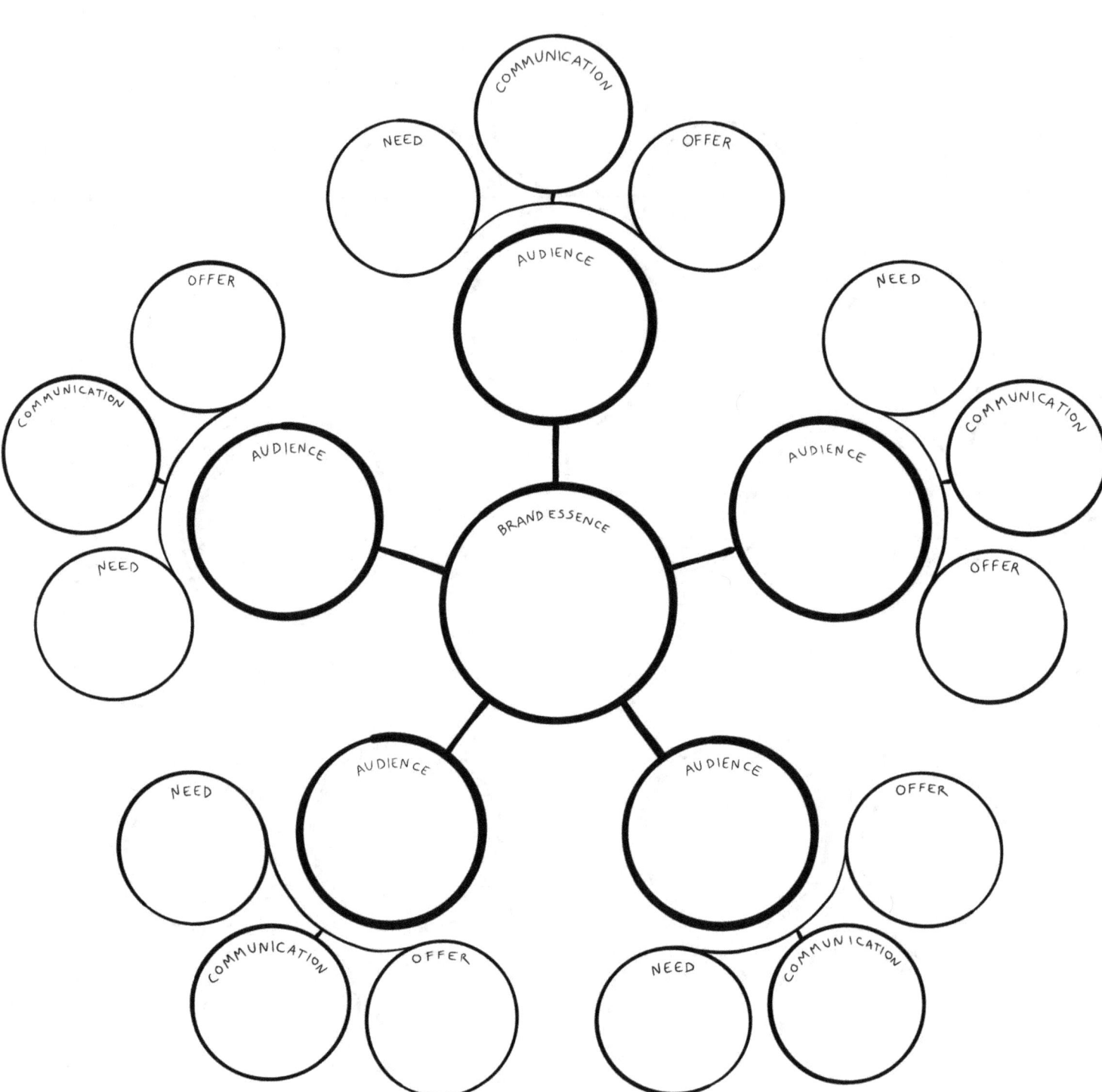

WHO IS YOUR AUDIENCE?

PROJECT:_____   DATE:_____

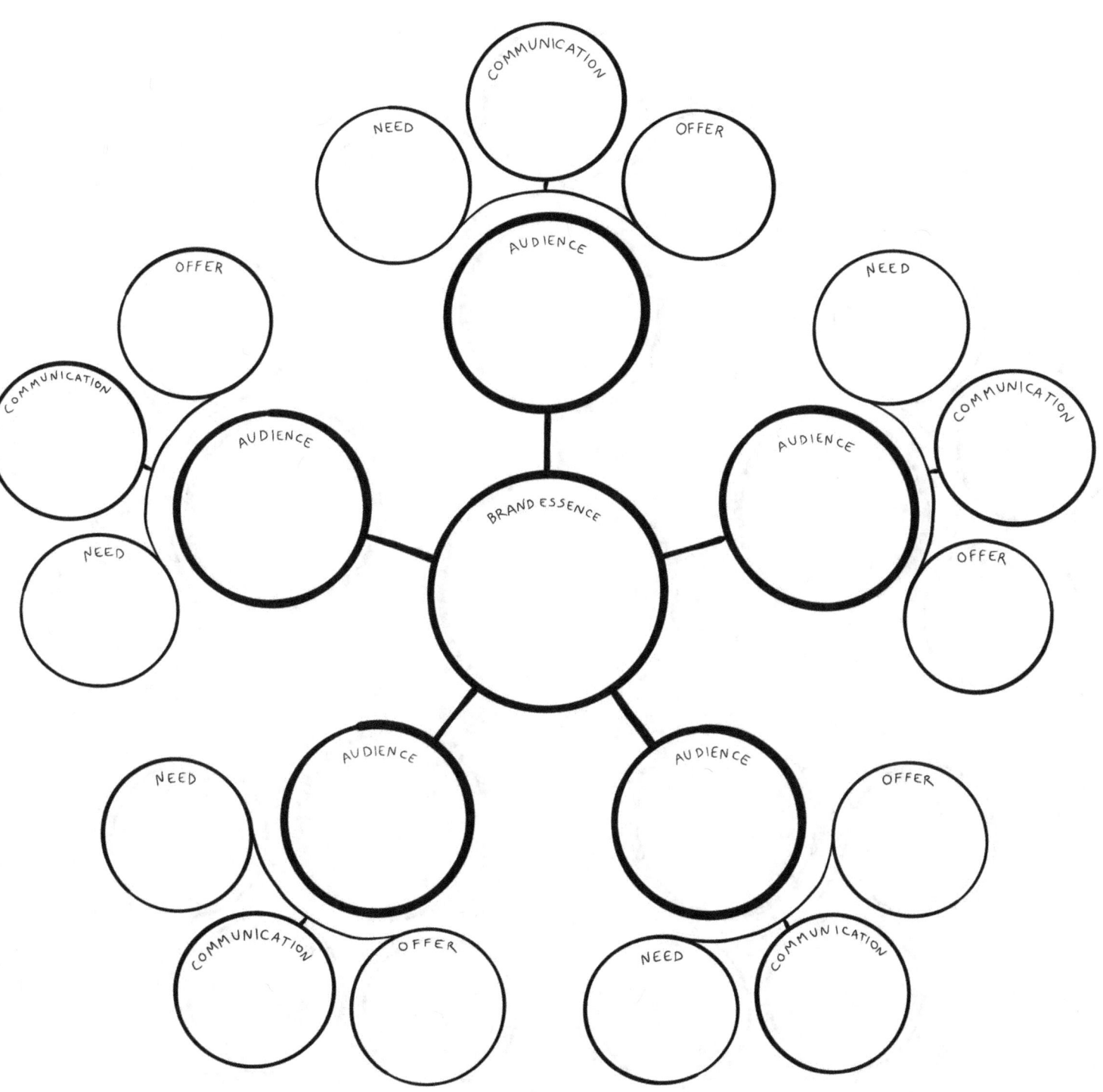

WHO IS YOUR AUDIENCE?

PROJECT:_____   DATE:_____

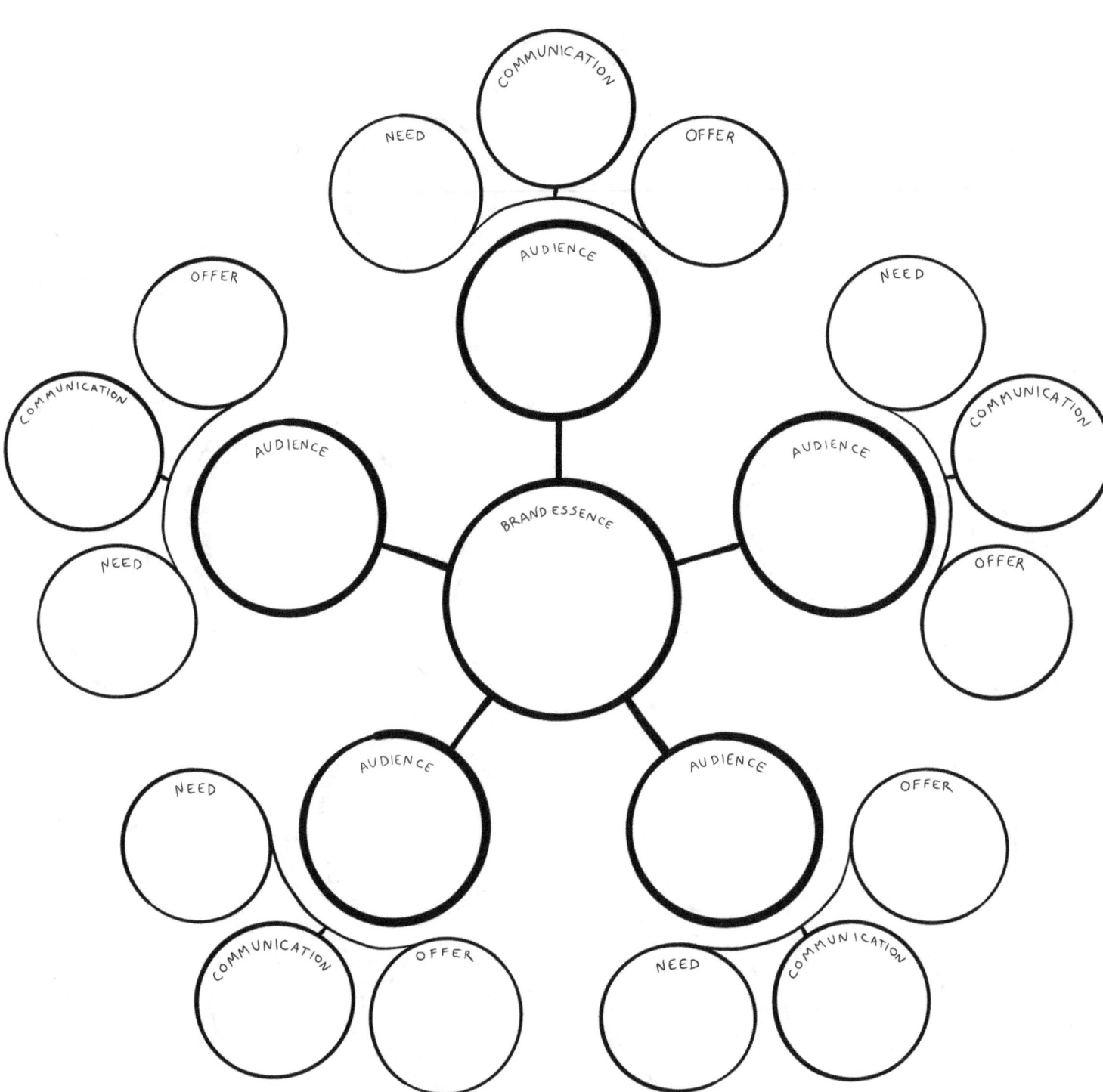

WHO IS YOUR AUDIENCE?

PROJECT:_____   DATE:_____

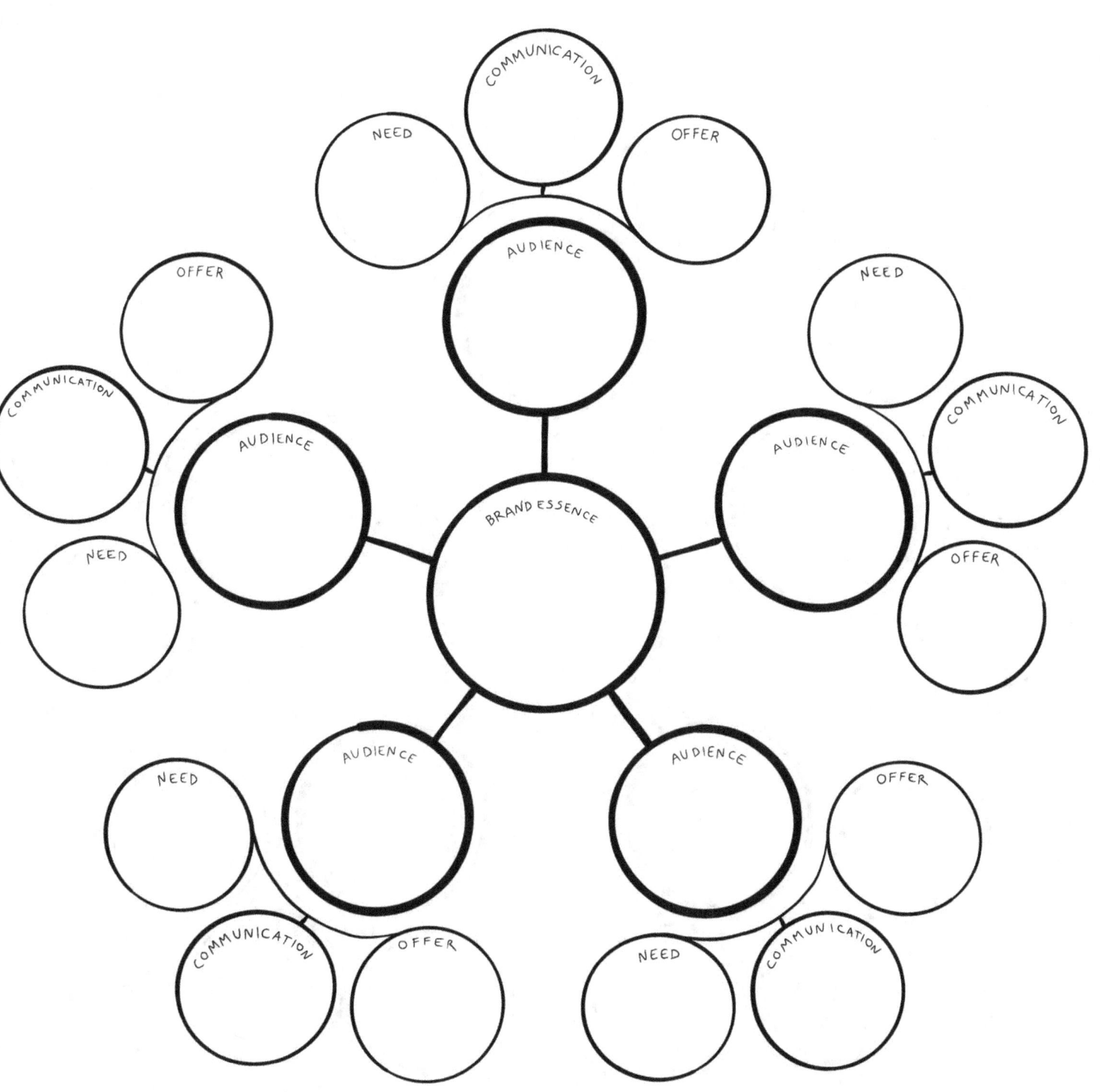

WHO IS YOUR AUDIENCE?

PROJECT:_____   DATE:_____

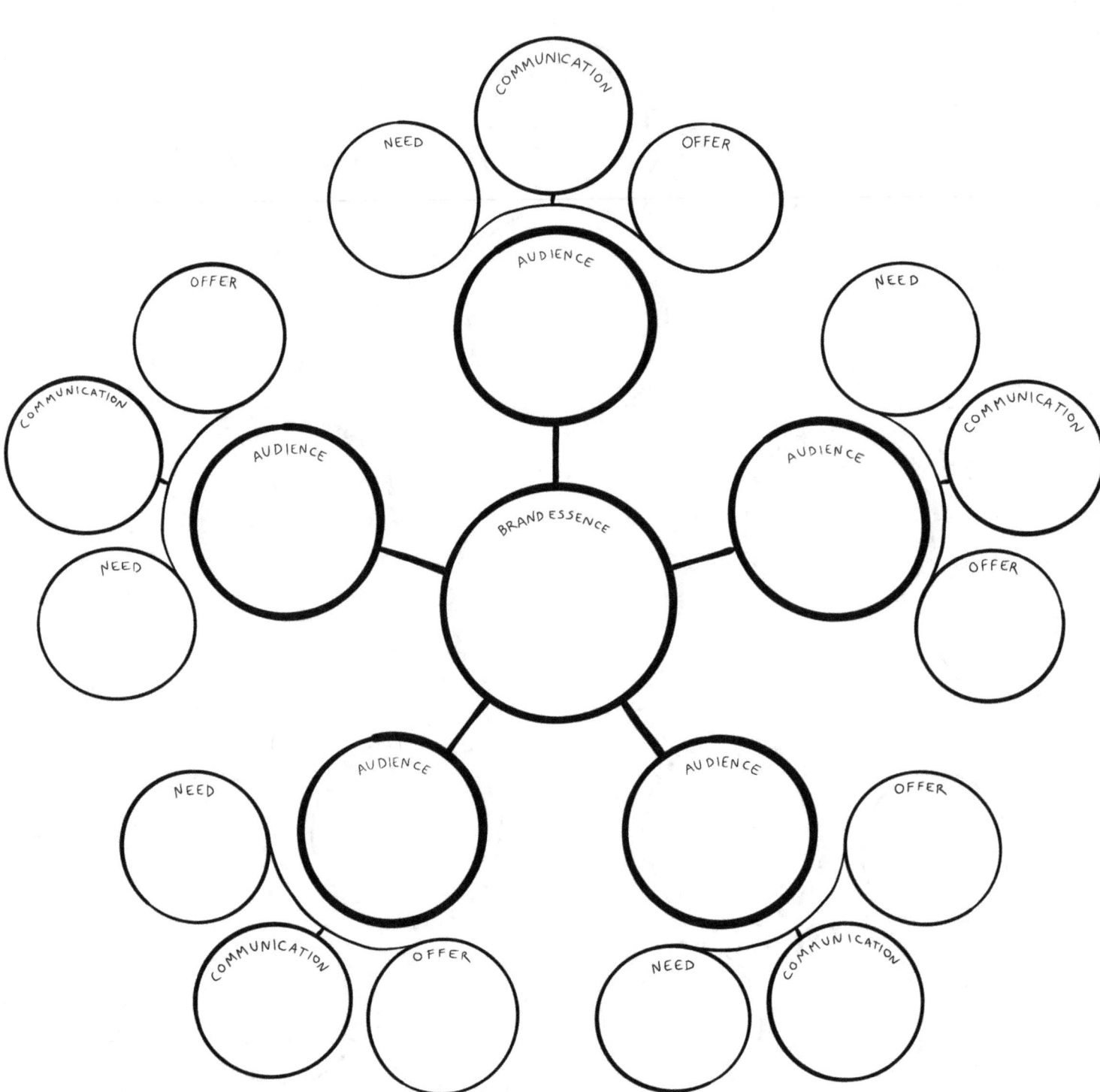

WHO IS YOUR AUDIENCE?

PROJECT:_____   DATE:_____

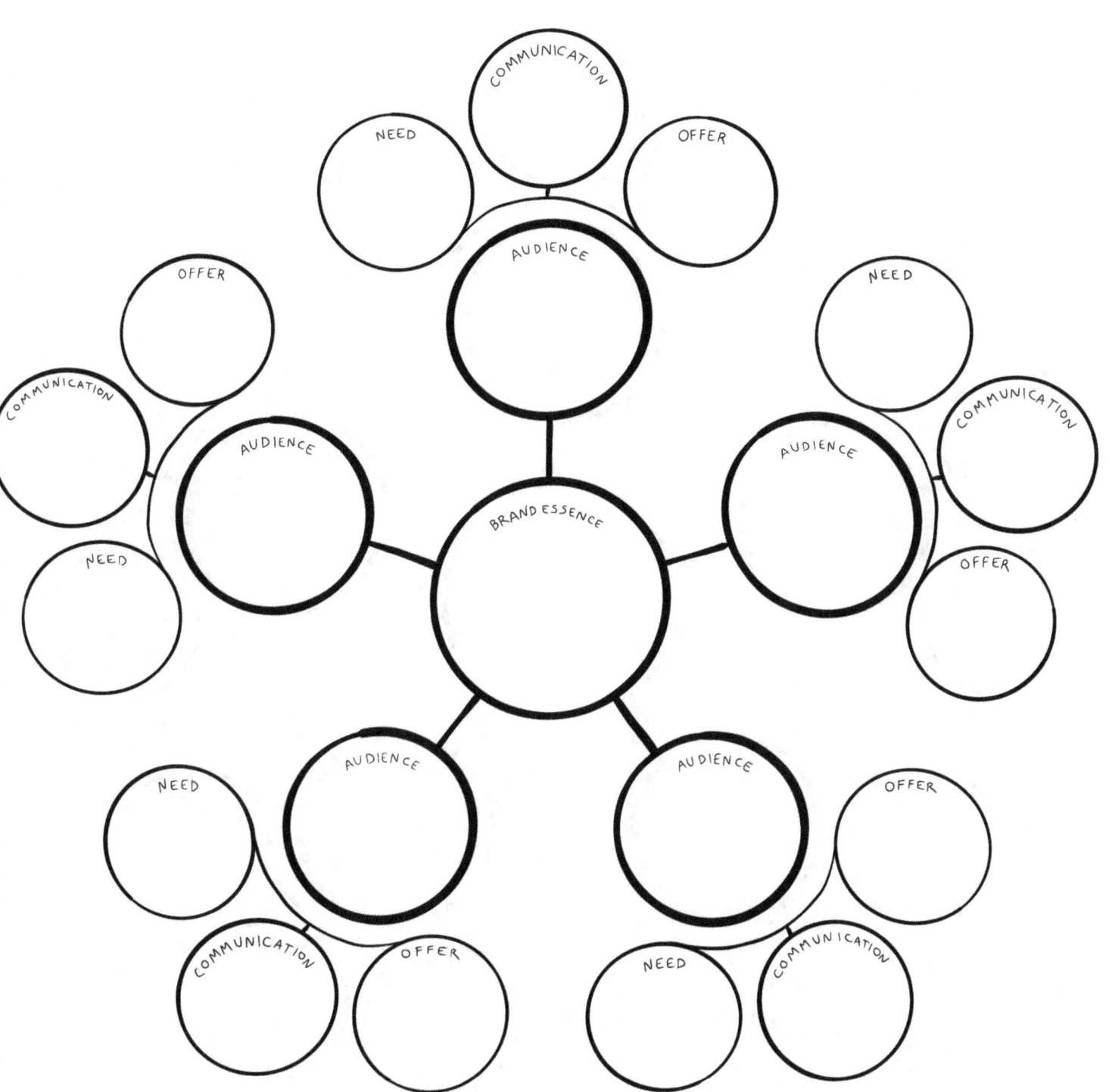

WHO IS YOUR AUDIENCE?

PROJECT:_____   DATE:_____

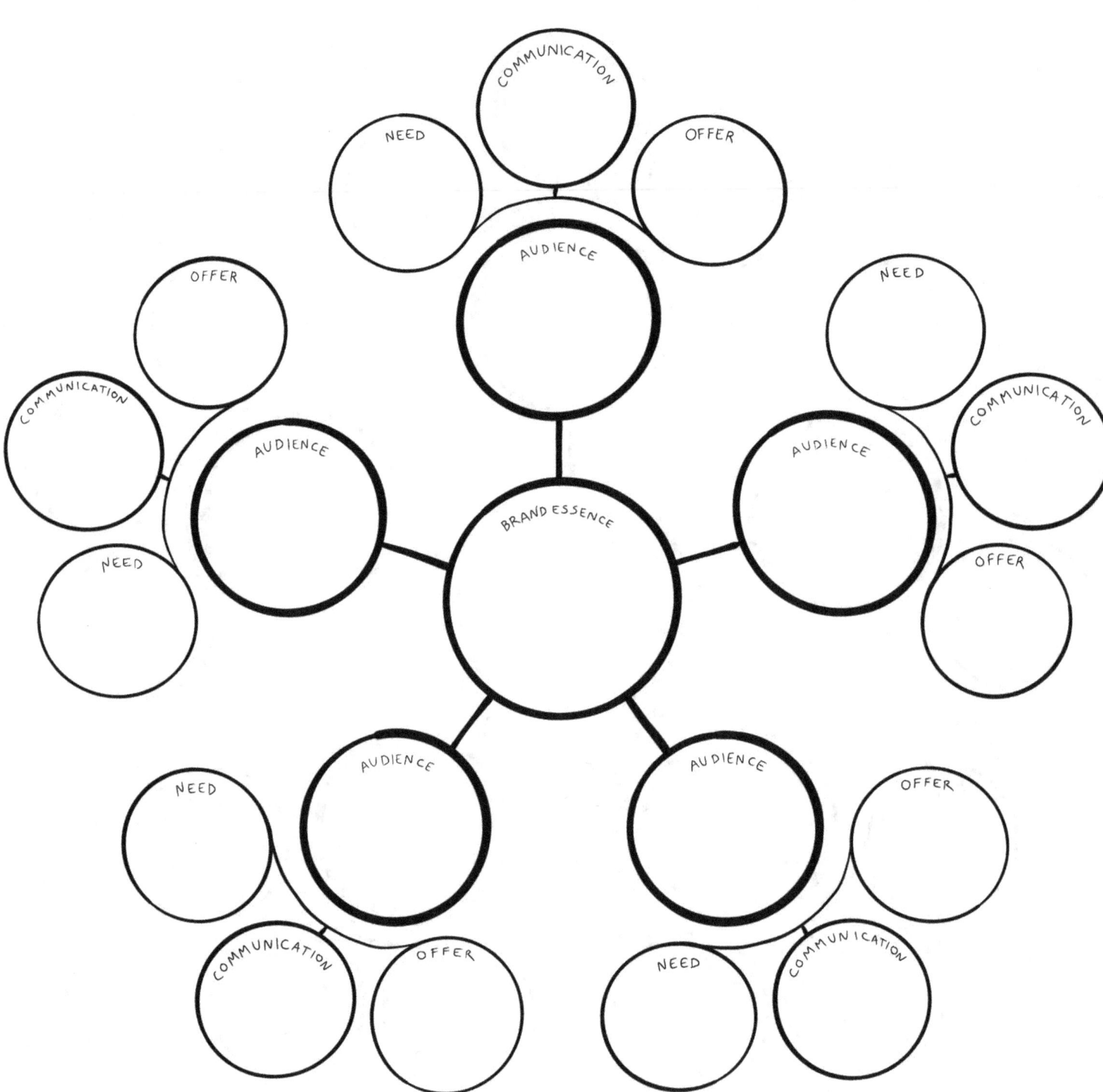

WHO IS YOUR AUDIENCE?

PROJECT:_____   DATE:_____

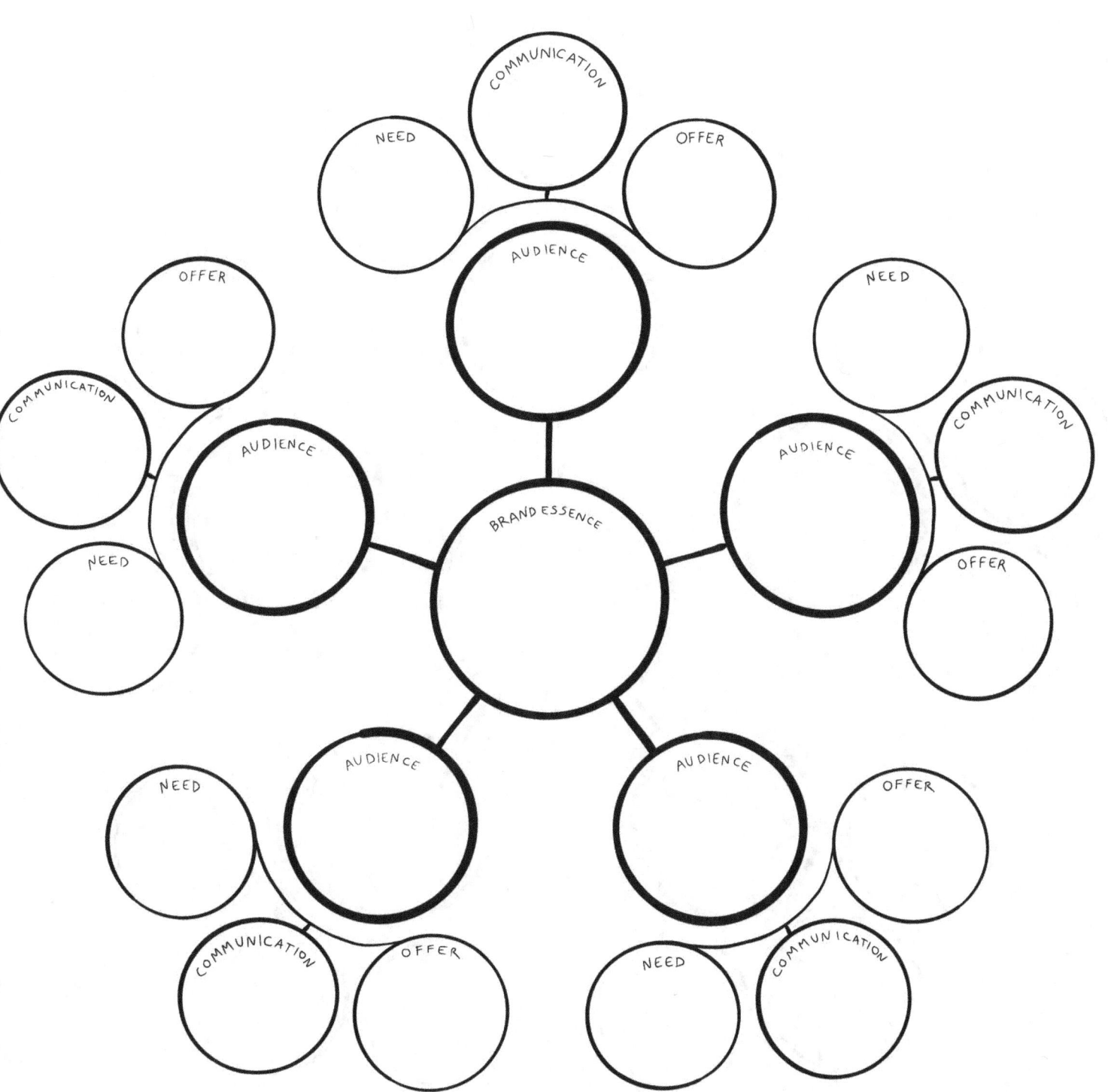

WHO IS YOUR AUDIENCE?

PROJECT:_____   DATE:_____

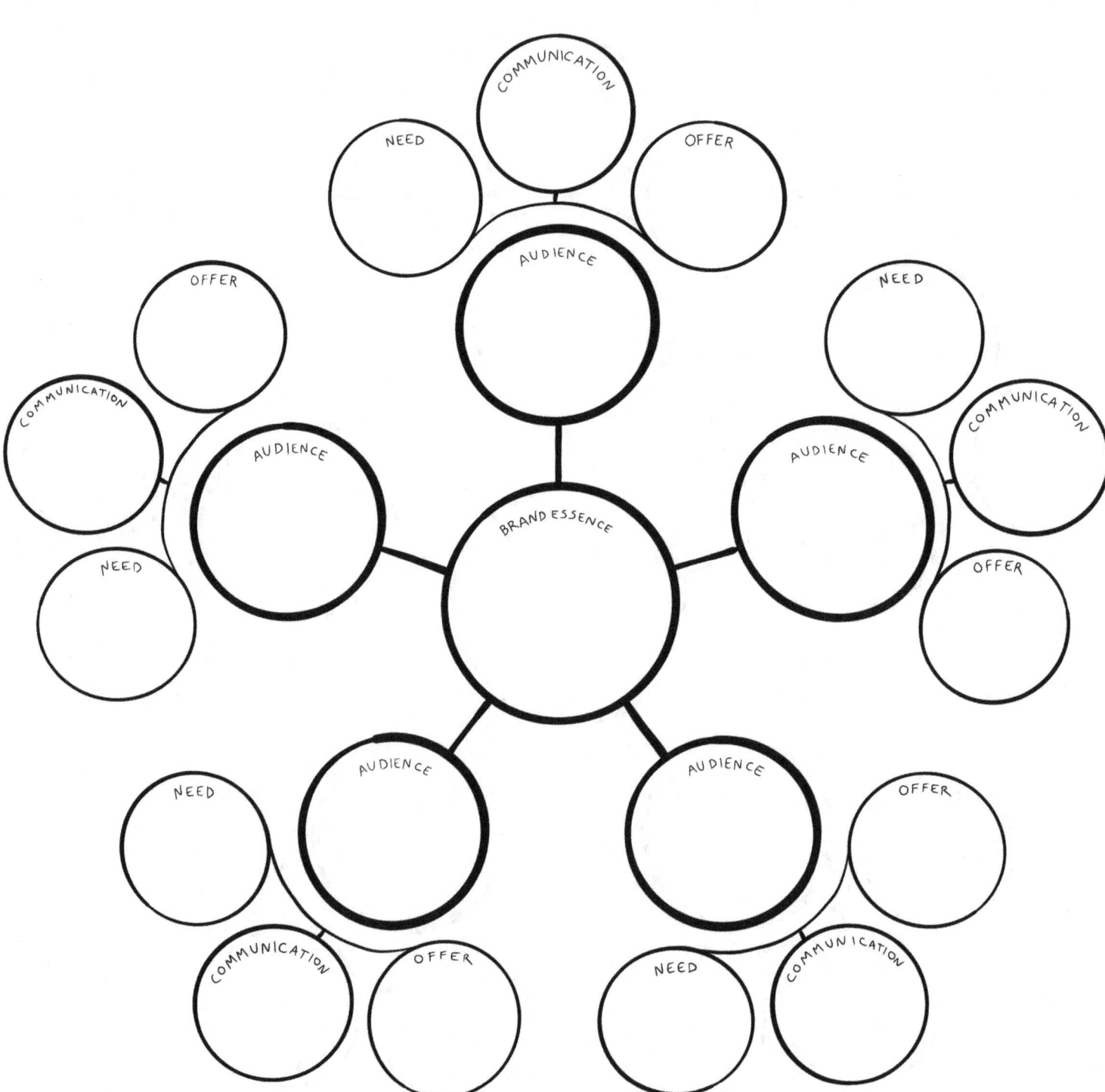

WHO IS YOUR AUDIENCE?

PROJECT:_____   DATE:_____

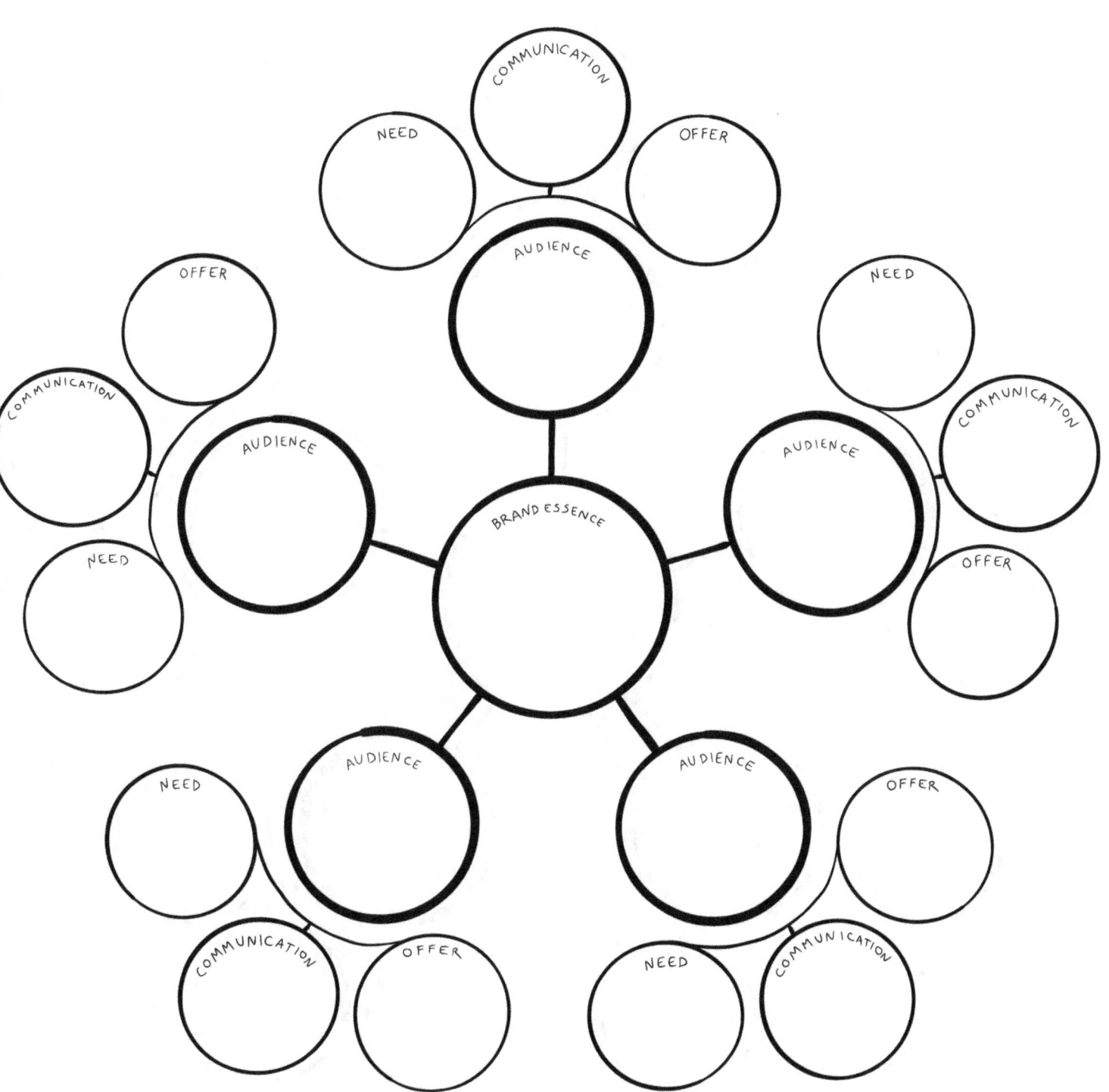

WHO IS YOUR AUDIENCE?

PROJECT:_____   DATE:_____

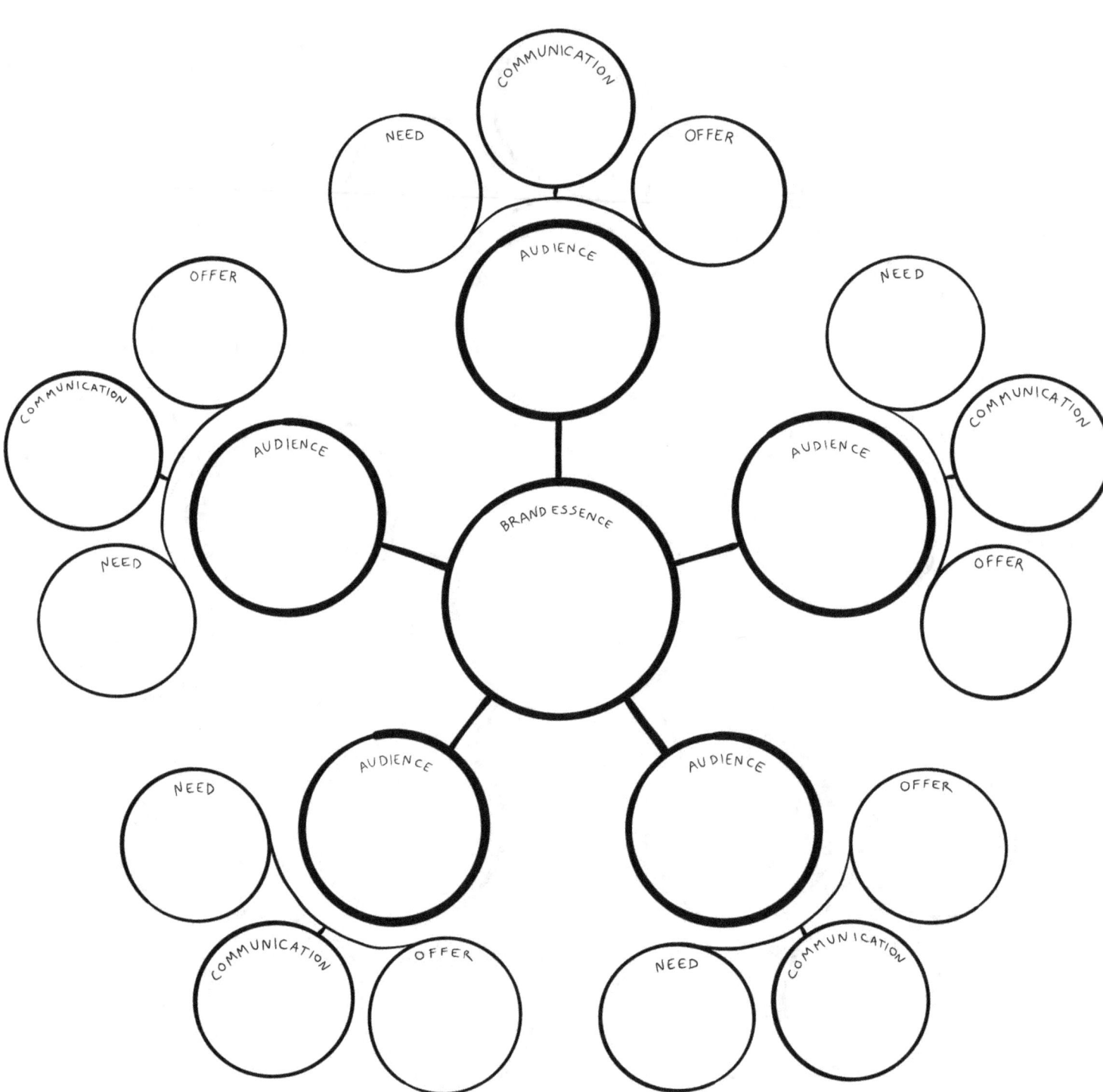

WHO IS YOUR AUDIENCE?

PROJECT:_____   DATE:_____

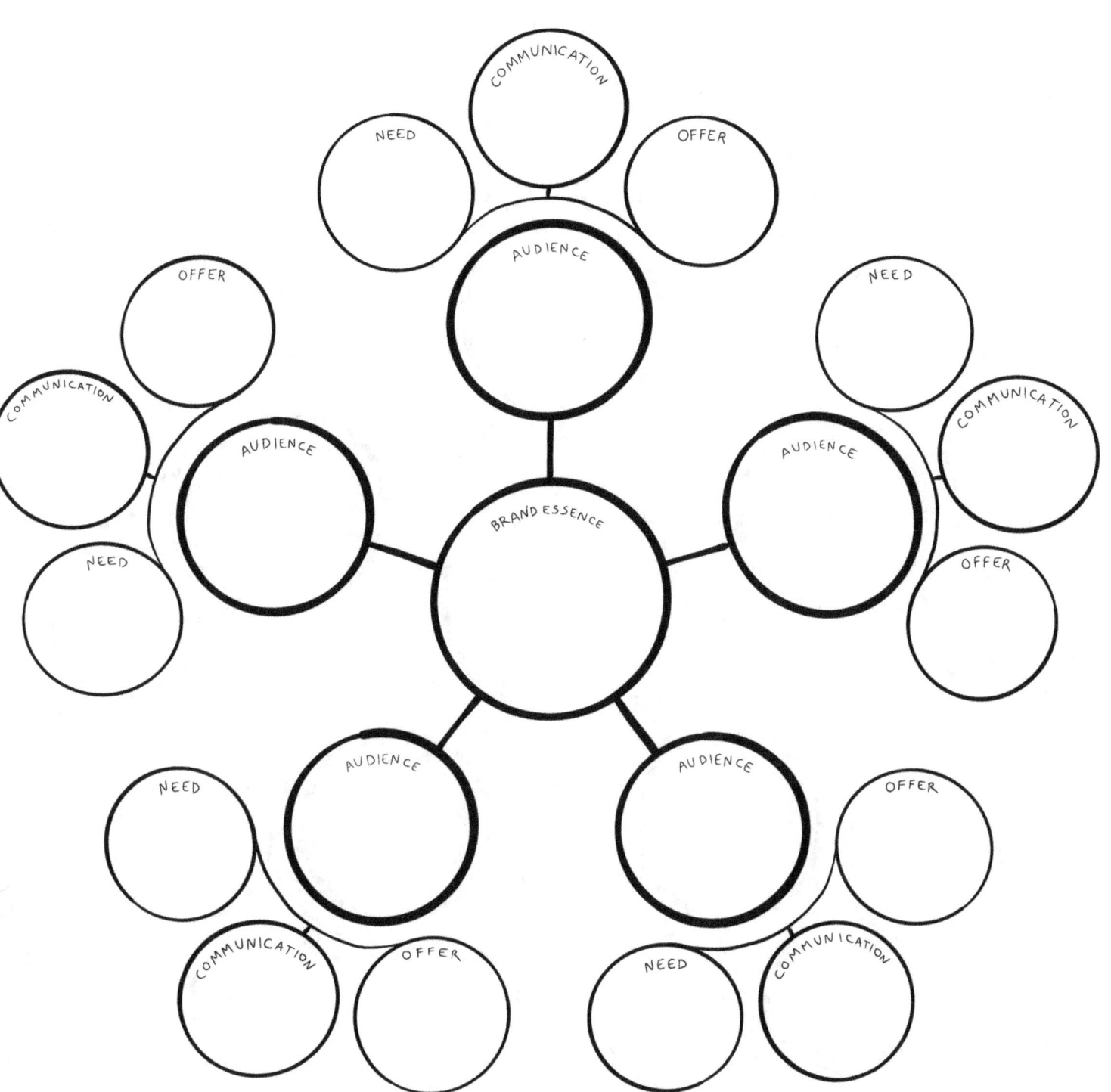

WHO IS YOUR AUDIENCE?

PROJECT: _____   DATE: _____

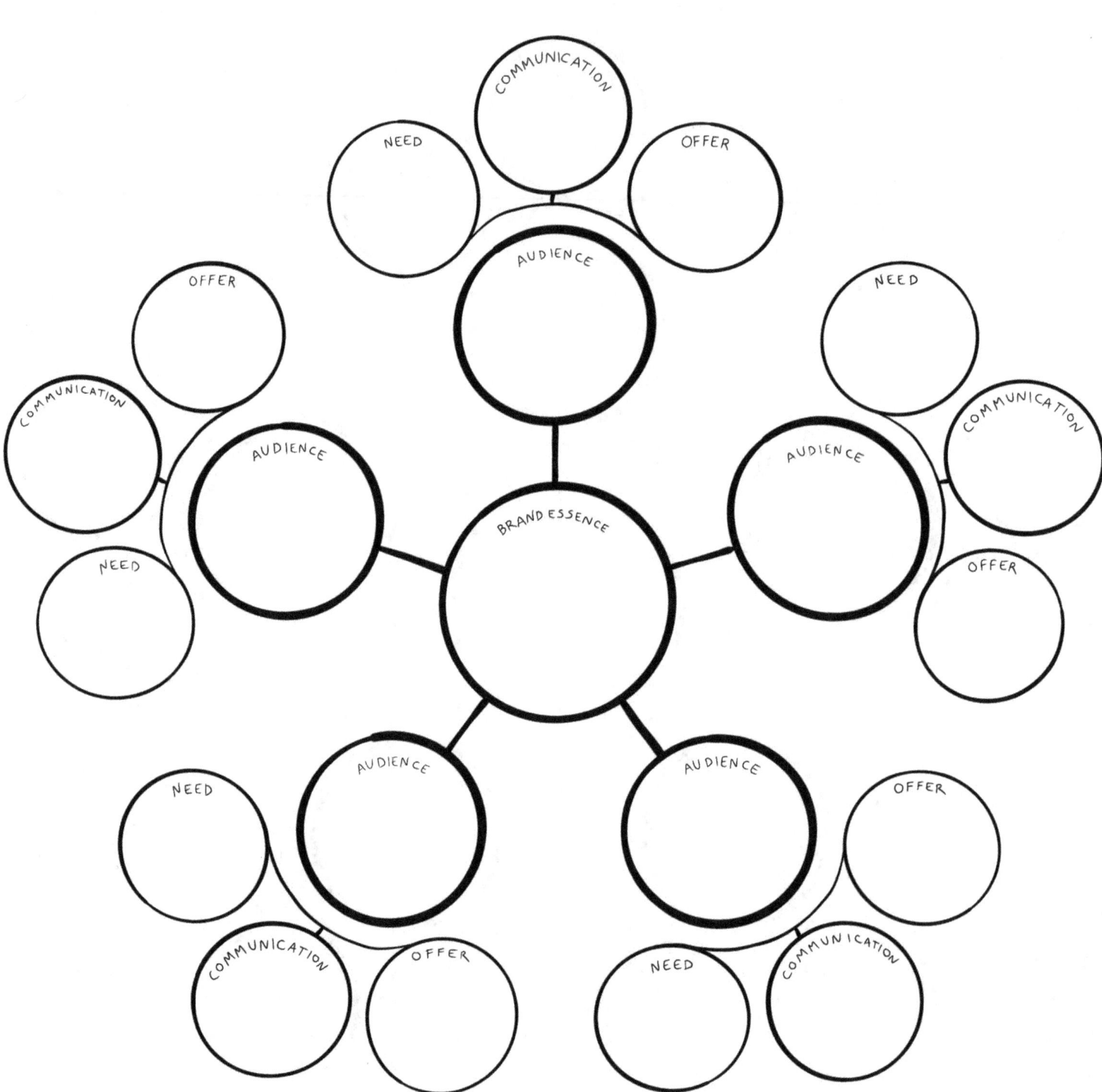

WHO IS YOUR AUDIENCE?

PROJECT:_____   DATE:_____

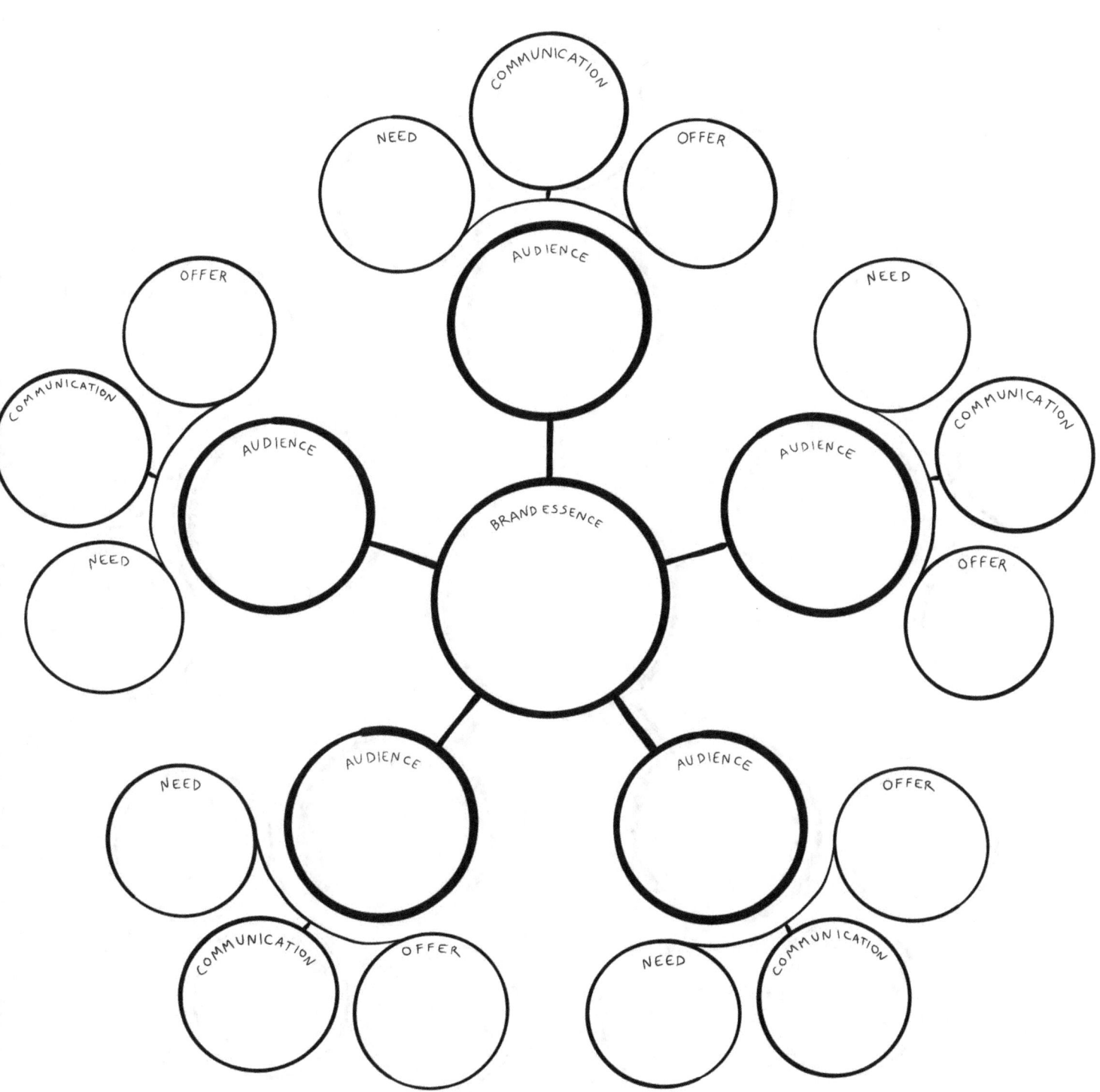

WHO IS YOUR AUDIENCE?

PROJECT:_____   DATE:_____

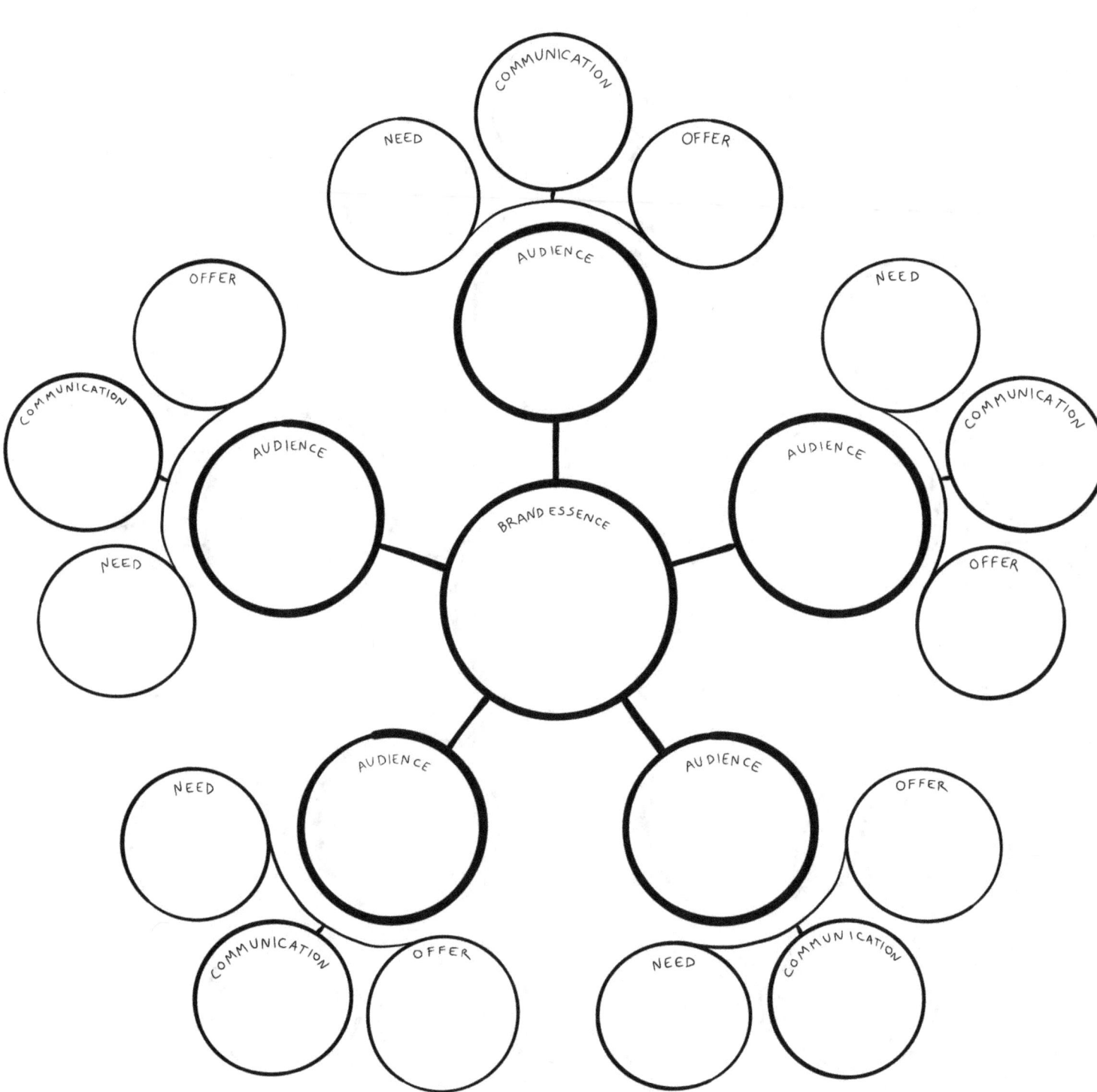

WHO IS YOUR AUDIENCE?

PROJECT:_____   DATE:_____

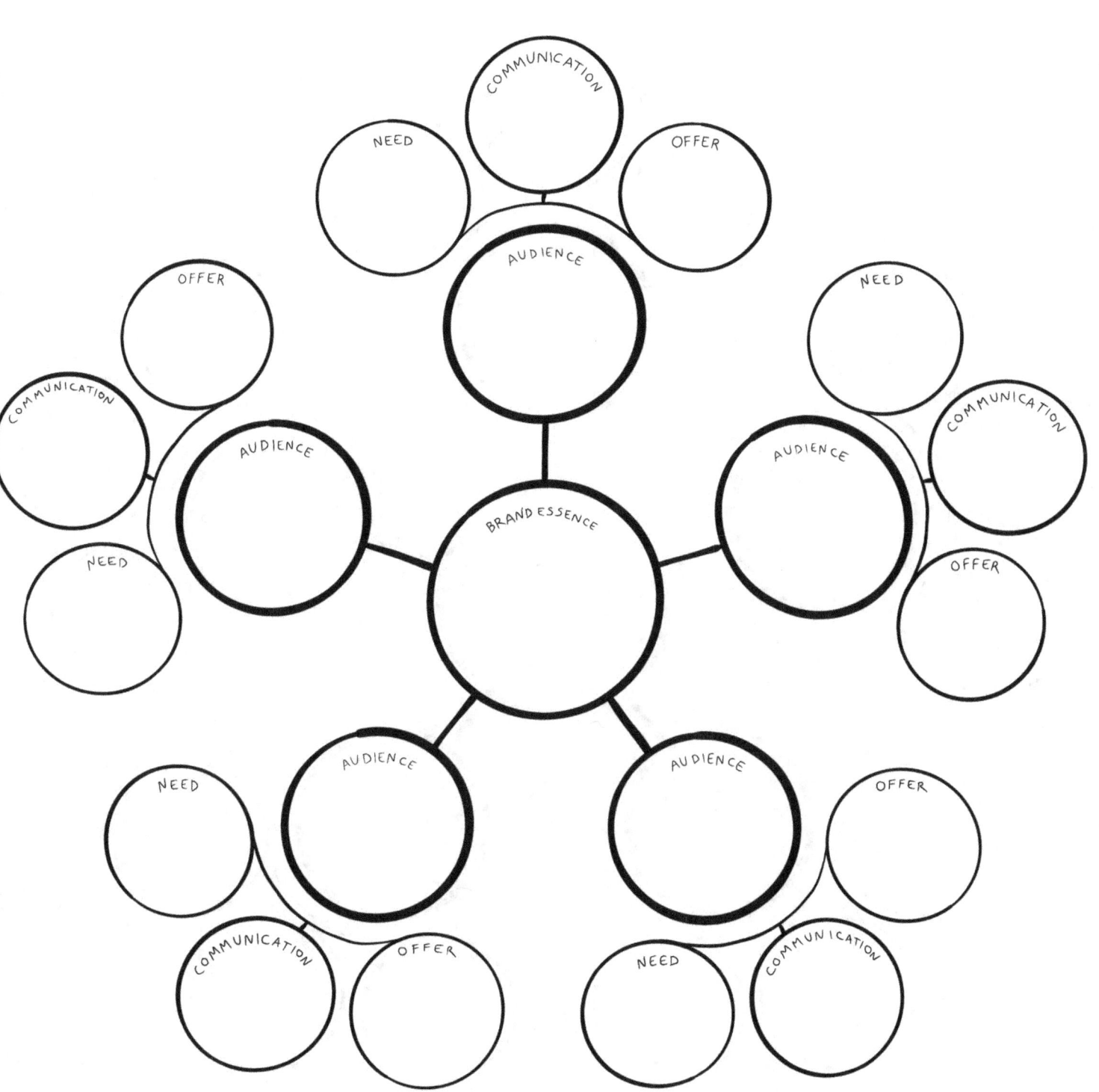

WHO IS YOUR AUDIENCE?

PROJECT:_____   DATE:_____

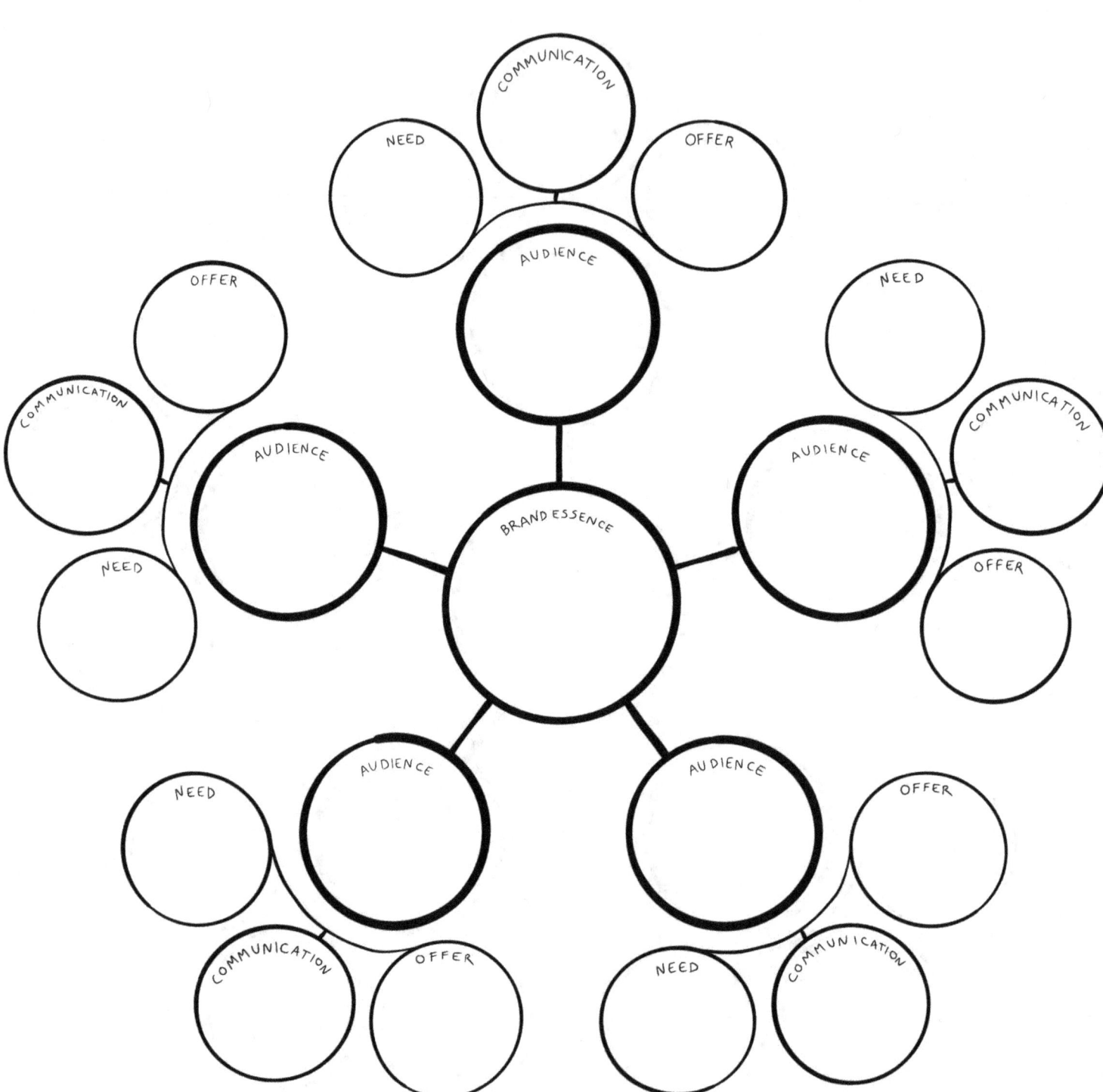

WHO IS YOUR AUDIENCE?

PROJECT:_____   DATE:_____

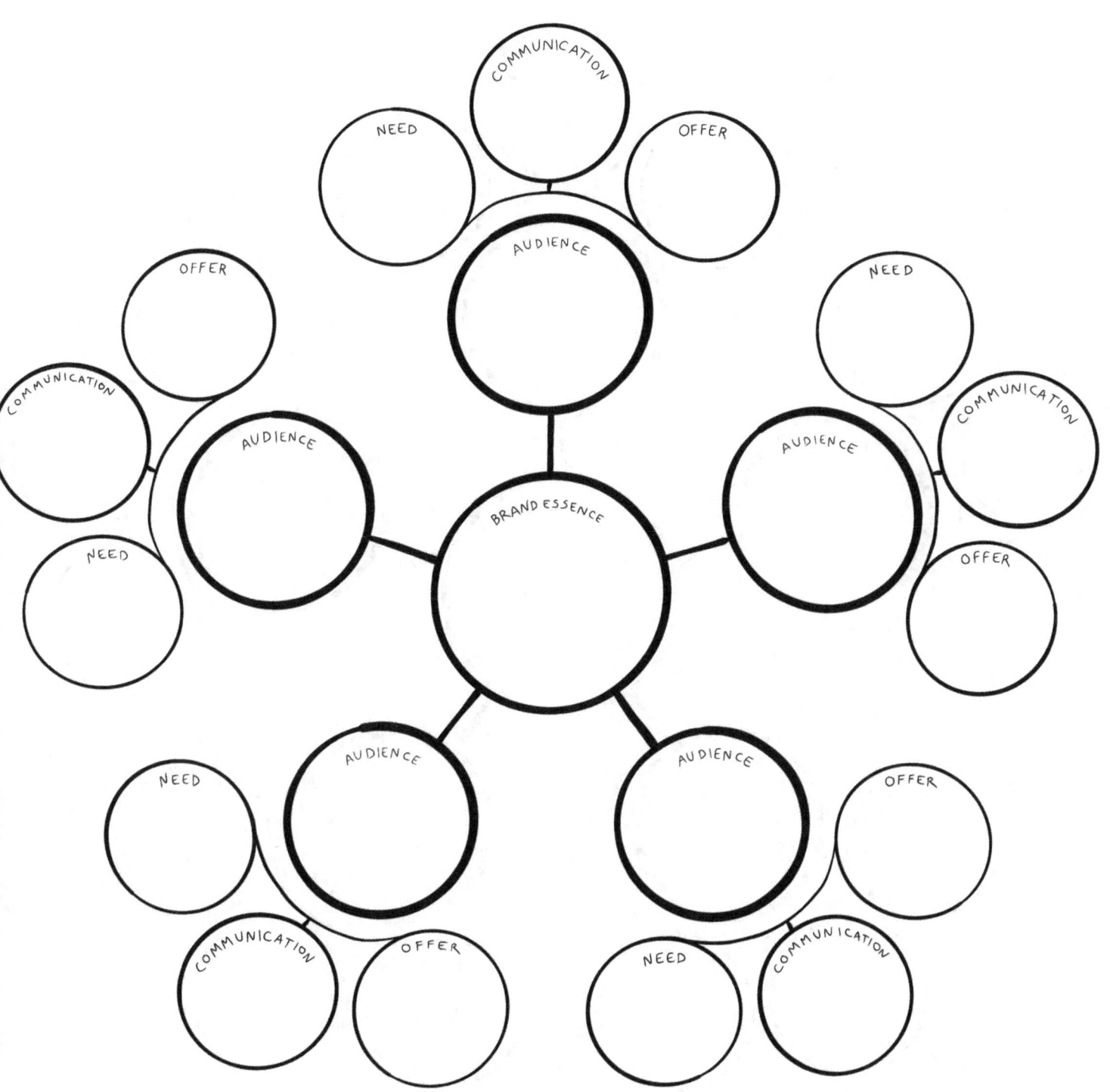

WHO IS YOUR AUDIENCE?

PROJECT:_____   DATE:_____

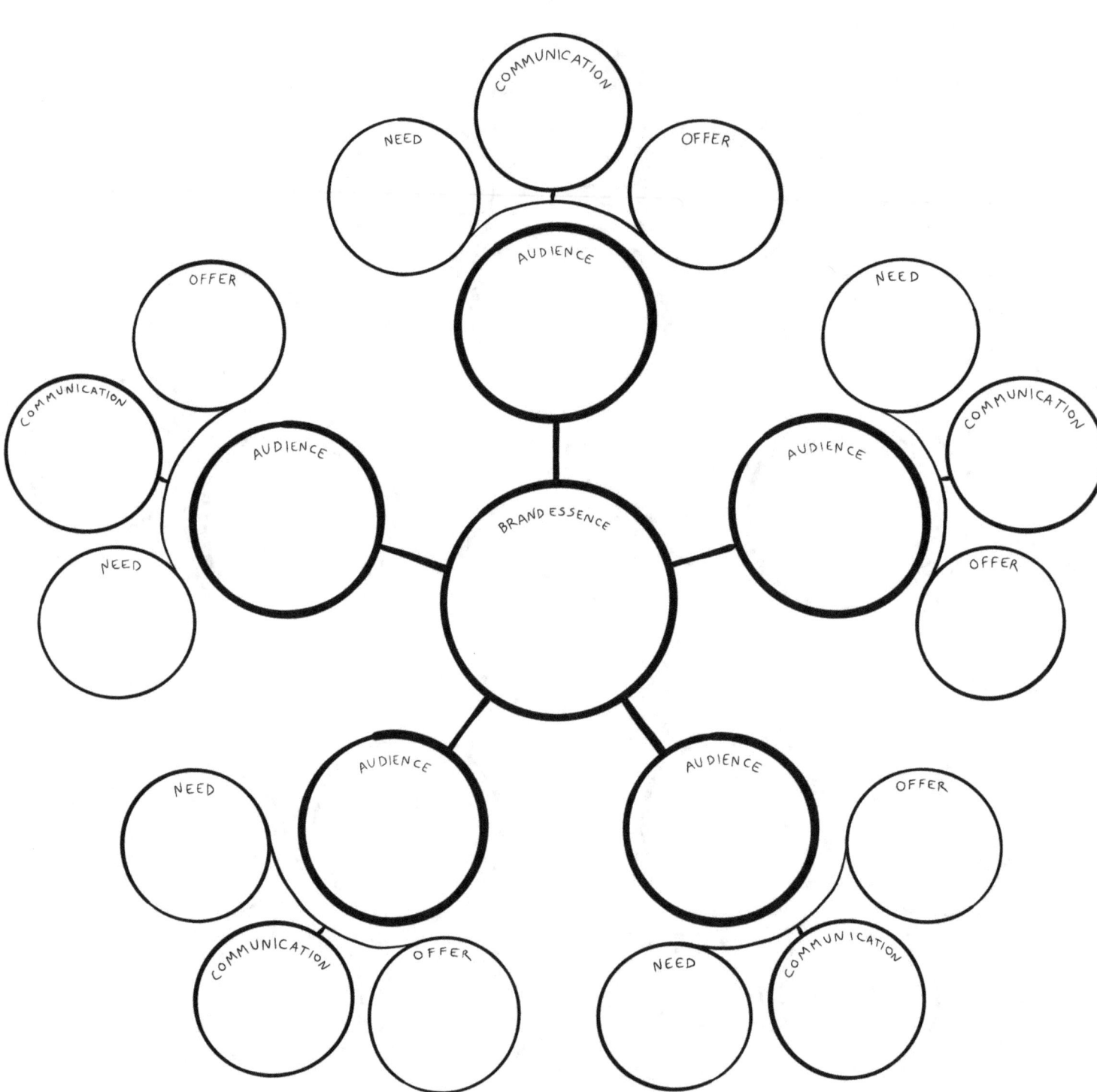

WHO IS YOUR AUDIENCE?

PROJECT:_____   DATE:_____

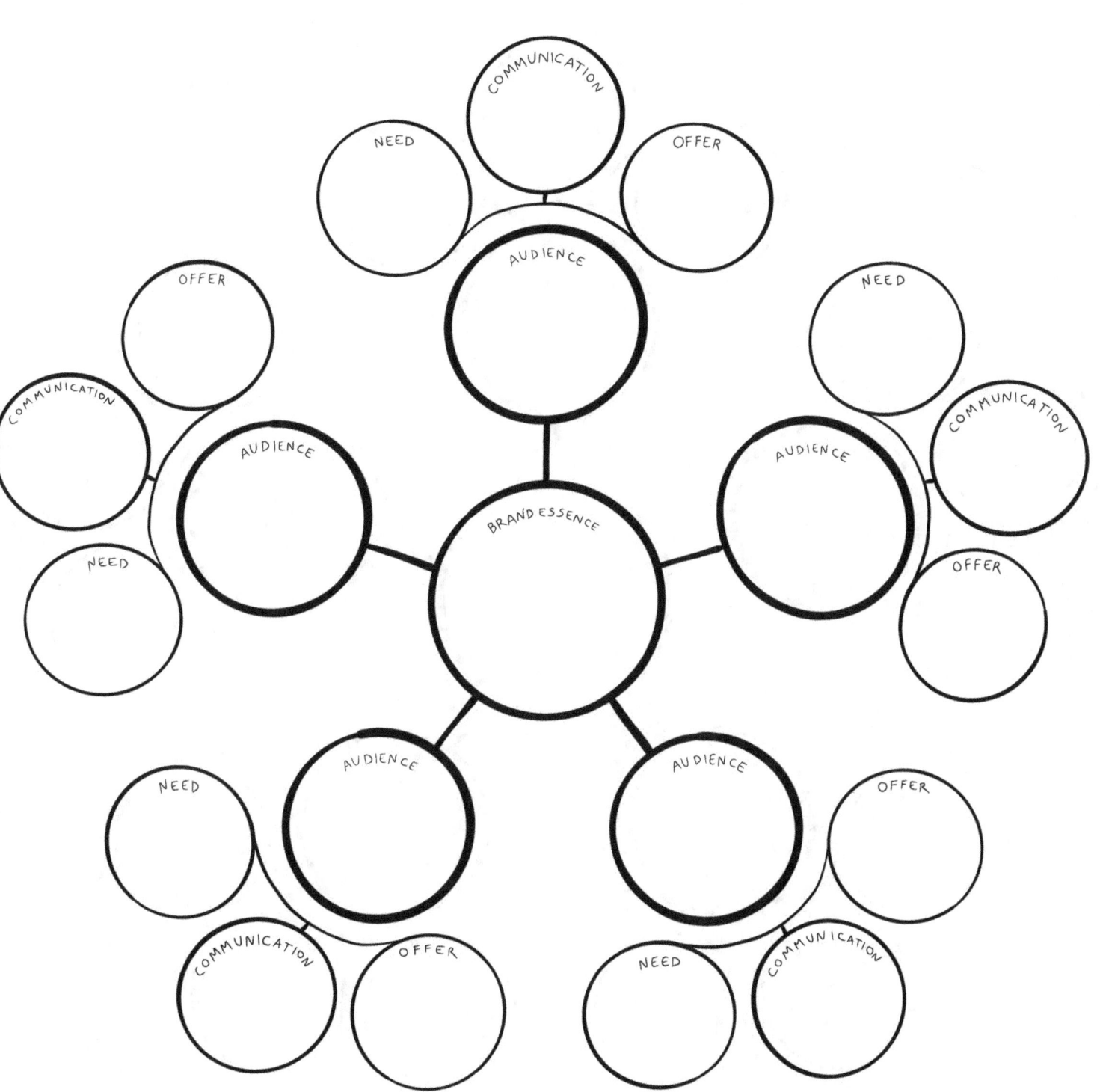

WHO IS YOUR AUDIENCE?

PROJECT:_____   DATE:_____

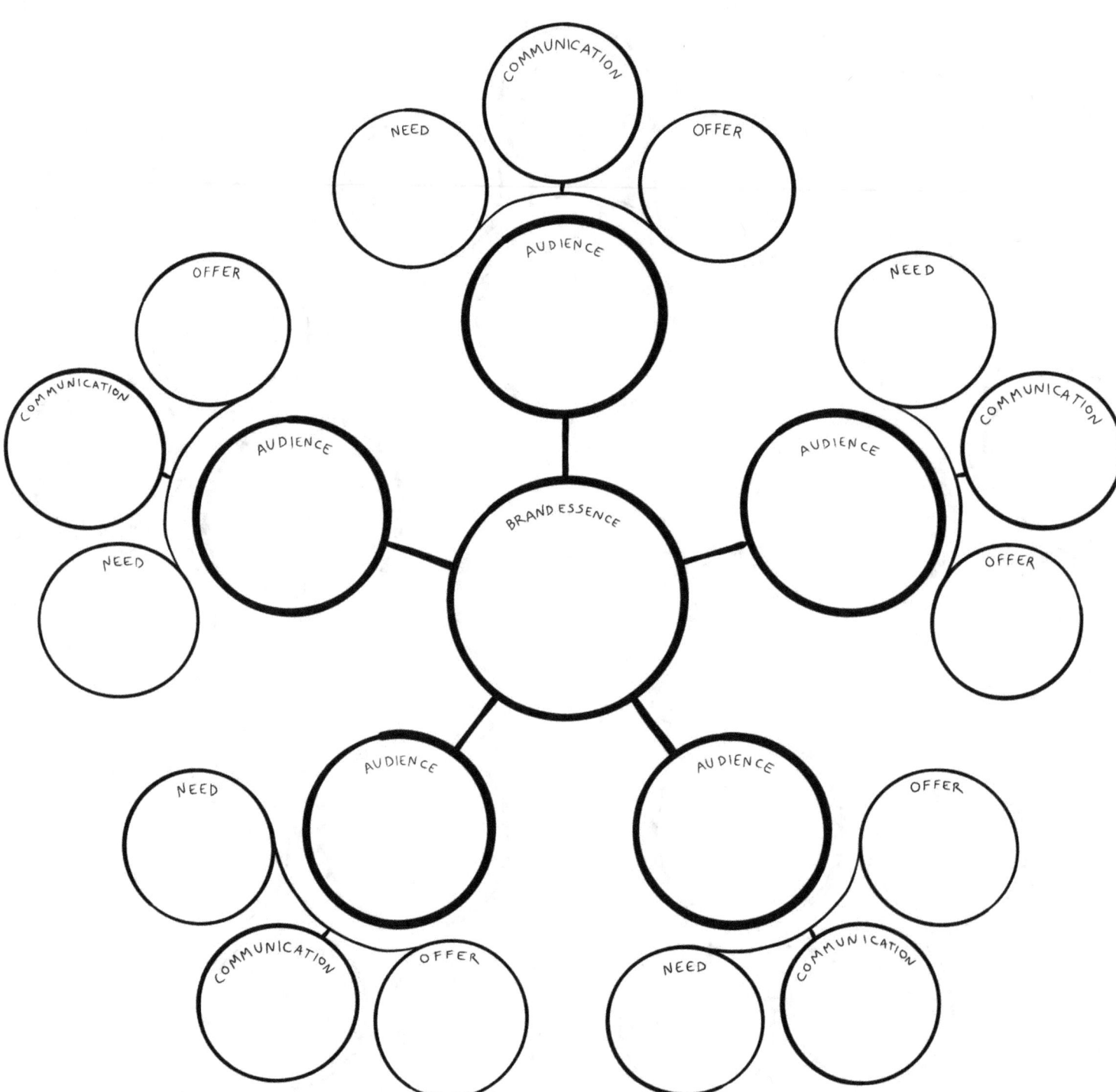

WHO IS YOUR AUDIENCE?

PROJECT:_____   DATE:_____

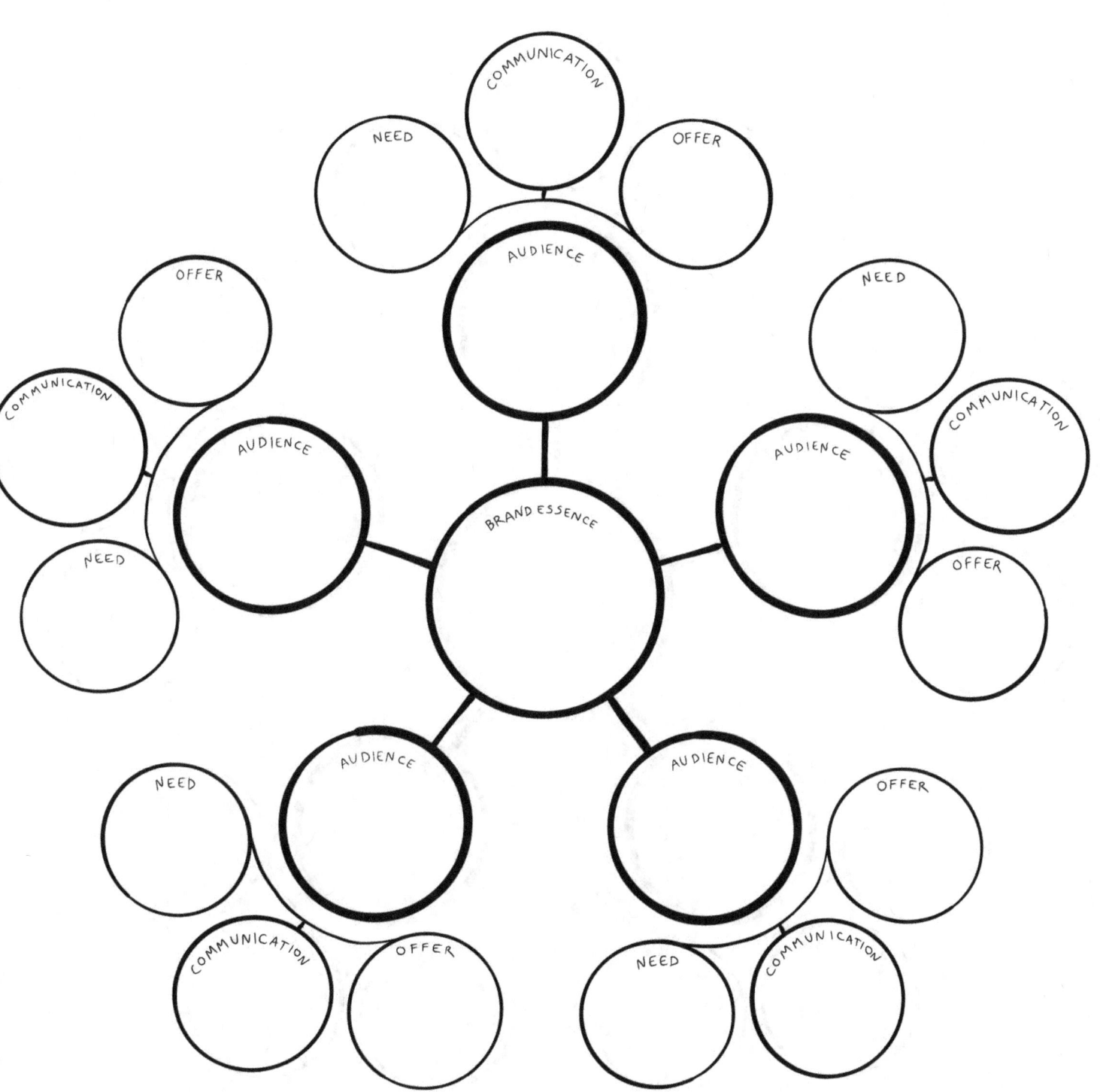

WHO IS YOUR AUDIENCE?

PROJECT:_____   DATE:_____

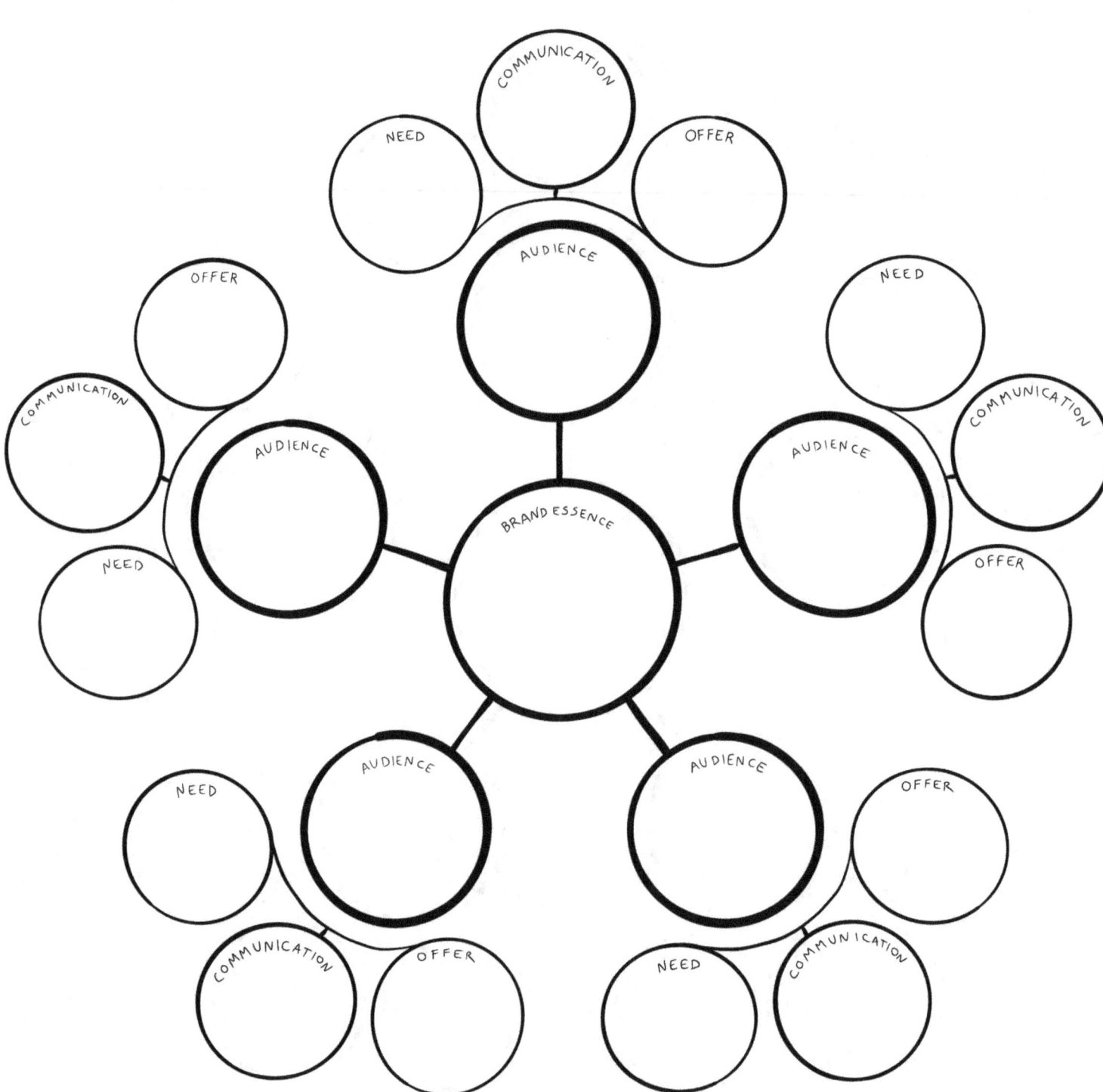

WHO IS YOUR AUDIENCE?

PROJECT:_____   DATE:_____

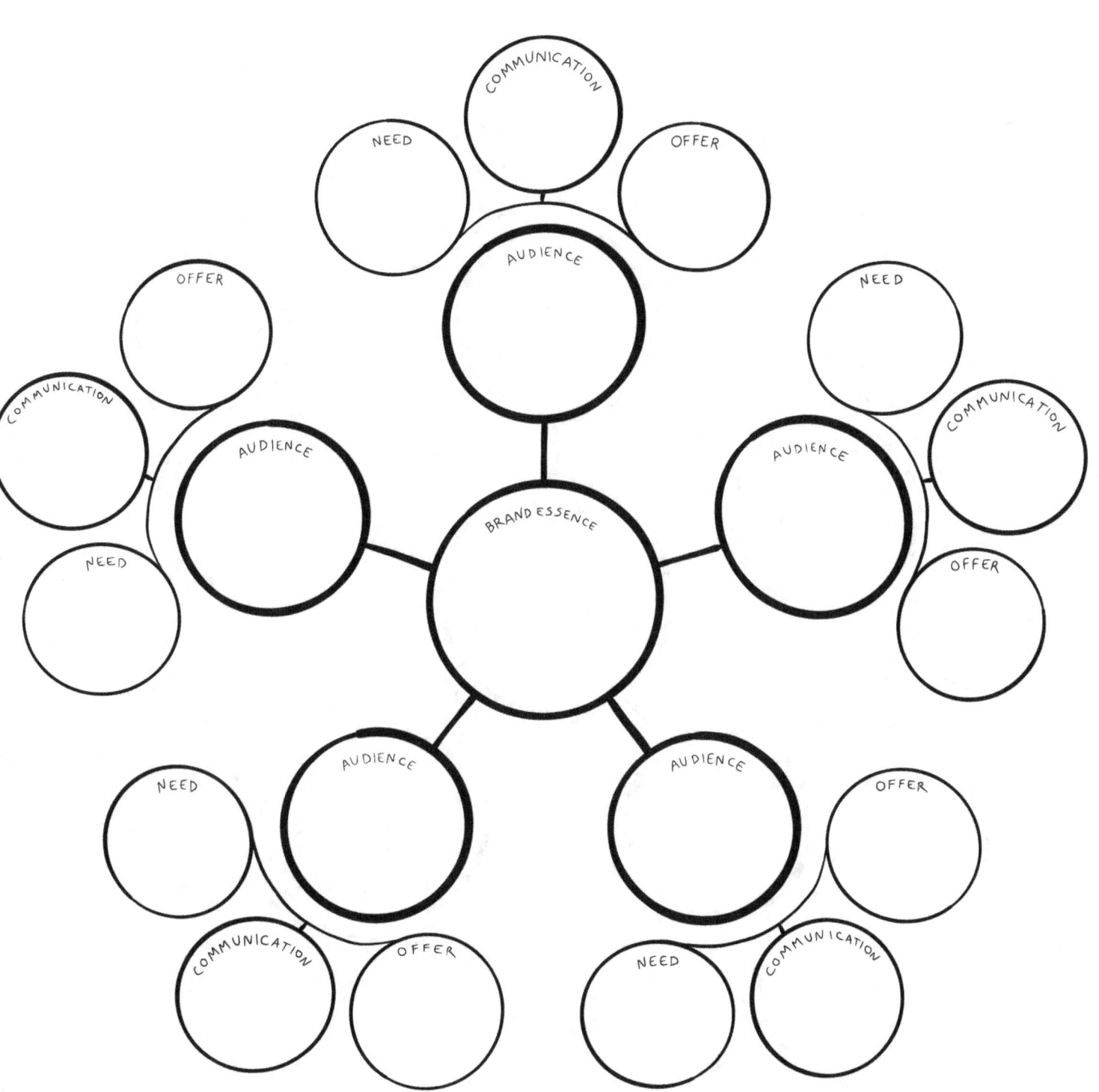

WHO IS YOUR AUDIENCE?

PROJECT:_____   DATE:_____

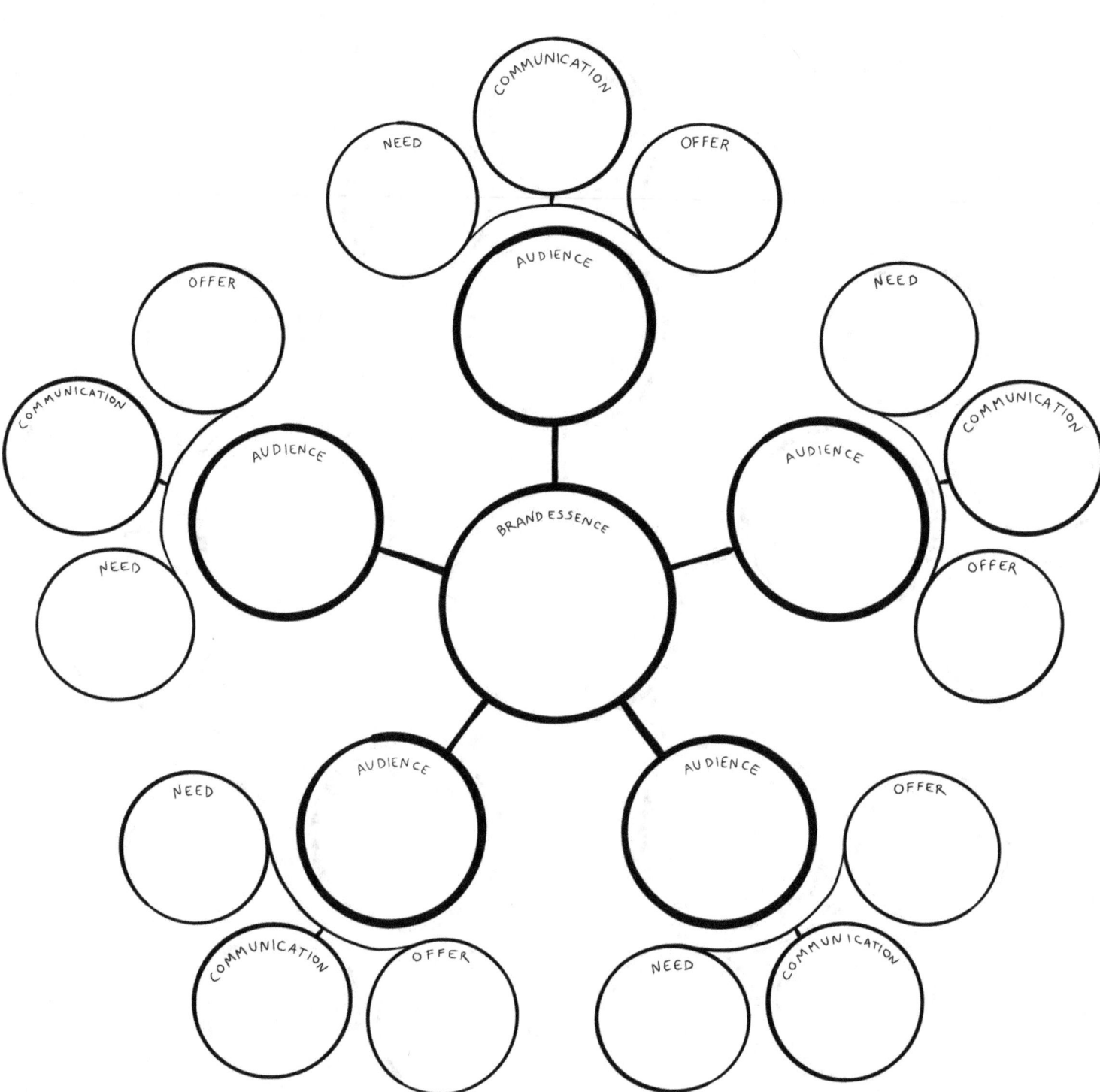

WHO IS YOUR AUDIENCE?

PROJECT:_____   DATE:_____

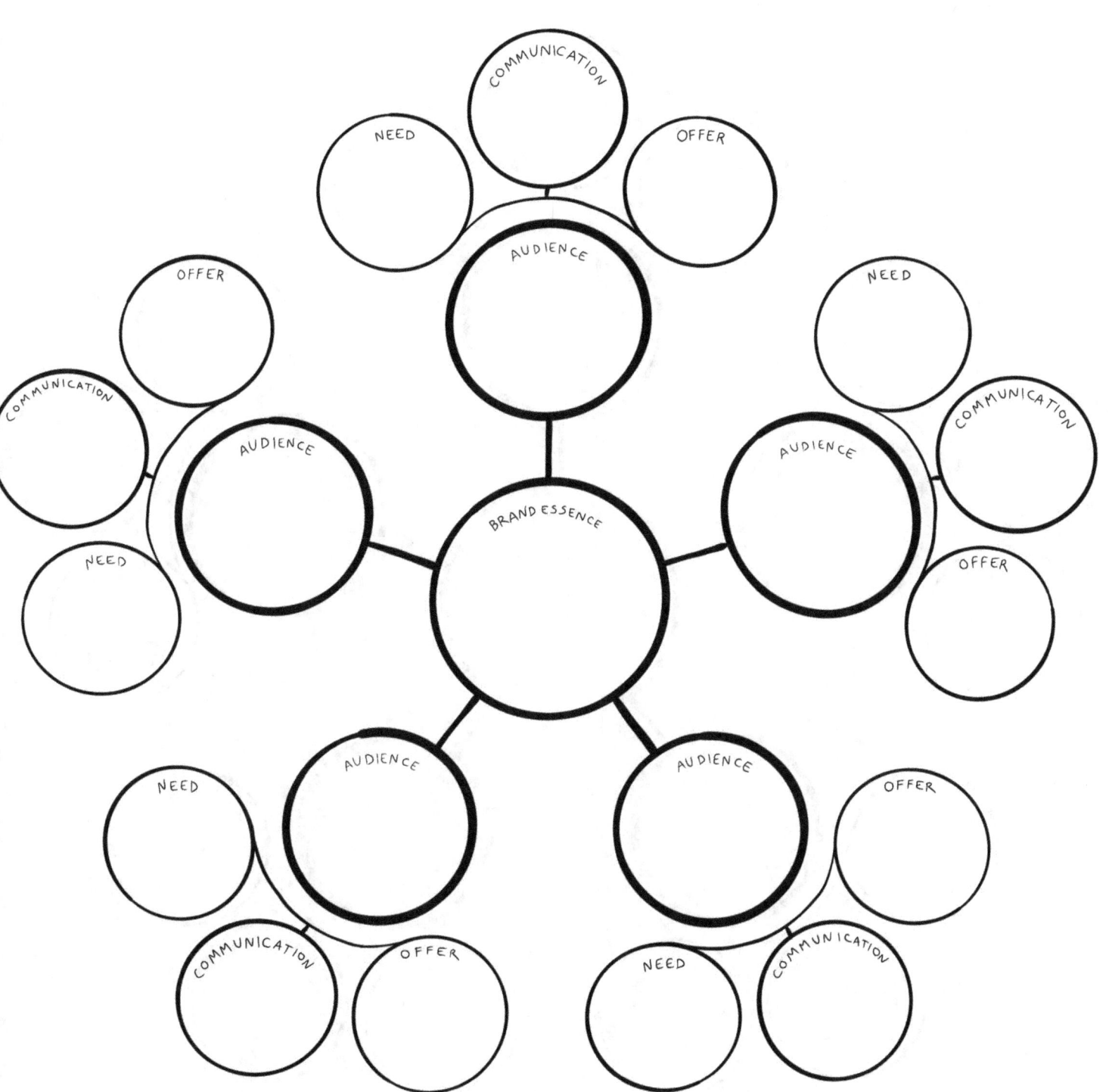

WHO IS YOUR AUDIENCE?

PROJECT:_____   DATE:_____

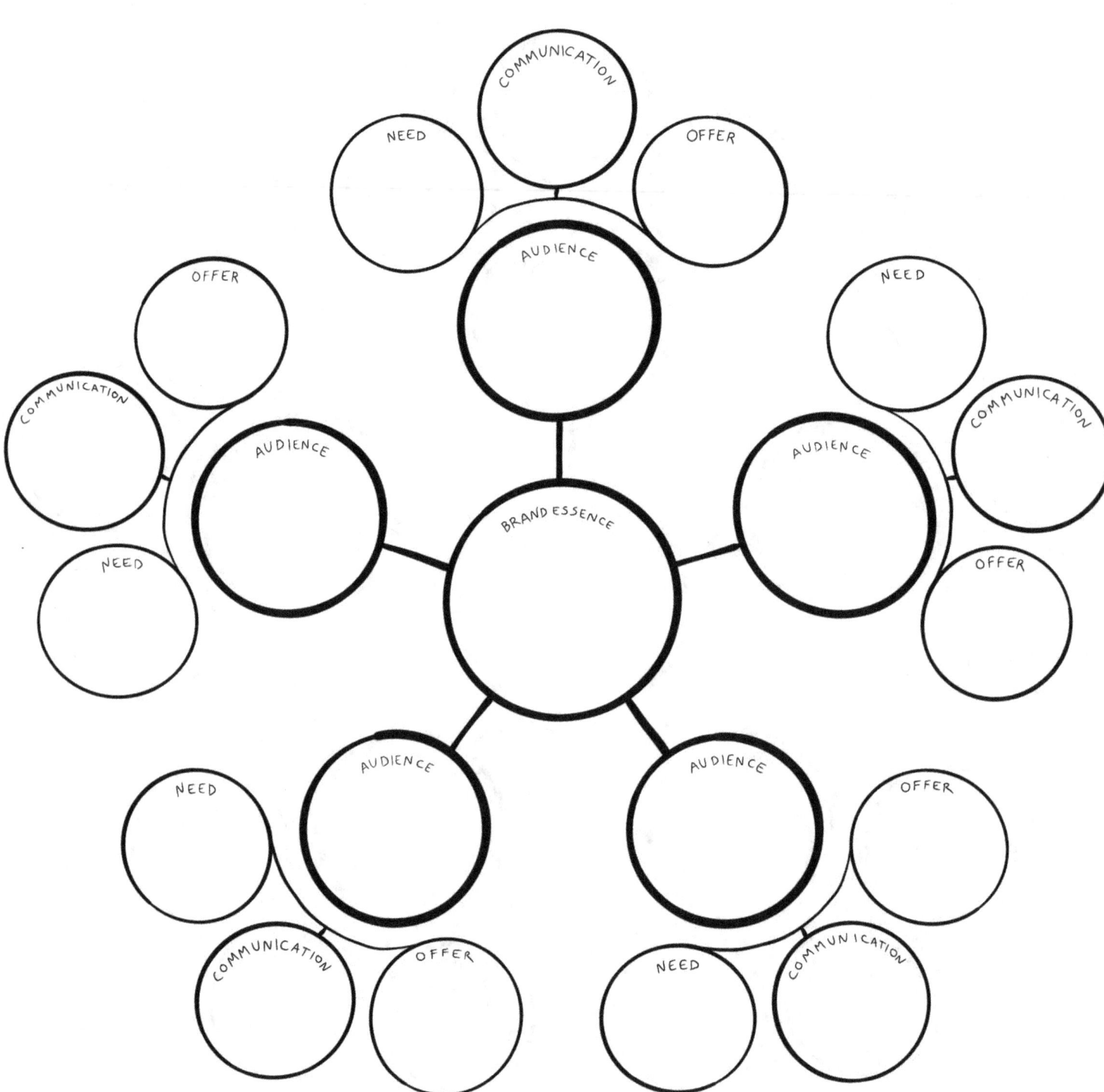

WHO IS YOUR AUDIENCE?

PROJECT: _____   DATE: _____

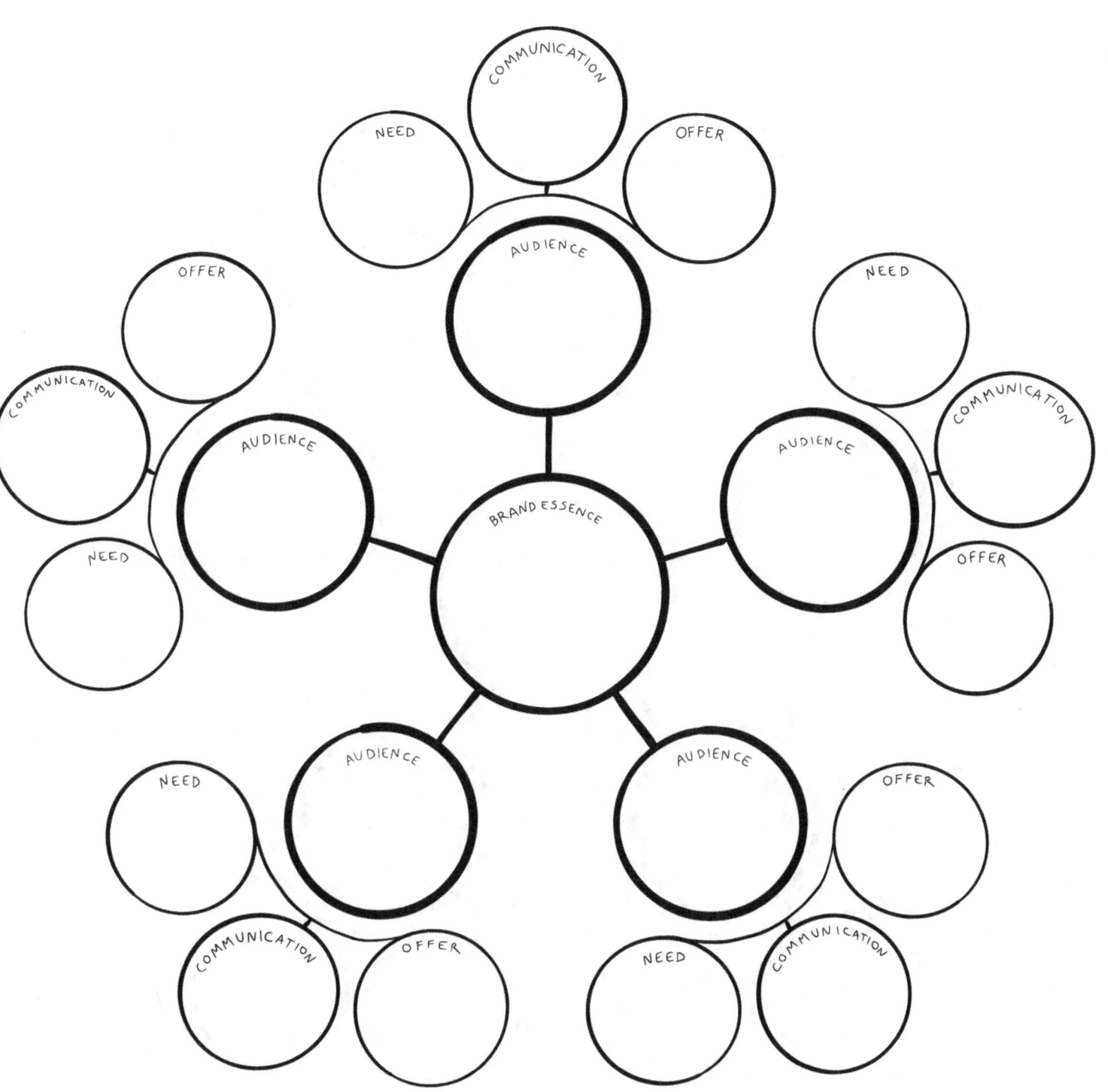

WHO IS YOUR AUDIENCE?

PROJECT:_____   DATE:_____

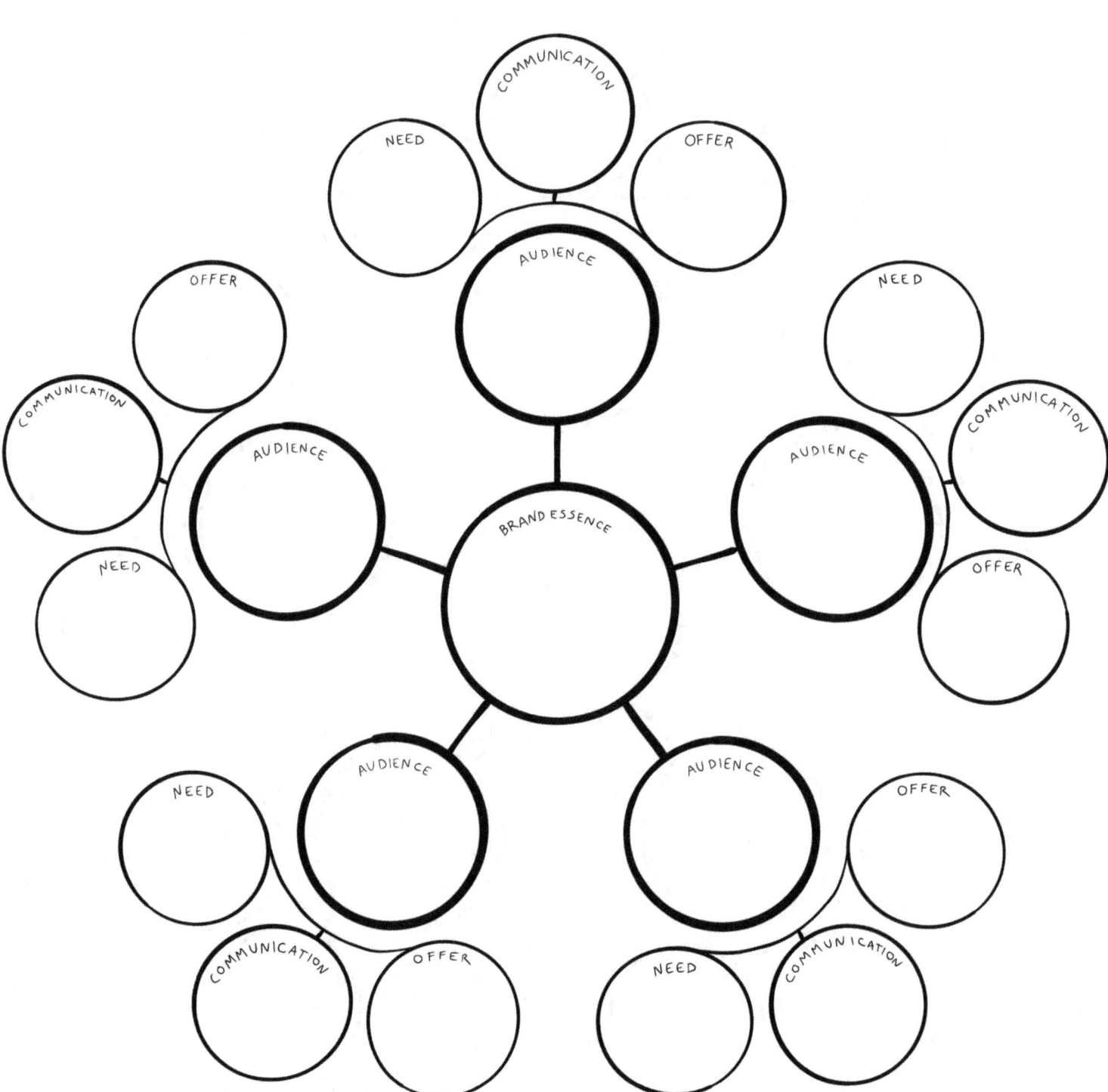

WHO IS YOUR AUDIENCE?

PROJECT:_____   DATE:_____

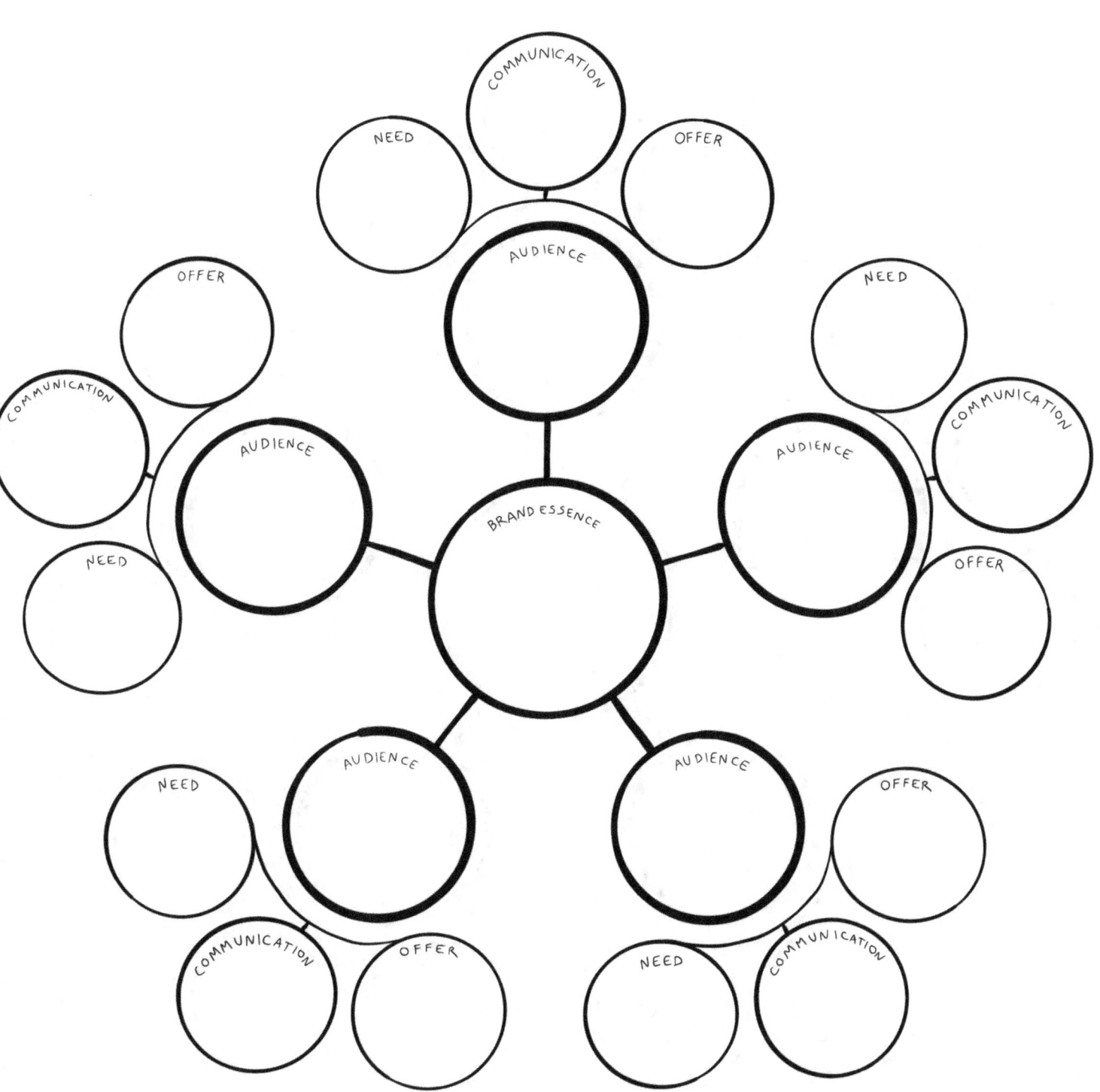

WHO IS YOUR AUDIENCE?

PROJECT:_____   DATE:_____

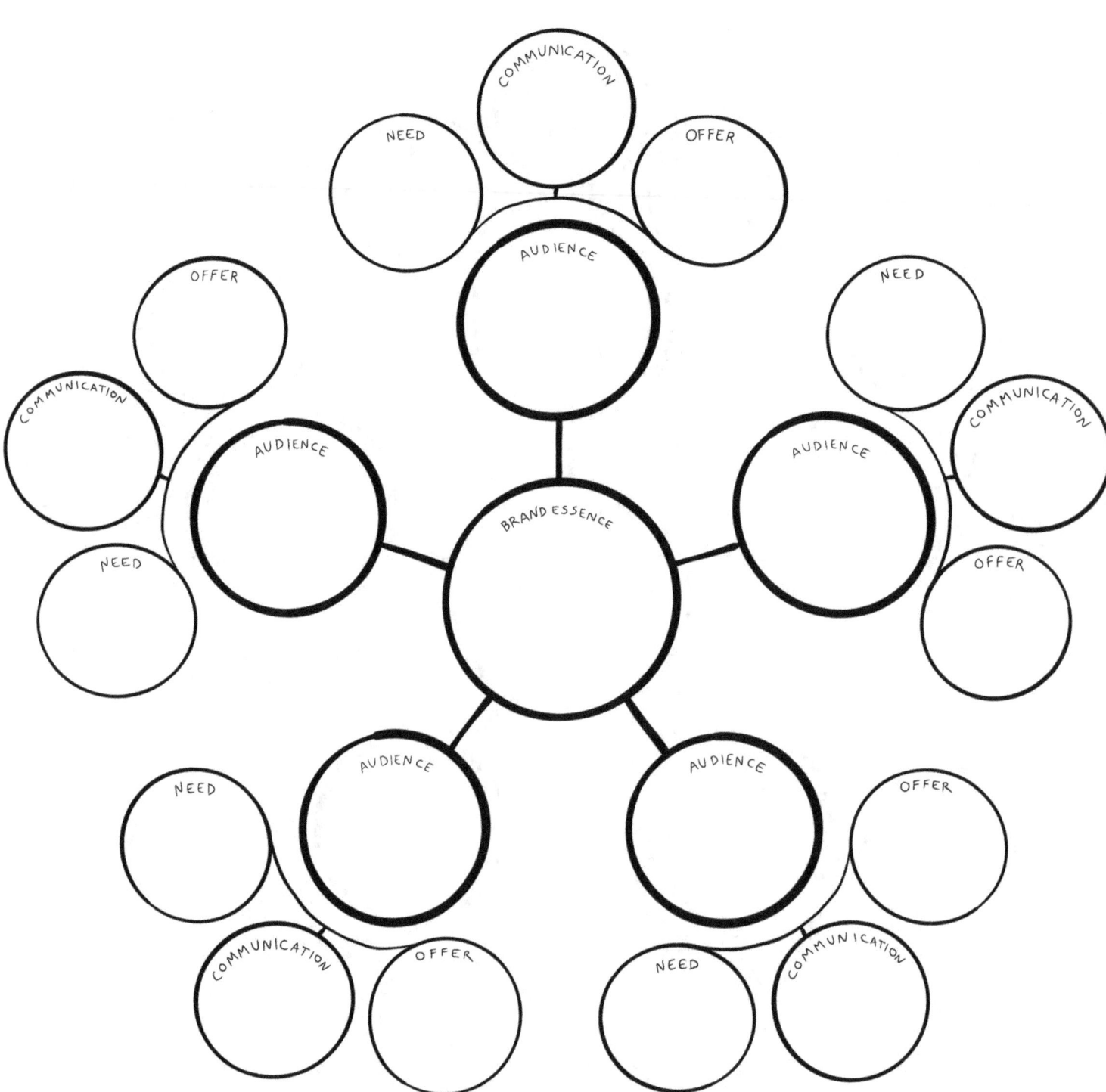

WHO IS YOUR AUDIENCE?

PROJECT:_____   DATE:_____

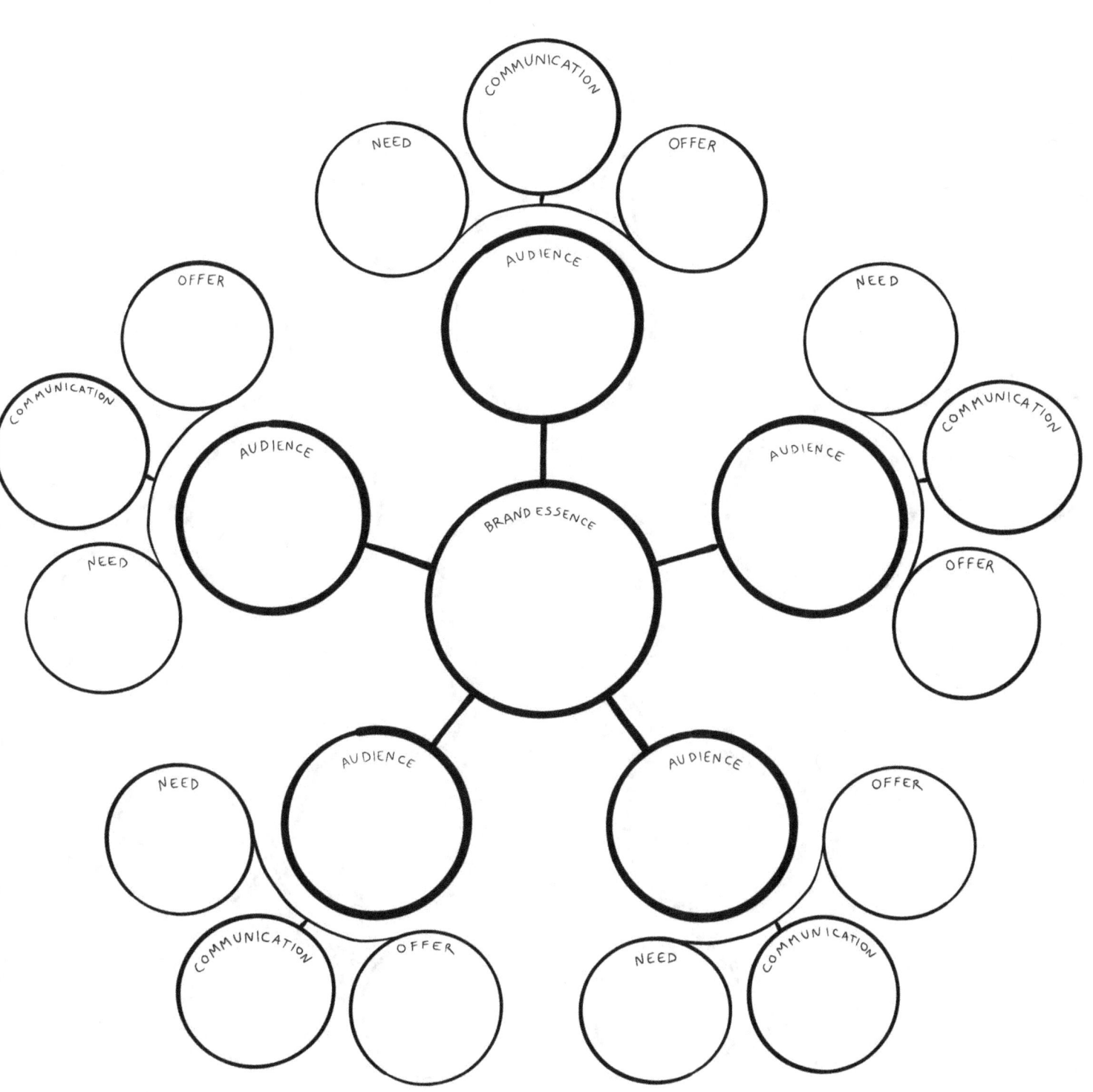

WHO IS YOUR AUDIENCE?

PROJECT:_____   DATE:_____

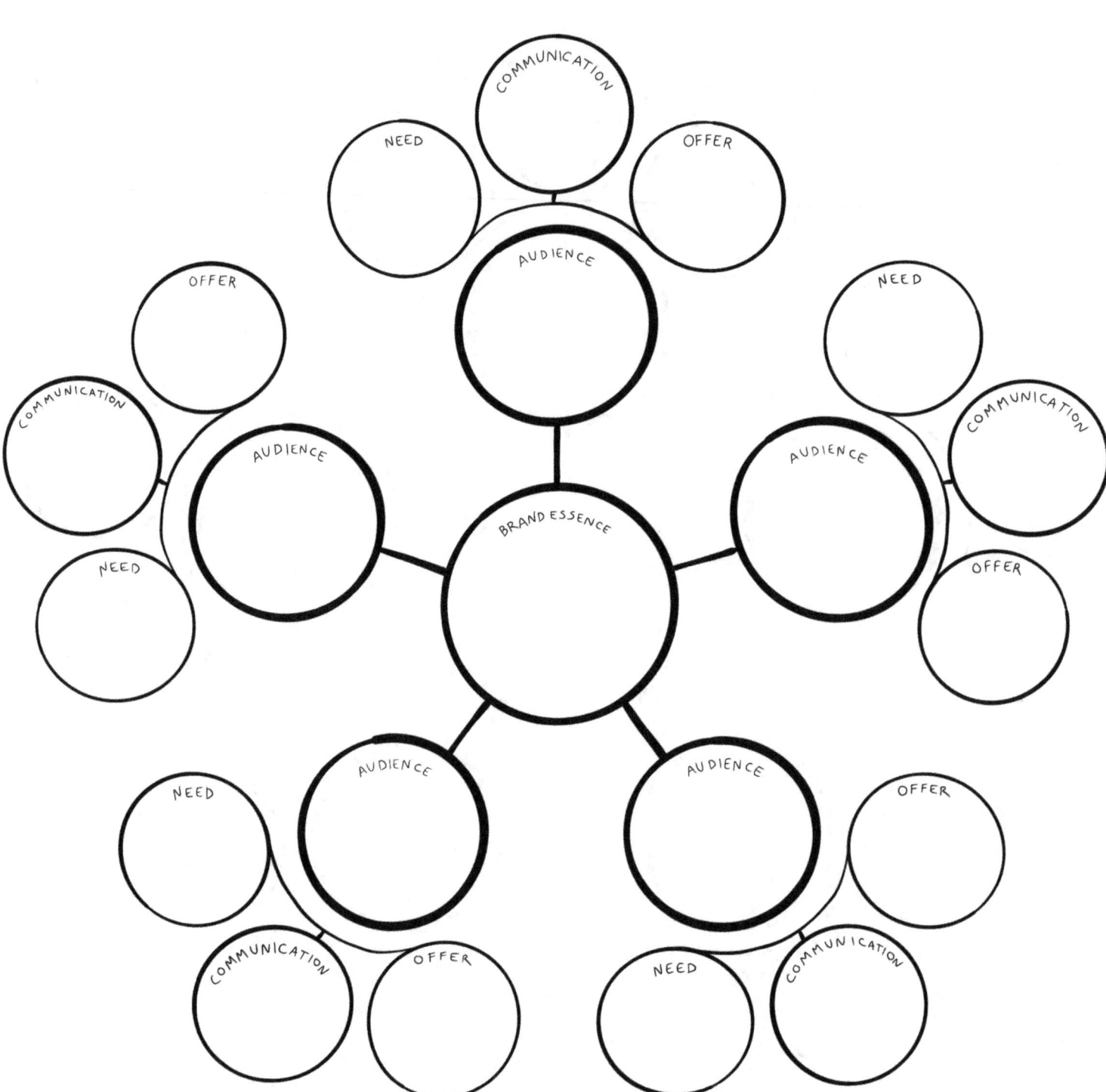

WHO IS YOUR AUDIENCE?

PROJECT:_____   DATE:_____

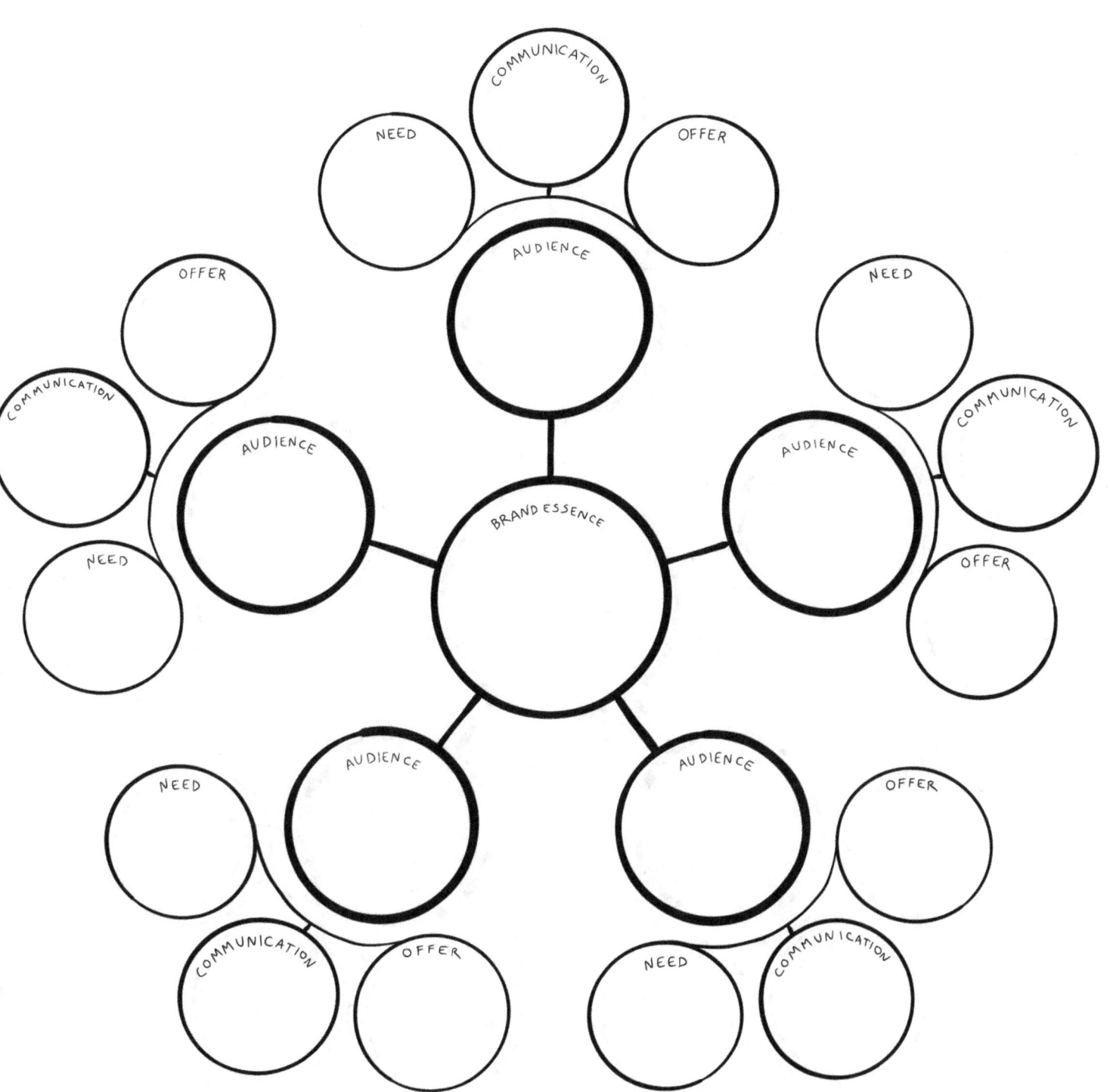

WHO IS YOUR AUDIENCE?

PROJECT:_____   DATE:_____

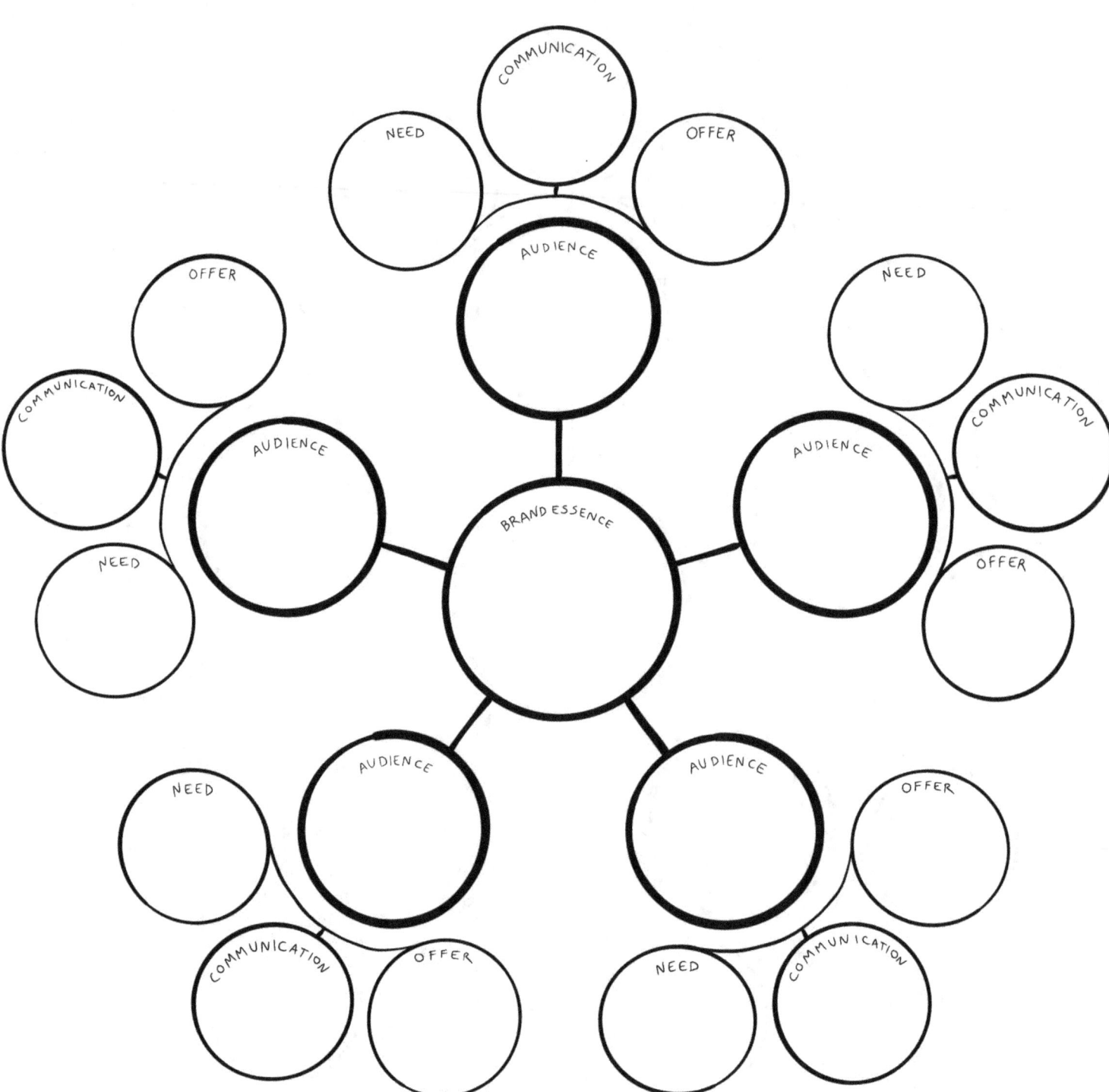

WHO IS YOUR AUDIENCE?

PROJECT:_____   DATE:_____

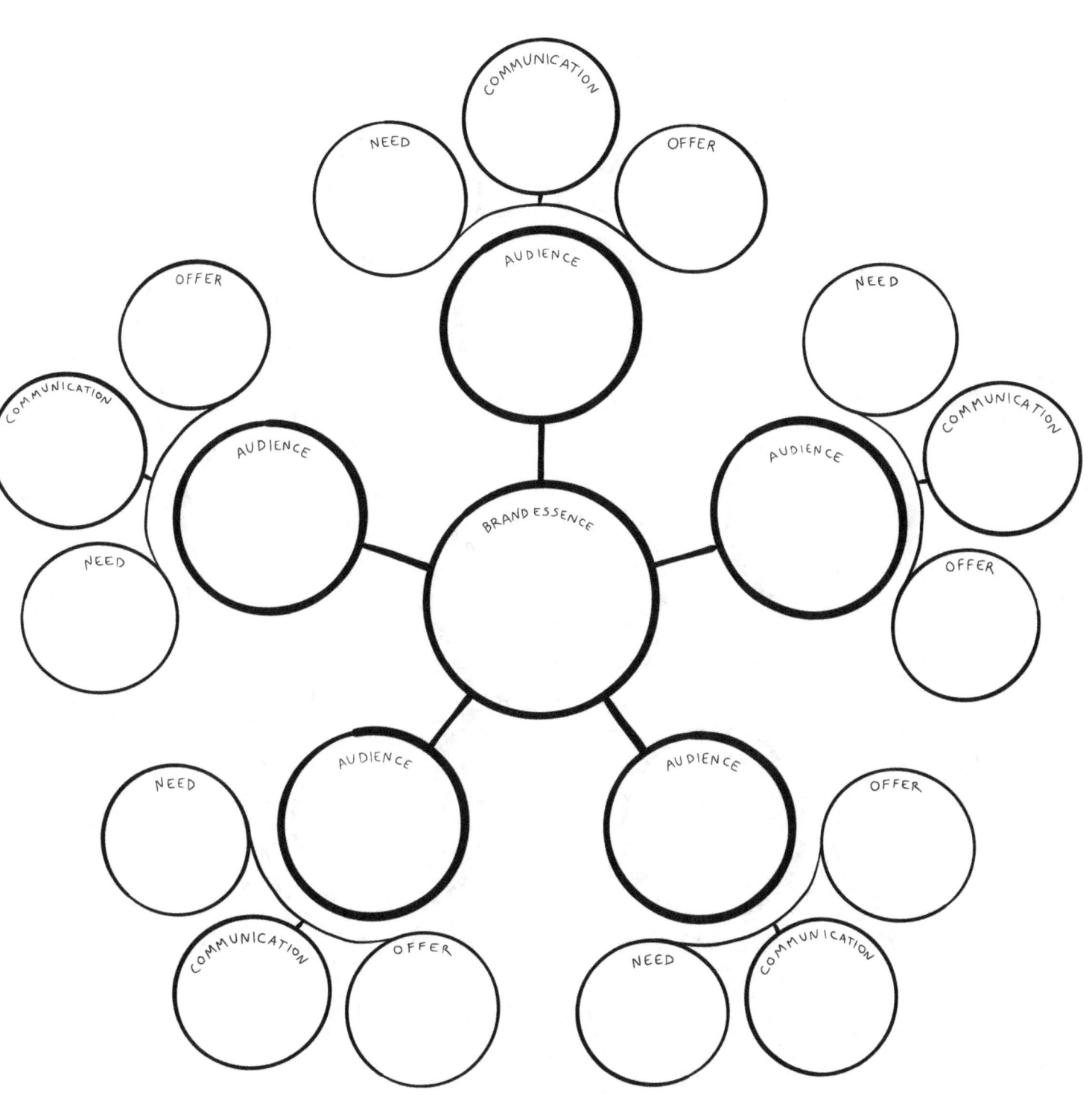

WHO IS YOUR AUDIENCE?

PROJECT:_____   DATE:_____

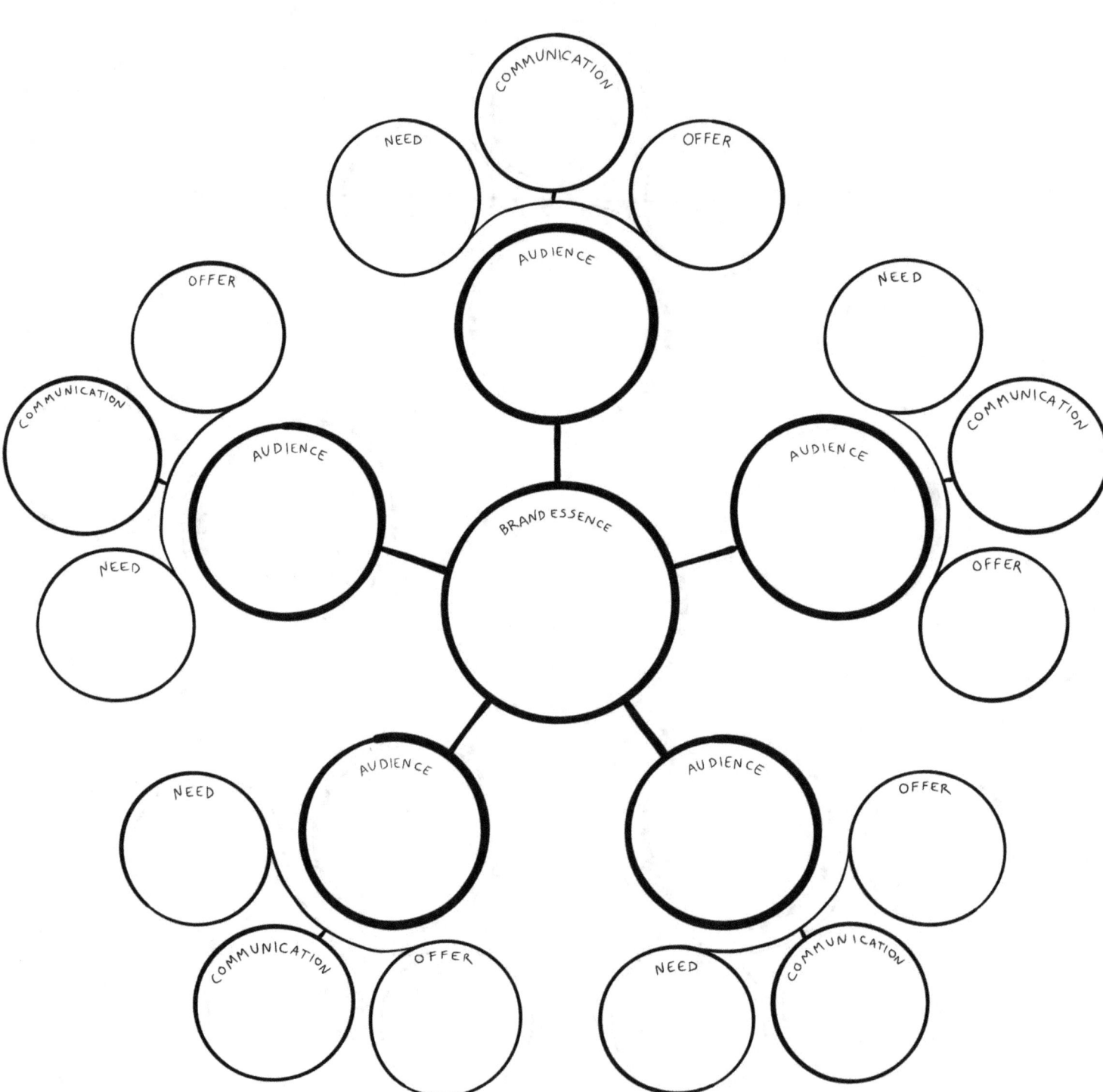

WHO IS YOUR AUDIENCE?

PROJECT:_____   DATE:_____

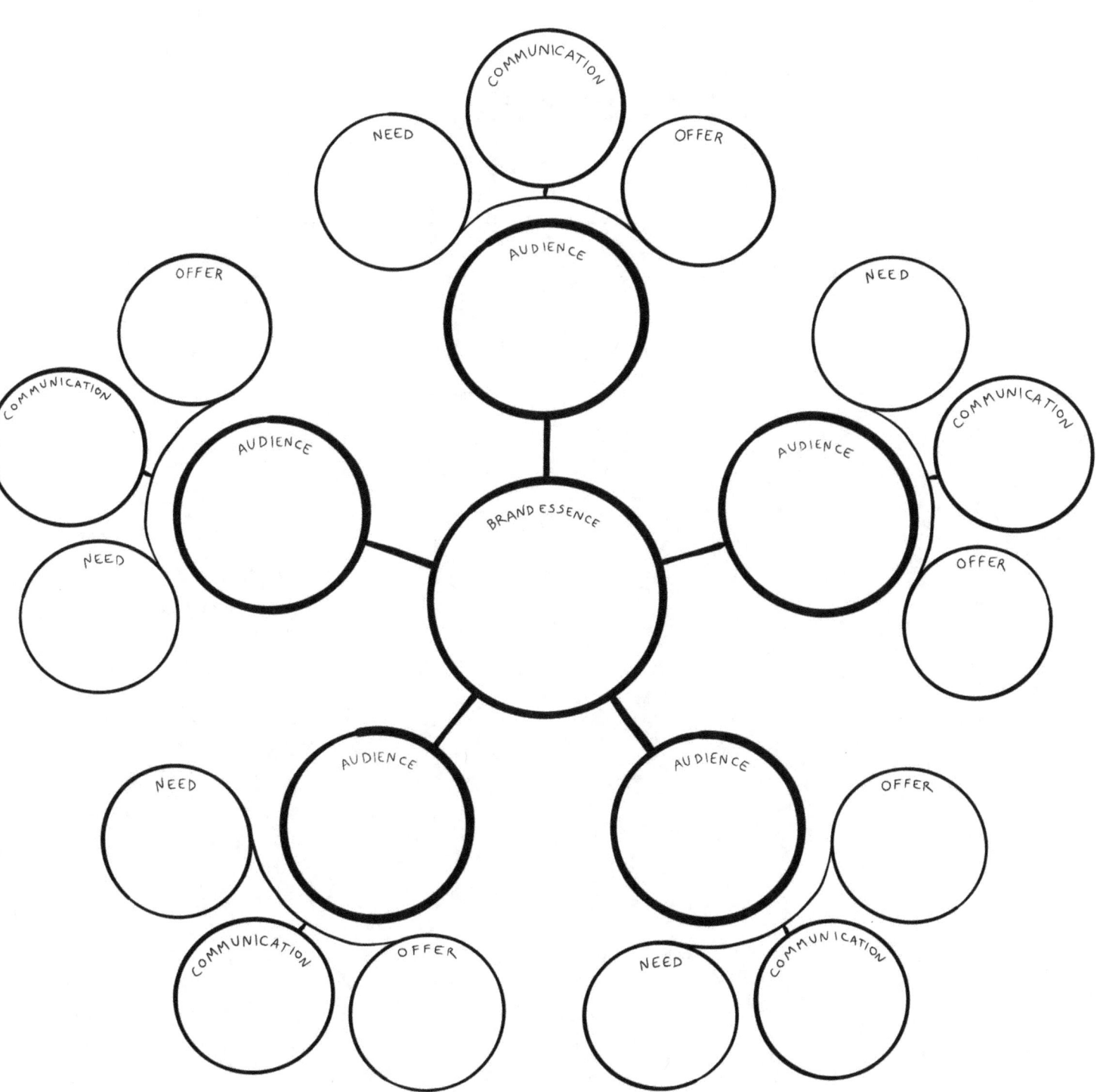

Takeaway notes:

_____

_____

_____

_____

_____

Year of use:

_____